# What Your Colleagues Are Saying . . .

Slow down to go fast. Joanne Quinn and her colleagues take the guess work out of Deep Learning by showing how we can transform our schools into Deep Learning cultures steeped in rigor and joy. This is the rare book that concretely shows how to build classrooms and schools infused with Deep Learning. Chock-full with resources, tips, rubrics, and more, this book provides both a road map and a set of tools that will accelerate the work of educators around the world who are transforming our industrial-age structures into passion-filled deeper learning environments.

**—Jal Mehta**
Professor of Education
Harvard Graduate School of Education

At a time when many schools are searching for ways to ensure equity in academic and developmental outcomes, this book will be a helpful guide and an invaluable resource. *Dive Into Deep Learning* provides educators with practical insights that can be applied at the classroom, school, and district level, to assess the impact of strategies aimed at developing the higher-order thinking skills of students. Written in a clear, accessible manner, this book will be a helpful guide to educators who seek to ensure that they are meeting the needs of all of their students.

**—Pedro Noguera**
Distinguished Professor of Education
Faculty Director, Center for the Transformation of Schools
UCLA Graduate School of Education & Information Studies

Drawing on experiences, expertise, and evidence from a "living laboratory" consisting of educators from across the globe, Quinn and her colleagues paint a clear picture of how to construct Deep Learning in ways that impact *all* students. The examples shared throughout this book not only demonstrate the different ways in which Deep Learning can be realized, but they also provide evidence of impact in places where it's actually occurring. This book is a must-read for teams who are collaborating in an effort to make significant improvements in educational settings.

**—Jenni Donohoo**
Project Manager
Council of Ontario Directors of Education (CODE)

Joanne Quinn, Joanne McEachen, Michael Fullan, Mag Gardner, and Max Drummy have created a critical companion to *Deep Learning: Engage the World Change the World.* Having done a masterful job laying out the need for educators, schools, and districts to embrace and move to a continuous improving system that embraces deeper learning, the authors have now have taken the critical next step in the process. It's one thing to document the need; the real trick is providing practical solutions. In this companion, Quinn and her colleagues have given educators a practical guide to implementing lasting change for improvement. This should be required reading (and implementing) in districts throughout the country.

**—Rick Miller**
Executive Director
CORE Districts

The perennial question of school and system improvement is *how* do we do this work? We're convinced of the *why*—yes, we want to make a profound difference in the learning lives of young people—and we know the *what*—a knowledge-rich curriculum that attends to the needs of diverse learners—but please explain *how* to do this work well. This is a page turner for leaders and teachers, laying out with clarity and precision how to create powerful learning environments for deeper learning.

**—Bruce Armstrong**
Special Advisor, Teaching and Learning
Victoria Department of Education, Australia

*Dive into*

# DEEP LEARNING
## Tools for Engagement

*This book is dedicated to all the deep learners and leaders who*
Engage the World and Change the World *for the better.*

# Dive into
# DEEP LEARNING
## Tools for Engagement

**JOANNE QUINN**
**JOANNE McEACHEN**
**MICHAEL FULLAN**
**MAG GARDNER**
**MAX DRUMMY**

FOR INFORMATION:

Corwin
A SAGE Company
2455 Teller Road
Thousand Oaks, California 91320
(800) 233-9936
www.corwin.com

SAGE Publications Ltd.
1 Oliver's Yard
55 City Road
London EC1Y 1SP
United Kingdom

SAGE Publications India Pvt. Ltd.
B 1/I 1 Mohan Cooperative Industrial Area
Mathura Road, New Delhi 110 044
India

SAGE Publications Asia-Pacific Pte. Ltd.
18 Cross Street #10-10/11/12
China Square Central
Singapore 048423

Publisher: Arnis Burvikovs
Development Editor: Desirée A. Bartlett
Senior Editorial Assistant: Eliza B. Erickson
Production Editor: Melanie Birdsall
Copy Editor: Erin Livingston
Typesetter: C&M Digitals (P) Ltd.
Proofreader: Ellen Brink
Indexer: Molly Hall
Cover Designer: Gail Buschman
Graphic Design: Trudy Lane, Mira Design
Marketing Manager: Sharon Pendergast

Printed in the United States of America

*Library of Congress Cataloging-in-Publication Data*

Names: Quinn, Joanne, author.

Title: Dive into deep learning : tools for engagement / Joanne Quinn, Joanne McEachen, Michael Fullan, Mag Gardner, Max Drummy.

Description: Thousand Oaks, California : Corwin, 2020. | Includes bibliographical references.

Identifiers: LCCN 2019027253 | ISBN 9781544361376 (paperback) | ISBN 9781544385402 (pdf)

Subjects: LCSH: Educational change. | Educational planning. | School improvement programs. | Motivation in education. | Curriculum enrichment.

Classification: LCC LB2806 .Q56 2020 | DDC 370.15/23—dc23

LC record available at https://lccn.loc.gov/2019027253

This book is printed on acid-free paper.

22 23 10 9 8 7

# Contents

## Chapter 04

## Chapter 05

# Section Four. Designing Deep Learning 141

## Chapter 08

# Section Five. Assessment Practices    187

Chapter 09

# Section Six. Building Capacity for Deep Learning    199

Chapter 10

**"** One of the most exciting findings
has been the unbridled optimism
of students, teachers, and leaders
who describe a renewed energy,
passion, and liberation. **"**

—*DEEP LEARNING: ENGAGE THE WORLD
CHANGE THE WORLD*, P. 46

# SECTION 01

## Dive Into Deep Learning

Adobe Stock/Robert Kneschke

> "If we want learners who can thrive in turbulent and complex times, apply thinking to new situations and change the world, then we must reimagine learning: what's important to be learned, how learning is fostered, where learning happens, and how we measure success. . . . We call this new conceptualization . . . Deep Learning. "

—DEEP LEARNING: ENGAGE THE WORLD
CHANGE THE WORLD, P. 13

# Chapter 01
# Good at Learning and Good at Life

Deep Learning puts the joy back into learning for students and adults alike, and it's spreading rapidly because it is meaningful, gives purpose, and unleashes potential. The need for Deep Learning is no longer a debate. Now is the time to transform learning. Our students desperately need it, and the world needs it to survive and thrive. The challenge is how to make this shift for *all* students in *all* classrooms. Shifting practices in classrooms means a re-culturing for students, teachers, leaders, and families. Everyone must embrace new roles and understandings.

In our book, *Deep Learning: Engage the World Change the World* (Fullan, Quinn, & McEachen, 2018), we laid the foundation for transforming schooling as we now know it. These ideas come from our partnership with over 1,500 schools in eight countries. Together with students and educators, we showed how and why traditional schooling is no longer up to the task of preparing students for the present, let alone the future. Students and teachers alike find current schooling less and less engaging as they proceed through the grade levels and as time passes. Some of them want to do something about it. These are the schools and systems that we are partnering with. The book, *Deep Learning*, contains many examples of what these new practices look like, and it provides a comprehensive, accessible framework for constructing the practices and establishing the conditions for moving in this direction.

Now, in this book, we provide the tools for constructing Deep Learning in your own situation, whether it be in one classroom or an entire school, local district, state, or country. Tools are only as good as the mindset using them, which is why we provide explanations and real examples. We also know that mindsets develop through actions, which is why in both books, we clearly present the ideas and examples that underpin what we can only call *The Deep Learning Movement*. If the reader is willing to do his or her part—work with others to engage in the new experiences, informed by the framework and tools—he or she will be amply rewarded. *Dive Into Deep Learning: Tools for Engagement* focuses on informed action that simultaneously develops know-how and mindset that will be essential for coping with and, indeed, shaping the future for the betterment of individuals and groups alike.

We encourage you to dig into our first book, *Deep Learning: Engage the World Change the World* (2018) to investigate the stories of students, teachers, and schools as they have engaged in this Deep Learning journey across our eight partner countries. Then move to this book, *Dive Into Deep Learning: Tools for Engagement*, as a guide to developing a comprehensive approach for mobilizing Deep Learning in your classroom, school, district, or system. It builds on the call to action described in our first Deep Learning book and overflows with practical supports, such as a framework, tools, and protocols. Inspiring vignettes and authentic examples bring the concepts to life and concretely illustrate how schools can shift to new practices. The facilitation guide provides a roadmap for building capacity in teachers, schools, districts, and systems to design Deep Learning, measure progress, and assess conditions needed to activate and sustain innovation.

In this chapter, let's investigate the *why* and the *what* of Deep Learning and how it comes to life.

## The Urgency

Looking at the landscape in 2019, it is important to acknowledge that the forces that are wracking the broader society have made their way into schools. Schools that continue to operate mostly in the early 20th-century mode in which they were created are not doing what is needed to counter these trends. Two findings led us to search for a way to transform learning. The first is the growing research indicating that conventional schools across most systems in the world are increasingly irrelevant for the majority of students. The Gallup Poll 2015 survey shows 76% engagement of students at Grade 5 and then a steep decline over time to 32% in Grade 10 (Stringer, 2018). Similarly, the Organisation for Economic Co-operation and Development's Programme for International Student Assessment (PISA) results from 78 countries show a steady decline in students' sense of belonging and connectedness at school from 2003 to 2015. The second finding is that stress and anxiety are rapidly increasing in most societies and are affecting younger and younger students across the board. These statistics should give us real pause.

At the same time, we need schools to respond to ever-growing demands; we must realize that schools are permeable institutions and thus are shaped heavily by changing external forces. There are a number of worrying global trends. The gap between the rich and the poor is enormous and on the rise. We make daily connections like never before, but those connections may be brief, superficial, and truncated. Jobs and the labor market are unpredictable and worrying to old and young alike. Technology and artificial intelligence will exponentially be interwoven into our lives with unknown (but certainly anxiety-producing) consequences. All of this generates more pervasive stress, illness, and apprehension. Cohesion lessens and the level of trust in society declines. Finally, much of what is emerging as "innovative" is often disconnected from the needs of students or relies on novelty rather than deep critical thought.

On the positive side, youth are not waiting for us to get it right—they are taking action. Recently, Greta Thunburg, a 15-year-old climate justice activist from Sweden, captured the world's attention at the United Nations Climate Change summit in Davos with her stark statements to world leaders: "I want you to panic. . . . You are stealing our future." Her words have galvanized protests by more than 1.5 million students in over 125 countries who are speaking out. In North America, youth leaders have emerged after the Parkland school shootings to galvanize action toward controlling gun violence, resulting in 67 gun control or gun violence prevention bills in the past year. Greta and the Parkland youth are two front-page examples of young people taking charge, but they are not isolated. In our Deep Learning work, we see thousands of daily examples across the globe where students (as change agents) display a deep desire to help humanity. This book is about how Deep Learning fosters such students and their teachers to unleash their potential to solve the complex issues facing us today and in the future.

## What Is Deep Learning?

*Deep Learning* is quality learning that sticks with you for life. Transforming learning on a global scale is ambitious, to say the least. For the last five years, we have partnered with clusters of schools and school systems across eight countries to build knowledge of new ways to implement learning with deeper goals. *Engage the world, change the world* is our mantra, formulated with our partner schools and systems around the world.

> " The Deep Learning competencies (6Cs) are at the heart of what's critical for learners today. "
>
> —*DEEP LEARNING: ENGAGE: THE WORLD CHANGE THE WORLD, P. 139*

The first step in reimagining learning was to identify six Global Competencies (6Cs) that describe the skills and attributes needed for learners to flourish as citizens of the world. In our definition, *Deep Learning is the process of acquiring these six Global Competencies: Character, Citizenship, Collaboration, Communication, Creativity, and Critical Thinking.* As schools and teachers began to foster Deep Learning experiences, we discovered that

> " Deep Learning is different in nature and scope than any other education innovation ever tried. It changes outcomes, in our case the 6Cs of global competencies: character, citizenship,

collaboration, communication, creativity, and critical thinking; and it changes learning by focusing on personally and collectively meaningful matters, and by delving into them in a way that alters forever the roles of students, teachers, families, and others. 🙸

—*DEEP LEARNING: ENGAGE THE WORLD CHANGE THE WORLD*, P. XIII

Deep Learning, as we have developed it, is good for the individual and good for society. The uplifting news is that an increasing number of schools and systems—including students, teachers, leaders, and communities—are strongly attracted to Deep Learning. Deep Learning maximizes *learning* per se, and fosters *identity* or *connectedness*—these two elements work in tandem to develop students as citizens who are committed and skilled at an early age and onward to be active learners and change agents. The transformation of school systems is essential for individuals, so that they can cope with an ever-complex and challenging society, and for systems, so they can be effective in relating to the ever-more-complicated issues facing the world, such as growing inequality, climate deterioration, uncertainty of jobs, unpredictable technologies, and reduction of social cohesion and trust within and across the globe.

Our model represents a redefinition of the "moral imperative of education." Traditionally, we used to think that the moral imperative was restricted to raising the bar and closing the gap of academic achievement. Now it is becoming increasingly clear that the sole focus on academic achievement is distorting what is needed in educating people for the complex world we now occupy. An emphasis on academic achievement by itself will not be effective in educating students in high-poverty environments or serving students of higher socioeconomic status (SES) who are struggling with increasing anxiety and stress. The redefinition of the moral imperative includes academic achievement, which we call *learning*, and identity, which we call *connectedness.* Deep Learning should then be thought of as representing good learning and good connectedness. The focus is on becoming good at learning and good at life and their synergistic development in individuals and in groups. This synergy is what we would call *well-being*.

Deep Learning tackles issues of both well-being and equity. Deep Learning is good for all, but it is especially effective for those most disconnected from schooling because it shifts the learning process to one that is authentic, engaging, and student centered. Well-being has gained worldwide attention in response to the growing anxiety and stress of our youth and the disengagement with traditional schooling. We define *well-being* as "having a sense of purpose, hope, belonging and meaning that is achieved when our cognitive, emotional, social, and physical needs are being met" (J. Clinton, personal communication, 2018). Our Deep Learning work is grounded in the fundamentals of neuroscience, promoting connectedness and belonging while working on problems relevant to life circumstances. As noted by child psychiatrist Jean Clinton,

> A focus on the 6Cs immunizes and protects against social and emotional difficulties thus building positive mental health and resilience . . . [and] levels the playing field for kids from challenging backgrounds.

—JEAN CLINTON, "CONNECTION THROUGH," JUNE 2017

Student-centered authentic learning attacks the emerging issues of both well-being and equity. We are seeing more and more students from both advantaged and disadvantaged circumstances flourishing. We describe this as the *equity hypothesis*. In our Deep Learning work, the old notion that students who struggle with school must focus only on mastering the foundations of literacy and numeracy are being replaced with effective experiences that bolster foundational literacy and numeracy skills and simultaneously immerse students in authentic tasks that engage them deeply while providing meaningful ways to learn critical skills.

> When students fully engage with the 6Cs, those students who come from disadvantage have a profound and deeper opportunity to engage in learning because they are able to bring their experiences and life knowledge, rather than being labelled as not having what we need them to know.

—JEAN CLINTON, PERSONAL COMMUNICATION, 2018

# Why Deep Learning Works

We are seeing that the nature of the Deep Learning tasks is intrinsically motivating for students as they delve into topics that are of real interest to them, have authentic meaning, and are more rigorous. It makes them want to persist and want to succeed. We are seeing that this combination of autonomy, belongingness, and meaningful work is building capacity in all students, but we have emerging evidence that it is catalytic for success in previously disadvantaged or under-engaged students who are beginning to flourish. We have scores of examples that show high impact. Our quest is to make Deep Learning the norm for the entire system so that all students thrive.

Six key features of Deep Learning are leading to massive transformation:

## 1 Whole Child—Whole System

Deep Learning is about developing all aspects of learners—both academic and socio-emotional—so that they thrive. It is not a project or program but a shift in both the outcomes of learning and the roles of teachers, leaders, families, and community.

## 2 Clarity of Outcomes

The six Global Competencies (6Cs) provide a comprehensive but clear vision for learning. They serve as a lens to deepen or amplify learning around selected curriculum goals.

## 3 Measurable

We have created tools to assess starting points and to measure progress in developing proficiency with the 6Cs.

## 4 Common Language

The related tools provide a shared language and precision about learning and practice among students, teachers, and families in the design and measurement of learning.

## 5 Co-Developed With Practitioners

The Deep Learning model has been co-developed with practitioners in eight countries using a common framework. Strong impact is noted in rural and urban areas as well as across advantaged and disadvantaged populations.

## 6 Action Orientation

We are not merely studying and reporting on Deep Learning but are building new knowledge about what works. We have assumed that examining and improving the world is an essential part of Deep Learning with a strong social connectedness. This connectedness makes it clear that Deep Learning is fundamentally a group phenomenon. Human beings are social beings.

These six features make our Deep Learning approach holistic and unique. What is most encouraging is that such learning is good for and attractive to all students, regardless of background and starting points.

## Systems Change and the Way Forward

The crucial challenge at hand is to change the culture of schooling. Those running school systems will need to move away from notions of command, control, and ordered change from above and, instead, work to create emergent systems that support teachers and students owning their learning and taking it in new directions. Students, teachers, principals, parents, and districts must push from the bottom and the middle. In this vision, districts (similar to modern learning organizations of all types) would be more horizontal than vertical, focusing less on prespecifying what everyone does and more on building platforms that connect and accelerate learning across the system. Districts could also create flexibility in all of the elements of schooling—they could permit multiage groupings, allow for courses that move across subjects, give credit for student opportunities in the field, lengthen the blocks of classes, give teachers time to collaborate, and much more. Such shifts would also create opportunities for teachers to engage in similar cycles of purpose and passion as their students, which would lessen burnout and increase the attractiveness of the profession.

This radical change involves defining and committing to a new moral imperative that displaces academic learning as the sole priority and replaces it with learning and connectedness as an integrated, synergistic capacity for all. In this way, learning and well-being become integrated as the new moral imperative. Being good at learning and good at life is essential to survival for individuals and for the collectivity of humankind. We believe an increase in specific, exciting learning experiences of the kind we have identified and fostered will create a breakthrough.

Deep Learning is about going deeper in knowledge, quality standards, assessment, and improvement of learning. But this will not be enough. The big problems are societal, not just individual. Small groups working in isolation will not suffice. Ultimately, Deep Learning is about the viability of the human race. This means that eventually all students must "engage the world" in order to "change the world"—to understand its evolving self and influence it for the better. This is for the good of individuals, collectivities, and the planet itself.

The question before us is, which path will we choose? We can continue to tinker with our existing models or transform schools as proactive Deep Learning agencies. Transforming learning would be good for all, but especially for those most disconnected from schooling. Creating such changes should also lessen the rates of depression and anxiety, while learning in the best sense of that concept will flourish, and, perhaps most importantly, we will produce the kinds of citizens who are equipped to take on the challenges of the rest of the 21st century, improving humankind as they learn. Combining learning and humanity is Deep Learning at its best.

## Getting Started

Use the six sections of the book to build the capacity of teachers, leaders, schools, and districts to mobilize and sustain Deep Learning.

**Section One** provides an overview of the *why*, *what*, and *how* of Deep Learning and then a detailed plan for how to best use this guide.

**Section Two** explores the Deep Learning Framework and details each of the components: the 6Cs of Character, Citizenship, Collaboration, Communication, Creativity, and Critical Thinking needed to flourish in the complex world; the Four Elements of Learning Design that activate Deep Learning experiences, including pedagogical practices, learning partnerships, learning environments, and leveraging digital; and the collaborative inquiry cycle that grounds both student learning and Deep Learning design.

**Section Three** introduces the Deep Learning Progressions, which provide detailed pathways to design and measure growth for each of the 6Cs. The chapters investigate how to use a learning progression to analyze student work, measure progress, and provide feedback to students. Student-friendly versions of the Deep Learning Progressions are introduced along with ways to engage students in monitoring and assessing their own learning

**Section Four** provides several Deep Learning vignettes and provides a Deep Learning Planning Template to facilitate the use of the Four Elements of Learning Design. The chapter provides a range of learning design samples and a process for analyzing the quality of learning designs using the Learning Design Rubric.

**Section Five** explores a process for the collaborative assessment of learning tasks. This process has proven to be powerful in enhancing learning results as well as shifting teacher practice.

**Section Six** focuses on building capacity for Deep Learning for teachers, schools, and districts. Chapters provide a teacher self-assessment tool, a school conditions rubric, and a district conditions rubric to assess the capacity of the school or district to support Deep Learning. Planning guides are provided for teachers, schools, and districts to move to action.

Each section draws upon rich examples and practices, featuring samples of Deep Learning designs, vignettes, and cases proven in field testing across the eight partner countries. Use these resources, and the result will be the creation of learning experiences that change the world by engaging the world in your own community and beyond.

Timing is crucial. We need teachers and leaders who are committed to humanity, good at networking, and ready to take action. This is the mindset you need to take full advantage of our tools for engagement.

**Now is the time to transform learning and life!**

> " The change lesson here is we need to change the *culture of learning*, not simply the trappings or structures. It cannot be done by policies or mandates. Transformation will only occur when we engage in the work of facilitating new processes for learning. "

*—DEEP LEARNING: ENGAGE THE WORLD CHANGE THE WORLD, P. 26*

# Chapter 02
# How to Use This Guide

Tools give us precision and clarity, but it's the common language and practices that shift the culture because they foster the conversation. The *Dive Into Deep Learning: Tools for Engagement* guide provides teachers, schools, and districts with step-by-step experiences to build the knowledge and skills needed to foster Deep Learning.

## Getting Started

### 1 Read

*Deep Learning: Engage the World Change the World*

First, review the big ideas of Deep Learning in the first book and then use the tools and protocols in this guide to help you focus and take action. Consider a book study format to examine the ideas and examples and then explore how they fit your classroom, school, or district.

### 2 Organize

Learning Partners, Teams, or Networks

Get started based on the needs of your organization. Here are some ways individuals, schools, and districts have formed learning teams.

Role Alike Learning Partners

While individuals may use the tools and approaches independently, collaborative learning teams accelerate and deepen the shift toward new practices. Grade teams, departments, or interest networks of like-minded colleagues can explore the protocols and tools to deepen knowledge and skills in designing and assessing Deep Learning.

Schools

Use the guide to build capacity for Deep Learning with interested groups of staff or as a focus for the entire school. Forming a leadership team accelerates progress as members learn from the work and from each other and apply the ideas and approaches in the classroom.

Developing a high-trust culture of learning is essential for innovation to flourish and is amplified as people learn from and with each other.

District Networks and Teams

Create teams/networks from schools who will learn, apply, and share insights at each step of the journey. Investigate the protocols, apply the ideas in classrooms, and then share findings to accelerate the spread of Deep Learning.

 ## Dive In

*Tools for Engagement* Guide

Use the protocols, vignettes, mini-cases, and examples to extend opportunities to work collaboratively, build new relationships, and learn from the work, individually and collectively.

# Organization of the Guide

The book is organized into six sections with twelve chapters:

| | |
|---|---|
| Section One: | Diving Into Deep Learning |
| Section Two: | A Framework for Deep Learning |
| Section Three: | Learning Progressions |
| Section Four: | Designing Deep Learning |
| Section Five: | Assessment Practices |
| Section Six: | Building Capacity for Deep Learning |

Incorporated in the *Tools for Engagement* guide are 44 protocols. The Deep Learning process begins with the engagement of staff in common experiences. Protocols are used to facilitate dialogue and critical thinking about Deep Learning. With each chapter, participants develop a greater understanding of Deep Learning by using the set of tools and resources. Figure 2.1 provides an overview of more than 100 tools, organizers, vignettes, examples, and case studies that will help you investigate Deep Learning.

Chapters are organized into four sections:

 ## Key Concepts
An overview of key concepts, research, and practices are included at the beginning of each chapter.

 ## Protocols
Each protocol provides a learning strategy to dig into the tools and processes of Deep Learning. They are designed to foster

powerful professional conversations that build skills, knowledge, and insights into practice. Each protocol is described in detail and includes powerful instructional strategies to encourage interaction between colleagues. Each protocol is organized in five sections:

- Purpose: specific learning outcomes for the experience
- Process: steps to facilitate collaborative learning
- Organizers: to record, analyze, or synthesize ideas and insights
- Time: range of time suggested for the learning experience
- Resources: references to pertinent videos and documents

### 3 Tools
Deep Learning Progressions, rubrics, and processes

### 4 Resources
*Vignettes,* which describe Deep Learning experiences, and *Examples* of learning designs from a range of grades and content areas captured using the Learning Design Planning Template

FIGURE 2.1

## Tools for Engagement in Deep Learning

| Global Competencies | Designing Deep Learning | Building Capacity for Deep Learning |
| --- | --- | --- |
| **Tools** | | |
| Deep Learning Progressions:<br><br>• Character<br>• Citizenship<br>• Collaboration<br>• Communication<br>• Creativity<br>• Critical Thinking<br><br>Student-Friendly Deep Learning Progressions:<br><br>• Character<br>• Citizenship<br>• Collaboration<br>• Communication<br>• Creativity<br>• Critical Thinking<br><br>Student Self-Assessment Tool | Learning Design:<br><br>• Rubric<br>• Planning Template<br>• Coaching Tool | • Teacher Self-Assessment Tool<br>• Simple Conversation Guide<br><br>Rubrics:<br><br>• School Conditions<br>• District Conditions |

*(Continued)*

FIGURE 2.1 (Continued)

| Global Competencies | Designing Deep Learning | Building Capacity for Deep Learning |
| --- | --- | --- |
| **Organizers** | | |
| • What's Deep About Deep Learning?<br>• Snapshots of Practice 6Cs Observation<br>• Four As Organizer | • The Four Elements Notetaker<br>• The Four Elements Learning Design Organizer<br>• Four Elements in Action Organizer<br>• Y Chart Organizer<br>• Deep Learning Framework Placemat<br>• Venn Diagram Organizer<br>• Learning Design Rubric Organizer<br>• Looking for Evidence of Pedagogical Practices Organizer<br>• Reflecting on Student Performance<br>• Norms for Assessing a Deep Learning Task<br>• Learning Design Observation | • Deep Listening Exchange Organizer<br>• Teacher Action Plan Organizer<br>• Graffiti Organizer<br>• School Conditions Rubric: Key Ideas Organizer<br>• 100-Day School Deep Learning Plan<br>• Three-Step Interview Organizer<br>• What? So What? Organizer<br>• District Profile of School Conditions Rubric Ratings Organizer<br>• District Deep Learning Plan |
| **Resources** | | |
| Vignettes:<br><br>• Bee the Change<br>• Ask Yourself: So What?<br>• Learning to Juggle Life's Demands<br>• No Planet B<br>• Daily Deep Learning Fitness for the Mind<br>• Learning Outside the Box<br>• The Sky Is Not the Limit<br>• Student-Friendly Language: Meet Them Where They're At | • Four Elements of Learning Design Poster<br><br>Deep Learning Design Examples:<br><br>• Learning About Landmarks, Grade 2<br>• Exploring World Peace, Grade 4<br>• Exploring Poverty: A Sustainable Approach, Grade 6<br>• Speed Dating: Critical Thinking and Writing, Grade 10 English<br>• Vulnerable Populations and Economic Activity, Grade 12 Economics<br><br>Case Studies:<br><br>• Introduction to Collaborative Inquiry<br>• Reflective Practice: A Grade 9 Classroom<br>• Who's Afraid of Algebra? | Case Studies:<br><br>• Mobilizing a Districtwide Shift to Deep Learning |

# Building Capacity for Deep Learning

While there will always be the teacher outliers, the pioneers who are able to transcend the system and create pockets of excellence, we are interested in how to help large numbers of teachers—ultimately all teachers in a school, district, or jurisdiction—take on the new pedagogies that foster Deep Learning. We cannot rely on individual teachers to turn the tide one by one, but rather, need an approach that mobilizes whole schools, districts, and systems to rethink their practices and provides models for that reflection and action planning. Schools that are on the move toward building precision in Deep Learning begin by cultivating a culture of learning for both the educators and the students. If the teachers and leaders are not thinking deeply, it's unlikely they will create those conditions for their students. The schools and districts that are cultivating cultures of learning and moving most quickly with the new pedagogies build capacity using a range of strategies.

## Four Strategies to Build Capacity

- Establish norms and relationships that foster transparency of practice
- Build common language and skills in using a research-based instructional repertoire
- Create intentional mechanisms for identifying and sharing innovative practices
- Provide sustained opportunities for teachers to build their capacity—knowledge and skills—in using the new practices with feedback and support

## Cultivating a Culture of Learning

Everyone needs to feel safe and supported in order to take risks and change the way they do things. An important way to build an environment that is safe and innovative is to co-develop norms because they provide a common language of respect and build consistency of practice. Protocol 29 provides a process for co-developing norms for collaborative assessment.

## Role of Facilitators

The role of facilitator is critical to the success of Deep Learning in classrooms and for adults. Facilitators, whether in formal or informal roles, act as lead learners and serve as activators, culture builders, and connectors.

Key roles facilitators may take on include
- Clarifying the purpose of the work together
- Establishing a set of norms for working together
- Organizing the learning sessions—dates, times, locations
- Understanding and facilitating the protocols for each session
- Accessing necessary resources
- Encouraging participation by all
- Resolving issues or challenges
- Communicating regularly with team members

## Role of Learning Participants

Participants take on five key roles as part of the learning team to
- Represent a range of perspectives
- Share expertise
- Be transparent
- Participate fully
- Apply new understandings and share insights

Use the tools and protocols to explore Deep Learning and dive into transforming learning in your classrooms, schools, or districts!

**"** It's not about pilots or bolt-on programs, but rather it's a rethinking of the learning process. **"**

*—DEEP LEARNING: ENGAGE THE WORLD CHANGE THE WORLD, P. 117*

# SECTION 02

# A Framework for Deep Learning

**"** What we propose here is moving Deep Learning from the margins of practice for a few students . . . to being the foundation of learning for all. **"**

—*DEEP LEARNING: ENGAGE THE WORLD CHANGE THE WORLD*, P. 55

# CHAPTER 03
# The Deep Learning Framework

Such massive transformation from traditional to Deep Learning calls for a model that can guide action without constraining it, that is comprehensive but not unwieldy. We set out with our partners to develop such a model. Five years ago, we proposed an initial framework and then deepened and validated it together through action and reflection. We populated the model with scores of examples and vignettes that illustrated practice but also gave us insight into the theory of Deep Learning and into strategies for initiating, implementing, and spreading it. To twist Kurt Lewin's observation, we say, "There is nothing as theoretical as good practice." When you have a good idea, you need a theory of change. When you have a complex idea, you need a theory of action. *Tools for engagement* is our theory of action for mobilizing a social movement to help scores of schools, districts, and systems.

## The Deep Learning Framework

We developed the Deep Learning Framework, a set of planning and measurement tools and a collaborative learning process that enables the design of learning experiences steeped in new knowledge creation and real-life problem solving. Shifting the learning outcomes radically changes pedagogical practices as well as the conditions under which Deep Learning flourishes. Working coherently at all levels to make shifts in learning conditions, pedagogy, and outcomes unleashes the potential for all students to thrive in a complex world. The Deep Learning Framework and tools, used together, support the rapid spread of Deep Learning that can be adapted to the varied contexts of schools, districts, and systems and provide concrete ways to shift practice. The framework and processes have been validated through practice over the past five years, with new insights and strategies uncovered and disseminated globally. Creating a knowledge-building global community of practice has been a key focus.

Figure 3.1 depicts the four layers of the Deep Learning Framework as circles of support. There are three key components. First, there must be clarity about the learning goals and what it means to be a deep learner—namely, to become proficient in the Global Competencies (6Cs) over time. Second, Deep Learning will be fostered across all classrooms only if we can define the learning process that makes it possible for teachers, leaders, students, and families to shift their thinking and practices. Third, it will happen in whole schools and systems only if we create the conditions for innovation, growth, and a culture of learning for all.

FIGURE 3.1

## The Deep Learning Framework

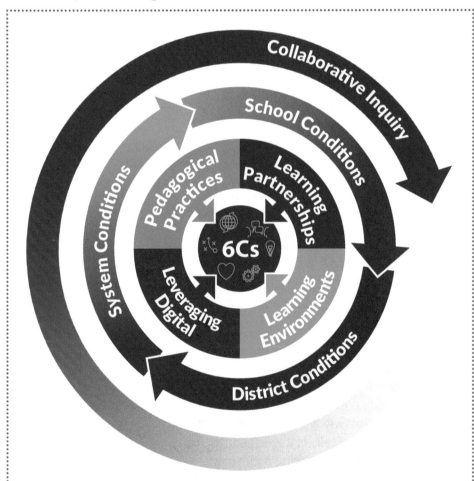

**Layer 1** Global Competencies at the center provide clarity about what it means to be a Deep Learner.

**Layer 2** Four Elements of Learning Design provide a process that makes it easy for teachers, students, leaders, and families to shift their thinking and practices.

**Layer 3** Conditions for mobilizing Deep Learning describe the conditions needed at each level—school, district/municipality, and system—to foster innovation, growth, and a culture of learning.

**Layer 4** Collaborative inquiry surrounds each layer—a process for continuous improvement.

Each of the core components is supported by a set of tools and processes described in Figure 3.2.

FIGURE 3.2

# The Deep Learning Framework: Tools and Processes

| Layer | Purpose | Tools |
|---|---|---|
| **01** Six Global Competencies for Deep Learning | The first circle of support at the center of the framework is Deep Learning, represented by the six Global Competencies, also known as the 6Cs: Character, Citizenship, Creativity, Critical Thinking, Collaboration, and Communication. <br><br> Deep Learning is defined *as the process of acquiring these six Global Competencies*. These competencies describe the increasing complexity of thinking and problem solving, collaborative skills, self-knowledge, and responsibility that underlie character and the ability to feel empathy and take action that makes one a global citizen. Building clarity about the learning outcomes in this layer is necessary if teachers, students, and families are to build common language and expectations. <br><br> Tools called *Learning Progressions* provide a detailed description of the dimensions of each competency and a pathway to proficiency. The progressions are used to assess starting points, design learning, and measure progress. <br><br> These progressions have also been developed using student-friendly language so that students can assess and monitor their progress | Deep Learning Progressions: <br><br> • Citizenship <br> • Character <br> • Collaboration <br> • Communication <br> • Creativity <br> • Critical Thinking <br><br> Student-Friendly DL Progressions: <br><br> • Citizenship <br> • Character <br> • Collaboration <br> • Communication <br> • Creativity <br> • Critical Thinking <br><br> Student Self-Assessment Tool |
| **02** Four Elements of Deep Learning Design | The second layer of the framework identifies four elements to foster the design of Deep Learning experiences: pedagogical practices, learning partnerships, learning environments, and leveraging digital. Teachers and students combine these four elements with intentionality and precision to ensure that learning experiences have the complexity and depth to facilitate growth and scaffold the prerequisite skills to maximize success. As well, the elements lead to intentionality in building new relationships between and among teachers, students, and families and using digital to facilitate and amplify learning. | Learning Design Rubric <br><br> Learning Design Planning Template <br><br> Learning Design Coaching Tool |
| **03** Conditions That Build Capacity for Deep Learning | The third layer or circle of support describes the conditions that mobilize Deep Learning to spread exponentially across schools and districts. This set of conditions describes policies, practices, and actions that best foster the development of the 6Cs and Four Elements of Learning Design. The rubrics can be used to identify strengths and areas of improvement, guide improvement, assess progress, and foster whole-school, whole-district development. | Teacher Self-Assessment Tool <br><br> Deep Learning School Conditions Rubric <br><br> Deep Learning District Conditions Rubric |
| **04** Collaborative Inquiry Process | The framework's outer circle depicts a collaborative inquiry process that grounds the work and fosters the interaction effect of all layers. While pictured as an outer circle, it is not a final step but rather permeates each circle by creating powerful conversations at every stage of development. This process may be used by teachers to design Deep Learning experiences, by teams to moderate student work and growth, and by leaders to assess the conditions needed to foster Deep Learning at the school and system levels. | Collaborative Inquiry Process <br><br> Simple Conversation Guide |

The framework and tools travel well across contexts because they

- build on existing success,

- connect schools and districts to a global community of experts and practitioners,

- promote precision in learning design and evaluation,

- foster collaborative cultures that impact outcomes,

- accelerate positive change, and

- build momentum for whole school, whole district, and whole system change.

There is no one way to implement Deep Learning, but getting started accelerates when teachers collaborate within and across schools and when they have rich examples, protocols, and a process for working together. Connecting with those who share common goals helps with problem solving and produces a shared commitment to stick with new behaviors. This common focus on Deep Learning and the intentional sharing of practices leads to collective understanding and a realization by teachers and leaders that they are not working alone.

## Final Thoughts

We invite you to mobilize our tools and processes in the next chapters to make *your* vision of Deep Learning come to life. We have created a system for newcomers to connect with those who have also gone through the journey and to learn from their experiences. More than that, we have developed front-end modules to help newcomers get started and systems for ongoing support, led by ourselves as the originators but more and more by local leaders who have significant experience in using the ideas and tools. In short, *you* have to kick-start the process, but expect a community of learners to join you as you go.

In the next chapter, we explore the foundation of our Deep Learning Framework, the Global Competencies for Deep Learning (the 6Cs).

# Notes

_____

_____

_____

_____

_____

_____

_____

_____

_____

_____

_____

_____

_____

_____

_____

_____

_____

_____

_____

_____

_____

_____

_____

_____

> **"** As we do this work, we
> see cut across themes
> occurring spontaneously:
> *engage the world change
> the world*; *do good, learn
> more*; and *the world needs
> me*. Because these themes
> emerge from experiential
> Deep Learning, they are
> not superficial. . . . Our
> emerging discoveries are
> born from deep learners
> at work. **"**

—*DEEP LEARNING: ENGAGE THE WORLD
CHANGE THE WORLD*, PP. 163–164

# Chapter 04
# The Global Competencies for Deep Learning

Connectivity, societal changes, and the global dynamic are all forces for change in schools and learning. The world is becoming more complex, and the days of set knowledge and accomplishment based on memorizing content are over. We need students who possess a set of Global Competencies that enable them to be creative problem solvers who can collaborate effectively and pursue leadership for action. A recent article, "The Skills Companies Need Most in 2019," cited a need for job seekers to have increasingly complex technical competency, a deep understanding of analytics, perspicuous problem-solving skills, and strong interpersonal abilities. These Global Competencies need to be explicitly developed in students to prepare them for changes taking place now on an international scale.

The first step we took in reimagining learning was to be clear about the outcomes we want for students if they are to gain lifelong success. With our country partners, we asked the question "What is essential for students to know, be able to do, and to be like as human citizens?" The result was the identification of six Global Competencies (6Cs) that describe the skills and attributes needed for learners to flourish as citizens of the world. In our definition, *Deep Learning is the process of acquiring these six Global Competencies: Character, Citizenship, Collaboration, Communication, Creativity, and Critical Thinking.* These competencies encompass compassion, empathy, socio-emotional learning, entrepreneurialism, and related skills for functioning in a complex universe. When learners are immersed in the 6Cs, they learn more—much more—and this learning contributes to their own futures and often to the betterment of their communities and beyond.

## Defining the Competencies

Simply naming the competencies was a step toward clarity, but that alone did not help educators, students, or families to have a shared depth of understanding. The goal of our living laboratory with partner countries was to bring clarity to a set of concepts that are often referenced vaguely by educators.

For example, *Collaboration* is probably easily recognized by teachers, but ask 10 teachers what it means to be an effective collaborator and you will likely get 10 different answers. Then ask them how they measure the depth and quality of the Collaboration and the response becomes even fuzzier. As we investigated future-focused approaches, we found that Communication, Critical Thinking, Creativity, and Collaboration have been on 21st-century lists of skills for almost two decades, but with little robust implementation or effective ways to assess them beyond single classrooms. There have been few attempts at large-scale change in learning and teaching practices guided by the competencies.

In addition to Communication, Collaboration, Creativity, and Critical Thinking, we added Character and Citizenship. Character and Citizenship are proving to be game changers. The Character competency builds the internal qualities of learning to learn; having a positive stance toward life; grit, tenacity, perseverance, and resilience; and the ability to understand empathy and compassion and to act with integrity. The Citizenship competency develops the skills to interact with the external world in a way that builds a global perspective, allows one to act with empathy and compassion for diverse values and worldviews, contributes to human and environmental sustainability, and solves ambiguous, complex real-world problems. Character and Citizenship are foundational qualities that bring to life the skills and behaviors of Creativity, Communication, Collaboration, and Critical Thinking.

Each of the 6Cs is defined by specific dimensions, as shown in Figure 4.1.

## Unique Characteristics of the Global Competencies (6Cs)

Our 6Cs differ from traditional 21st-century lists in three crucial ways—comprehensiveness, precision, and measurability.

**Comprehensiveness**: The Global Competencies are robust and are defined in expansive ways that speak to all disciplines and levels of development. For example, developing Creativity has frequently been reserved for the arts; our Deep Learning Framework recognizes that all disciplines and all levels of growth should develop this crucial competency. Consider the advantage then, when all disciplines and all levels of learning embrace these comprehensive descriptions of competencies. Teachers and students from different subjects and different grades can have rich discussions using a common language. Over time, they experience how these competencies are relevant, and they see how the competencies are authentically and universally applied in the real world.

**Precision**: Making the competencies easy to put into action meant creating a more detailed set of attributes and skills for each competency and ways to measure their development. For each competency, a *Deep Learning Progression* was created. Each competency is broken down into four or five dimensions that provide a detailed picture of the skills, capabilities, and attitudes needed to develop that competency. It is the precise language that guides the learner on a clear pathway to improvement. The progression tools also serve as an anchor for professional dialogue and provide a common language to design and assess Deep Learning.

FIGURE 4.1

# Defining the Six Global Competencies for Deep Learning

### Character
- Proactive stance toward life and learning to learn
- Grit, tenacity, perseverance, and resilience
- Empathy, compassion, and integrity in action

### Citizenship
- A global perspective
- Commitment to human equity and well-being through empathy and compassion for diverse values and worldviews
- Genuine interest in human and environmental sustainability
- Solving ambiguous and complex problems in the real world to benefit citizens

### Collaboration
- Working interdependently as a team
- Interpersonal and team-related skills
- Social, emotional, and intercultural skills
- Managing team dynamics and challenges

### Communication
- Communication designed for audience and impact
- Message advocates a purpose and makes an impact
- Reflection to further develop and improve communication
- Voice and identity expressed to advance humanity

### Creativity
- Economic and social entrepreneurialism
- Asking the right inquiry questions
- Pursuing and expressing novel ideas and solutions
- Leadership to turn ideas into action

### Critical Thinking
- Evaluating information and arguments
- Making connections and identifying patterns
- Meaningful knowledge construction
- Experimenting, reflecting, and taking action on ideas in the real world

CHAPTER 04

**Measurability**: The Deep Learning Progressions are used by students and teachers to assess starting points, develop shared language about success, facilitate development, monitor progress, and measure learners' growth on a continuum over time. Sample progressions for each competency and ways to use them are described in Chapter 5.

## Global Competencies in Action

So, what do these competencies look like in action? Walk into schools and classrooms where Deep Learning is taking root and you will see students who are voraciously curious and asking questions of one another, teachers, families, and experts across the community or globe. There's a constant buzz of conversation as students grapple with real-life problems or investigate ideas so they can make sense of their world. Everyone is highly focused, and you will hear students articulate what they are doing and learning *and why*. They can describe the skills they are mastering and what it will take to get better. They take pride in describing their work for classmates or community members because it is authentic, meaningful, and relevant—it makes a difference. Learning relationships between and among students, families, educators, communities, and society as a whole are repositioned as they focus on a new set of outcomes. Explore a few authentic learning experiences described in the vignettes at the end of this chapter.

## Emerging Insights
### Traditional Versus Deep Learning

Once teachers began to use the 6Cs, they started to notice some important differences in how Deep Learning experiences are used and the outcomes of Deep Learning.

FIGURE 4.2

## Traditional Versus Deep Learning

| Traditional | Deep Learning |
| --- | --- |
| Teacher driven | Student led—teacher framed |
| Transmits existing knowledge | Connects students to real-world, authentic problem solving |
| Compliance oriented | Builds new relationships between and among learners, teachers, families, and community |
| Student is receiver of knowledge | Student is an inquirer and builds knowledge |
| Learning is impersonal | Learning connects meaningfully to student interest and voice |
| Student agency is unclear | Deepens human desire to connect with others to do good |

## Connecting the Dots Among Socio-Emotional Learning, Equity, and Well-Being

A massive shift is emerging from a fixation on standardized test scores to a focus on educating the whole child, equity, and well-being. A recent poll by

Gallup of 2000 district leaders in 2018 indicated that 88% of superintendents agree that student engagement is a key measure of school effectiveness; three quarters say that preparing students to be engaged citizens is a challenge for schools (Stringer, 2018). This shift from focusing on standardized testing to a focus on the whole child and engagement has jumped from 50% to 75% in the past year. When asked how they measured effectiveness of public schools in their communities, only 9% said that standardized tests were important—more popular choices were students' hopes for the future, student engagement, and high school graduation rates (Stringer, 2018). However, student engagement continues to be a problem; we noted earlier that student engagement drops from 74% of fifth graders to only 34% of twelfth graders. We are discovering that participating in Deep Learning results in not only higher engagement but also equitable outcomes and improved well-being for individuals and society.

When students are invited to demonstrate their learning differently and when learning environments include all students as contributors and agents of change, those who are most marginalized encounter hope for school success and begin to see themselves as efficacious. Teachers regularly report to us that students who have been traditionally underserved by schools and systems are thriving as never before. Socio-emotional well-being is not a program or event but is fostered when we create ways of being connected, valued, and safe.

## Deep Learning Connections to Literacy, Numeracy, and Curriculum Outcomes

One of the first questions from teachers is "How will I cover the curriculum if I take time for Deep Learning?" The most important thing to understand is that the 6Cs are not an add-on but rather a way of amplifying the learning. You might think of the 6Cs as a lens that you use to view the curriculum standards. For example, if you are teaching history, you could provide a very shallow coverage limited to dates and events as outlined in the textbook chapters. Using the Deep Learning approach, you might select one of the competencies (such as Critical Thinking) to intentionally pay attention to. When you view the curriculum standards with the question "How can I deepen the level of Critical Thinking?" you might have students explore not only the events but the implications and impact of those events on society and future events. We are seeing countless examples in which teachers begin with their current curriculum as a jumping-off point to go deeper. Deep Learning is not additional content but rather a refinement of the learning process that engages learners, amplifies their knowledge and skills, and drives thinking.

## Getting Started

Once educators, students, and their families experience the excitement and learning potential of Deep Learning, they become more committed; as they interact with others, the contagion factor sets in. One of our principals shared the following advice for starting the Deep Learning journey.

> **Slow and steady is key—changing teacher pedagogy and mindsets around teaching and learning takes time. Start with a shared vision of what skills (6Cs/Global Competencies) students need to be successful in the future and articulate how you give students opportunities to learn/demonstrate these skills in schools. It is important to take time to celebrate the Deep Learning happening in your building—this allows you to build on those great ideas, refining the Deep Learning process and vision for learning.**
>
> **—FRANK BRADICA, PRINCIPAL**

The six protocols in this chapter are a great way to start powerful conversations flowing in your school, district, or community. Use them to explore what is possible, build a shared understanding of Deep Learning, and examine the 6Cs. It's time to find a learning partner or team and dive into Deep Learning!

## Final Thoughts

The definitions of the Global Competencies lead to greater specificity, a common language, and shared understanding of what they look like in practice. The definitions guide conversations and perspectives but are not sufficient for measuring growth on the competency. In Chapter 5, we introduce Deep Learning Progressions, which provide a description of the dimensions of each competency and possible pathways to build student proficiency.

Protocols

 ## Reimagining Learning

Engage learning partners or teams in considering the possibilities for transforming the learning process. The video provides a common experience and serves as a catalyst to unleash conversations about possibilities.

## ② What's Deep About Deep Learning?

Use the vignettes at the end of this chapter to build a shared understanding of attributes of Deep Learning and a vision of what's changing for students and teachers in this new way of learning.

## ③ Global Competencies for Deep Learning

Strategies for fostering Deep Learning are provided to stimulate conversations that bring to the surface your beliefs and assumptions about learning.

## ④ Snapshots of Practice

Teacher quotes offer a jumping-off point to extend knowledge about Deep Learning in powerful conversations.

## ⑤ Going Deeper With Deep Learning

Explore the dimensions of each of the 6Cs and compare them to the approaches in your school and classrooms.

## ⑥ Teacher Voices About Deep Learning

Examine a range of Deep Learning experiences (captured in video) to develop your understanding of what the competencies look like in practice. Choose age levels that will most resonate with your teaching.

## Vignettes

Bee the Change

Ask Yourself: So What?

Learning to Juggle Life's Demands

No Planet B

Daily Deep Learning: Fitness for the Mind

Learning Outside the Box

The Sky Is Not the Limit

Student-Friendly Language: Meet Them Where They're At

## For more information:

Read Chapters 1 and 2 from *Deep Learning: Engage the World Change the World.*

# 01 Reimagining Learning

**Purpose: Generate interest in future thinking using a common experience**

**Process: Think–Pair–Share**

**Time: 45 minutes**

Resource:
- Video at www.deep-learning .global: Rubik's Cube: A Question Waiting to Be Answered

**1** **View a video,** such as Rubik's Cube: A Question Waiting to Be Answered.

**2** **Think about**

- What ideas or possibilities excite you?
- What holds us back from seeing more of this learning in classrooms?

**3** **Pair up** and share your thinking.

**4** **Rotate and share** with a new partner.

**5** **Discuss** key ideas that emerge as a large group.

> ❝ Our best hope collectively is that deep learners inherit the world. ❞

*—DEEP LEARNING: ENGAGE THE WORLD*
*CHANGE THE WORLD, P. 164*

# 02 What's Deep About Deep Learning?

**Purpose: Build a shared understanding of the attributes of Deep Learning**

**Time: 30–60 minutes**

**Process: Share and Swap**

**1** **Select** and read one of the Deep Learning vignettes.

**2** **Consider**

- What attributes/characteristics make this a Deep Learning experience?
- What is changing in the roles of students and teachers in this example?

**3** **Meet up with a partner** and share a summary of your story and what makes it deep. (4 minutes)

**4** **Rotate to a new partner** and discuss what is changing for students and teachers.

**5** **Form a group of four** and synthesize what you have learned from all the stories using the organizer.

**Resources:**

Vignettes:

- Bee the Change
- Ask Yourself: So What?
- Learning to Juggle Life's Demands
- No Planet B
- Daily Deep Learning: Fitness for the Mind
- Learning Outside the Box
- The Sky Is Not the Limit
- Student-Friendly Language: Meet Them Where They're At

| What's deep? (attributes) | What's changing for students? | What's changing for teachers? |
| --- | --- | --- |
| | | |

# 03 Global Competencies for Deep Learning

**Purpose: Build a shared understanding of the Global Competencies—6Cs**

Time: **15–25 minutes**

Process: **Best C Debate**

**1** **Form a group of six** and review the descriptors of the six Global Competencies (see Figure 4.1).

**2** **Provide an example.** Each group member takes responsibility for one Competency and provides an example of what that Competency might look like and sound like in practice or how it is being developed in his or her classroom or school.

**3** **Share** the examples within the group of six.

**4** **Debate** which "C" might best prepare students for the future.

Character

Communication

Creativity

Citizenship

Collaboration

Critical Thinking

# DEFINING THE SIX GLOBAL COMPETENCIES FOR DEEP LEARNING

## Character

- Proactive stance toward life and learning to learn
- Grit, tenacity, perseverance, and resilience
- Empathy, compassion, and integrity in action

## Citizenship

- A global perspective
- Commitment to human equity and well-being through empathy and compassion for diverse values and worldviews
- Genuine interest in human and environmental sustainability
- Solving ambiguous and complex problems in the real world to benefit citizens

## Collaboration

- Working interdependently as a team
- Interpersonal and team-related skills
- Social, emotional, and intercultural skills
- Managing team dynamics and challenges

## Communication

- Communication designed for audience and impact
- Message advocates a purpose and makes an impact
- Reflection to further develop and improve communication
- Voice and identity expressed to advance humanity

## Creativity

- Economic and social entrepreneurialism
- Asking the right inquiry questions
- Pursuing and expressing novel ideas and solutions
- Leadership to turn ideas into action

## Critical Thinking

- Evaluating information and arguments
- Making connections and identifying patterns
- Meaningful knowledge construction
- Experimenting, reflecting, and taking action on ideas in the real world

# 04 Snapshots of Practice

Purpose: **Examine the Global Competencies in action**

Process: **Global Competencies in Action**

**1** **Select a video** of classroom practice (www.deep-learning .global) and look for examples of the Global Competencies (6Cs).

**2** **Record evidence** of what the Competency looks like in practice in the observation template.

**3** **Share your findings** and discuss how the Competencies can be developed.

**4** **Think about a lesson or unit** you will teach soon and consider ways you could include one or more of the 6Cs in the learning design.

Time: **30–45 minutes**

Resources:
Videos at www.deep-learning.global:
- The Enigma Mission, Wooranna Park, Australia
- Deep Learning With Robotics, Uruguay
- Project Root, USA
- Eat Fit, Canada
- Kindergartners as Experts, USA

" Students have untapped potential, but given voice and choice through Deep Learning, we see them influencing dramatic changes to organizations, society, and pedagogy. "

—*DEEP LEARNING: ENGAGE THE WORLD CHANGE THE WORLD, P. 47*

# Snapshots of Practice—6Cs Observation Organizer

| Communication | Creativity | Critical Thinking |
|---|---|---|
| | | |

| Character | Citizenship | Collaboration |
|---|---|---|
| | | |

CHAPTER 04

# 05  Going Deeper With Deep Learning

**Purpose: Extend thinking about what is deep about Deep Learning**

**Time: 15–30 minutes**

**Process: Strategies for Activating Deep Learning and the Four As**

**1** **Provide copies** of the Strategies for Activating Deep Learning.

**2** **Invite** participants to silently read and jot their responses using the Four As organizer.

**3** **Discuss** responses in groups.

## STRATEGIES FOR ACTIVATING DEEP LEARNING

What are your reactions to the following Deep Learning strategies?

→ Support learners to be "infiltrators" and shapers of the future

→ Teach students to be problem designers—shift the thinking from "what is" to "what could be"

→ Rather than just asking students to solve a problem, support them in getting involved beyond the classroom

→ Foster the mindset that we're all perpetual amateurs who always have room to learn and grow

→ Include all children in Deep Learning opportunities, especially those underserved by the current system

→ Believe that children will exceed all our expectations

→ Recognize that innovation and creativity are intrinsic elements of our humanity and let them shine

Source: Roosegaarde, D., in *Deep Learning: Engage the World Change the World*, p. 14

# Four As Organizer

## Agreements

What strategy do I agree with? Why?

## Aspirations

What strategy would I aspire to? Why?

## Argument

What strategy might someone argue with? Why?

## Assumptions

Identify a strategy that holds hidden assumptions. What are they and how might this be concerning?

# 06 Teacher Voices About Deep Learning

**Purpose: Connect with other teachers' experiences of Deep Learning**

**Time: 20–30 minutes**

**Process: Using Knowledge-Building Prompts**

**1** **Form small groups.**

**2** **Choose a quote.** Individually, choose a teacher's quote (on opposite page) and respond to it by using one of the Knowledge-Building prompts.

**3** **Build.** Each member builds on the thinking by using a prompt.

**4** **Share and repeat.** The next member shares their quote and the process is repeated. See a sample conversation.

" It allowed me, as a teacher, to see my students in a whole new light. It reaffirms what I've always believed: Our youth is the key to our future." **MICHELLE HOWE, CANADA**

" Teachers are observing older students developing deeper understanding and tolerance as a result of their role as peer-to-peer teachers." **KAHUKURA CLUSTER, NEW ZEALAND**

" What we experience time and time again is that we give people back their professionalism." **JELLE MARCHAND AND ANNEMARIE ES, NETHERLANDS**

" This has taught me that creativity requires the safety of being allowed to fail. If failure is not an option, students will not risk enough to be creative; instead, they will submit what they think the teachers wants to see so they can be "successful." **ANDREW BRADSHAW, CANADA**

# TEACHERS' QUOTES ABOUT DEEP LEARNING

"I noticed how the boys affirmed and recognized each other for the different skill sets that they each brought to the group. It wasn't all about who academically had the most to offer; they also gained status in the group from other life experiences, like previous building projects they had worked on." **PARAMATTA SCHOOL TEAM, AUSTRALIA**

"Having meaningful collaboration and an opportunity to reflect on what we're doing and why we're doing it is key." **LAURA WHITE, CANADA**

"Starting small and getting buy-in—I totally get that—and we have a fearless attitude that you don't have to have it all figured out." **TEACHER, USA**

"It was great to see students tackling real world issues and coming up with their own original solutions." **RNPS, AUSTRALIA**

"My students finished this project feeling more engaged and confident and that they had gained important skills that they can use in the future." **J. WILKINSON, CANADA**

"Our weather balloon project was a successful multidisciplinary module. Eventually, it included more school subjects, and more teachers participated than designed at the beginning." **AKI KUKKONEN, JANNE NIEMINE, & JUSSI ROMS, FINLAND**

"We found that even though our project was mainly based on Collaboration, because of the scope of the project, it hit on all other Competencies effectively." **RYAN DUFRANE, ALICIA MORRALLEE, & JEREMY MAHONEY, CANADA**

"I am amazed by how the technology impacts children's learning— not only the motivation but they are learning new things without even noticing it." **TEACHER, URUGUAY**

"I have taught lower elementary for 10 years now and have never been a part of anything as meaningful and important as this . . . I have seen my first graders rise to the challenge of empathizing with others from all around the world when inherently they are still at a very egocentric age." **KEVIN HALL & MADELINE PARTHUM, USA**

## KNOWLEDGE-BUILDING PROMPTS

I wonder . . .

I still need to understand . . .

My theory is . . .

Building on this idea . . .

This does not explain . . .

We need evidence for . . .

I would want to investigate . . .

A promising idea . . .

Another way of looking at it . . .

An example might be . . .

A comparison/analogy is . . .

Another way of saying this is . . .

# SAMPLE KNOWLEDGE-BUILDING DISCUSSION

**Person A:** I chose this quote: "What we experience time and time again is that we give people back their professionalism." Another way of saying this is that the Deep Learning supports teachers as thinkers, as contributors.

**Person B:** My theory is that if you treat teachers respectfully, allow them to come together to share their ideas and reflect on their practice that helps them to become better teachers.

**Person C:** An example might be when we worked on the Invention Convention last year; we were provided some release time, we got together frequently to plan, and we all felt like we came away learning a lot . . . and so did the kids!

**Person D:** A promising idea would be to take the work we did last year with that project and see if we could apply it to this Deep Learning work. It might allow us to refine it even more.

**Person B:** Yes! Building on that idea . . . if we collect more evidence along the way, especially when we are reflecting on the learning, it might show how we grow professionally.

CHAPTER 04

# Bee the Change

There is a hive of Deep Learning happening at Bessborough School. When Nick Mattatall, principal, and his lead team attended the NPDL Capacity Building Institute, they were inspired by a Deep Learning task that was conducted in a Grade 3 class more than 1,200 miles away. That task encouraged students to embrace competencies like Citizenship, Collaboration, and Critical Thinking by exploring the dwindling bee population.

Mattatall and his team examined the task and redesigned it for their school. Grade 6 teacher Julie Gautreau asked the students how they could protect the bees. The students buzzed with ideas. She says, "When the students realized that one third of everything we eat comes from pollinators, the students decided that they had to do something to raise awareness." So, the class set off to conduct research and communicate their learning. They created 3D models, Minecraft bee hive tours, and bee hotels. They led a showcase to parents, partnered with other classes, and even replicated bee dances using Spheros (a robotic sphere). All students, even those struggling with attendance issues, were excited about the learning. Gautreau says, "The students were fully engaged. . . . This was their baby! My role as a teacher changed!"

> "Failure should not be the end. It should be the beginning of the learning." Student

> "This challenge was a great opportunity for creative people to thrive, but also a terrifying experience for noncreative people." Student

Another class learned about the UN 17 Sustainable Development Goals and collected more than 20,000 single-use plastic bags and applied a design process to prototype something useful. Students got creative and made mats, chairs, kites, hair accessories, flip flops, kites, and lamp shades. They even made plastic bag clothing and hosted a fashion show for the rest of the school.

Soon, the whole school was stung by the Deep Learning bug. In the following year, Mattatal led a schoolwide gardening day involving partners from Tree Canada. They transformed their school grounds by planting fruit trees, berries, rhubarb, tomatoes, and flowers. Fruits and vegetables were then shared with their neighbours and foodbanks and used in the school's breakfast program. The students made bi-weekly floral deliveries to the local seniors' residence. Seeds were harvested, dried, and used in bird feeders. Families watered the gardens through the summer months. The schoolwide Deep Learning experience quickly evolved into communitywide engagement and learning.

Throughout these Deep Learning experiences, the Bessborough teachers fulfilled the curriculum expectations. For example, in Grade 7, students learn about sustainability. In Grade 4, students learn about habitats. And, math was not forgotten. Mattatall explains, "Some classes took a field trip to the local apiary and learned about bee keeping. They learned how to make algorithmic calculations to maximize pollination. Talk about real-life math!"

They say that when a bee finds a good source of nectar, it returns to the hive and does a "waggle dance" to communicate its location to its bee peers. In the New Pedagogies for Deep Learning global network, this example gives rise to our own kind of "waggle dance" and encourages all of us to be the change we wish to see for all kids in the world.

# Ask Yourself:
# So What?

Deep Learning isn't just about teaching what is relevant or building skills to prepare for a changing world. It's about reminding the students of their relevance in the world and how they can make a difference. Teachers who shift to an activator stance have created a habit of asking themselves an important question: "So, what real difference will this make?" In Terri Kirkey's classroom, learners drive their own sense of learning and purpose. Let's take a closer look at how she cultivates this.

Creating an interactive and mutually respectful learning environment is foundational to Terri's work. Terri creates a culture of inquiry by reviewing the purpose and practice of knowledge-building circles. Protocols that reinforce collaboration, growth mindset, and curiosity set the tone for asking questions, wondering, and exploring. This past year, their big question centred around "How can we use our learning to make a difference?" From the get-go, the message to students is *this learning matters and you matter*.

To feed this question of making a difference, students turn to various resources and partners beyond the teacher. And they are regularly reminded that they, too, bring critical experiences and knowledge to contribute to the classroom dynamic. Terri explains, "Student curiosities, questions, and ideas drove the direction of the learning. We "shared our brains" and celebrated the experts in our very own room. Students had many opportunities to share their personal knowledge and connections. Students played an active role in the documentation on our Learning Journey Wall. They helped create printable slides to be posted and students facilitated the connections we made. Students were also involved in the learning goals and assessment by co-creating the success criteria." A strong sense of student ownership pervades the classroom.

> It all begins with a simple question: So what?

Students in this class see themselves as partners in the learning design and also as agents of change. Terri sums it up: As we approached new learning, we often asked the question *So what?* Why are we learning this? Can we connect this new learning to our past learning and/or experiences and how can it shape our learning for the future? We celebrated connections between what we already knew and what we learned. We began to recognize that these connections help us to deepen learning. We also noticed that it is better to learn collaboratively because we all have contributions to make. Through knowledge building and sharing, we learned that we can teach one another many things and together, we learn more!

When students see themselves as efficacious, they feel confident about sharing their learning more publicly. Terri explains, "Our learning journey has been shared and celebrated on our classroom blog but also on the school Twitter feed and in the school newsletter. Making our experiences visible to others helps initiate and then expand the conversation for students, their families, and our school community. It also shows that our learning experiences are linked to our schoolwide commitment to make a difference locally and globally."

It all begins with a simple question: So what?

# Learning to Juggle Life's Demands

Across New Zealand, young students participated in a nationwide shared Read Aloud and used digital tools such as Edmodo and Padlet to connect with students from all over the country. Edmodo allowed students to communicate with each other online in a contained, supervised community. Their chosen book was *Juggling With Mandarins*, written by New Zealander V. M. Jones. The literature provided a platform for developing Global Competencies in Communication, Critical Thinking and . . . life.

Students introduced themselves to peers from distant schools by using Padlet. Then teachers posed weekly tasks for six weeks. Some of these tasks involved typical communication and critical thinking approaches. For example, students were to write predictions about the book, interpret language, and visualize characters or analyze plot developments. Other tasks were more open-ended, like creating a Twitter profile for their fictional character or a dialogue between two characters using the texting feature.

> ## "If you are really passionate about something, then go ahead and do it."
>
> Student

Students also built on each other's thinking by responding to each other's texts. They learned how to constructively and politely disagree with each other while online—a relevant digital literacy skill for all of us. This back-and-forth naturally evolved into providing peer feedback. In one post, a student writes, "It looks like great work though unfortunately it is upside down. You can change this using. . . . Good luck!"

Literature is a launchpad for reflection, and students shared those insights in a safe online space. One student writes, "I chose this quote because it's true: You can't make an omelette without breaking eggs." The other replies, "I had never heard of that saying before, I had to look it up. I think it's true that you have to make sacrifices to something else in life. I find this very inspiring. Thanks for introducing this to me."

The learning stretched beyond Communication and Critical Thinking. This task provided a platform for students to share more personal thoughts. They used this opportunity to juggle life's questions. One student processed how she handled a painful friendship. Another shared insight that life doesn't always unfold as planned. Another student remarked, "I think it could be a life lesson for kids our age about how kids should not be afraid of their parents and let them know how they feel without being scared." This serves as another reminder that when you create an interactive learning environment and establish partnerships that foster trust and mutual respect, the learning goes well beyond the curriculum.

# No Planet B

The educators of Springlands School in New Zealand must have felt the weight of the world on their shoulders when they decided to initiate a schoolwide Deep Learning task for all 424 of their students. No Planet B was an integrated, cross-grade collaborative performance addressing the world's environmental challenges and spanned over seven weeks.

The educators tapped parents and partners to support the learning. Cultural advisors, dance teachers, a professional theatre company, and the University of Norway all contributed to mounting the production. One parent exclaimed, "As a parent of children growing up on this planet, I valued the opportunity for them to not only learn about some of the issues facing this planet but to have a voice to demonstrate their learning through song and dance and to demonstrate what they can do to really make a difference."

A local school and members of the community constituted the enthusiastic audience. As the deputy principal says, "The community was stunned and entertained with the quality and calibre of the performances. . . . They could not believe that the children of the school were able to achieve a performance of such a professional standard."

One teacher reported that despite the extra effort involved, it was well worth it. She says, "It has been exciting to watch the children truly engaged in this experience. They have driven their learning throughout the process, had authentic opportunities to problem solve and reflect, and have been empowered in the difference that they have made to themselves as learners and the shift in thinking created across our school community."

This is one more good example of Deep Learning. We are reminded that when young students demonstrate their boundless potential, the world is in good hands. It's our shared interest, after all. With our support to foster innovative and thoughtful future leaders, our vulnerable planet may not need a Planet B.

> When young students demonstrate their boundless potential, the world is in good hands.

# Daily Deep Learning: Fitness for the Mind

David McCully, a phys-ed teacher, had become frustrated over the years. His energetic fifteen-year-old boys were not demonstrating maturity in collaboration. In spite of his best efforts, they, just didn't seem to get it. He needed to try something different.

He asked the boys a question: "What makes a great teammate?" After some conversation, he cued up a Skype call with a professional athlete to chime in on the conversation and this hooked the students' interest. Students then articulated their own criteria, which included responsibility, respect, positive attitude, dedication, and selflessness. It was this list that became the students' shared reference point for the next month. They used this list to self-evaluate, set weekly goals, and reflect regularly. They also created videos to communicate these concepts, which encouraged them to use different skills than they normally used in phys-ed. A final reflective journal invited them to review their progress over their weekly surveys. Last, McCully asked students to identify others who could evaluate them on the way they collaborate. The boys chose contacts and others from inside and beyond the class to comment on the criteria they had formerly created.

> "You need these skills for your entire life."
> Student

That was a lightbulb moment for students. Until then, many students did not realize how they were presenting to others. One boy said, "It's allowed me to see the good stuff I do and the bad stuff I do." Another reflected, "You could be doing something damaging to other people and you don't know it." Others recognized that the skill of collaboration is transferable, that "relationships off the field are as important as on the field" and that "you need these skills for your entire life." In the fast-paced world of schools, we often assume that students understand our expectations. Especially at the secondary level, we assume they don't need concepts spelled out so plainly. McCully found that the explicit focus and breaking it down into component parts helped students to understand how their behaviors were affecting others.

This teacher's experience reminds us that Deep Learning can happen daily within a regular classroom setting. With explicit attention to the competencies and some regular opportunities for meaningful reflection, students can acquire deeper understanding that can get them in great shape for tackling future challenges.

# Learning Outside the Box

Grades 1 and 2 teacher Pamela Newton couldn't quite believe it herself. Her students were so engaged in saving the dwindling monarch butterfly population that they didn't bother with their video games anymore. She said, "One student who used to talk about his Xbox every day, cannot stop talking about monarch butterflies. He works on the garden at recess and eagerly looks for butterfly books in the library. It is exciting to see his curiosity captured."

But the engagement didn't end when the bell rang. Parents described how the learning spilled over into their homes. One parent reported, "Alex really enjoyed learning about monarch butterflies. She often came home and told all of us interesting facts that she learned about. It has also made an impact on me while whipper snipping yesterday, I avoided all of the milkweed." Another cheered, "I think you know, but Brooke LOVED everything about monarchs. We had lots of talk at home. I now get the daily report on what the caterpillars look like. I like how you tied in art and writing as well. The seed bombs and community involvement were awesome. I love the out-of-the-box learning and feel this study looked at so many things. The country study too . . . started with monarchs but covered so many other subjects. The book on YouTube is so cool. We have shared it with friends and relatives, and everyone is quite impressed."

> It is exciting to see his curiosity captured.

Newton easily found cross-curricular connections to generate a Deep Learning Task. The students Skyped with a butterfly expert and spoke to a contact in Mexico to learn more about the plight of the monarchs. They also studied local and global migration patterns and maps to learn about the dwindling monarch population (geography) and then studied the life cycle of butterflies (science). Propelled to take action, the students created information flyers with QR codes (media) and crafted seed bombs to sell in the community. They also composed a digital short-story book (language) to get the message across. They enhanced their community garden and measured tree stumps to attract more butterflies (math). The local newspaper soon caught wind of the student energy and featured them, further drawing attention to their campaign.

Give students a choice whether they want to feel empowered to make a difference in the real world or in the imaginary world and there is no contest. The real world wins every time. Step out of the box and they will put aside the games. There's a new way of learning and students are showing us they can lead the way.

# The Sky Is Not the Limit

When some teachers from a tiny elementary school in Finland launched into Deep Learning, they set their sights beyond the skies. Three classes of Grades 5 and 8 students engaged in a multidisciplinary module that covered physics, environment, and technology. The students designed a weather balloon that would soar into the atmosphere and collect data on temperature, humidity, windspeed, and atmospheric pressure, allowing the students to predict weather days in advance. The project was a bold undertaking and earned Veikkola School a prestigious international award.

Digital played a central role in the student learning. For example, students video-recorded their experiments and used 3D printing to fabricate special parts required for the balloon. They had to design equipment that would collect data and provide video while the balloon was in flight. They also facilitated real-time video and pictures that were shared on Instagram.

Ironically, designing the weather balloon wasn't the real challenge. It was learning how to navigate through bureaucracy to legally and safely launch the balloon. So teachers Aki Kukkonen, Janne Nieminen, and Jussi Roms tapped multiple partners, including an amateur radio league, the Finnish Metereological Institute and Transport Safety Agency, and the Lammi Biological Station at the University of Helsinki. Their professional expertise and access to resources and equipment enabled this lofty learning design to take flight. The teachers recognized the relevant life lessons these partners provided. "The project was not just to make the weather balloon fly, but to follow laws and to show pupils how much pre-work and partners a quality project needs." They added, "It was essential to learn how to find right partners, follow the instructions given by official authorities and cooperate with them all."

**From a small town school to the world and a little beyond . . .**

Check out a short video of the project: https://youtu.be/2kxciRZS06s

# Student-Friendly Language: Meet Them Where They're At

Mark Twain once said, "Don't use a five-dollar word when a fifty-cent word will do." It's with that approachable spirit that Michelle Howe teaches her secondary students. She uses "student-friendly" versions of the Deep Learning Progressions to explicitly engage them in her Grade 12 geography class, and it's made a real impact.

Student versions of the tools are available on the NPDL hub and are used throughout the global partnership with students as young as kindergarten. The accessible language allows students to develop a shared language and deeper understanding about the Global Competencies. These student-friendly progressions also allow them to self-assess and peer-assess. It all adds up to this: When students can deeply understand and apply concepts, their independence and confidence grow.

Howe focused on two Competencies: Critical Thinking and Creativity and used the student-friendly progressions throughout a monthlong learning experience. She started with a Google Form pre-assessment to determine students' strengths and needs. This gave her useful information to guide her instruction. Then at midpoint, students completed a self-assessment. That informed her teacher–student conferencing meetings and allowed her to provide specific feedback and guidance to each student. At the end of the project, Howe conducted a post-assessment using the rubrics. Students also did a self-assessment where they reflected on their Critical Thinking and Creativity. At every stage, the rubrics provide a clear lens and pathway to success. Howe says, "Depending on where they were in their process, as a class or in their own groups, we set up what criteria applied to their inquiry and discussed ways they could show and improve on their Critical Thinking and Creativity."

> Student friendly learning progressions illuminate the way for students, taking the intimidation out of learning life's important skills.

Student friendly learning progressions illuminate the way for students, taking the intimidation out of learning life's important skills. And when students get it, they appreciate it. As one student said, "Thank you for the opportunity to go out of my comfort zone and solve a seemingly impossible world issue.  It has told me I am capable of more than I thought."

**"** The role of the teacher is to create the conditions for invention rather than provide ready-made knowledge. **"**

—SEYMOUR PAPERT

# Chapter 05
# The Four Elements of Learning Design

Back in the sixties, at MIT, Seymour Papert was dismissed by academics when he suggested that children would use computers as instruments for learning and enhancing creativity, because computers were rare and so very expensive. Fast-forward 50 years—most adults and teens possess a handheld device far more powerful than those original mainframes and can connect themselves to knowledge, experts, and resources ubiquitously. So, the question becomes, "How do we shift from the kind of content-based learning of the last century to empowering teachers and students to create learning experiences that build on students' innate curiosity and desire to solve complex issues and impact the world?"

Change can be difficult, so we have identified four key elements of Deep Learning and an organizer that helps teachers design Deep Learning experiences. We know that we learn best when we have time for meaningful conversation, access to quality examples of practice, and time to experiment with effective feedback. In this chapter, you will explore a description of the Four Elements of Learning Design and view several videos of learning designs in action. So, gather some learning partners and prepare to investigate a simple but powerful way to start designing Deep Learning experiences.

When the Four Elements depicted in Figure 5.1 are integrated during the planning stage, they enable teachers and students to design learning experiences that are mapped to student strengths and needs; create new knowledge using authentic, relevant problem solving; and help students identify their talents, purpose, and passion. These Four Elements can be used by individuals and teams to promote powerful conversations, brainstorm ideas, and plan ways to deepen the learning. Imagine a group of teachers using the space around the graphic to capture their decisions about how to best address each of the design elements. Let's explore the essential features of each element and the decisions that impact the learning design.

FIGURE 5.1

## Four Elements of Learning Design

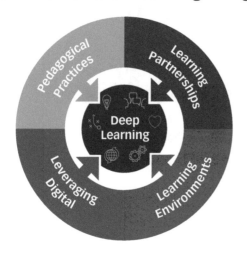

# Learning Partnerships

Dramatically new learning relationships that shift voice, control, and interactions are emerging and are at the heart of Deep Learning. Students and teachers aren't only partnering with one another but are also creatively finding ways to partner with others across classes, schools, and countries and with parents, experts, and the community. The new relationships have the potential to reframe learning by connecting learners to authentic opportunities locally, nationally, and globally. As learning becomes more relevant and authentic, it moves beyond the classroom walls and builds on interests and talents organically.

This new focus on relationships is an accelerator of learning but does not happen by chance. It requires the cultivation of new roles for students, teachers, families, and community.

## Students as Co-Designers and Co-Learners

Students are becoming increasingly engaged in determining, designing, and assessing their learning. This is accelerated when teachers feel confident in releasing control and invite student voice and agency. Students begin to take responsibility for their learning when they understand how they learn, how to give and receive feedback, and how to take action. Teachers facilitate this growth by linking learning to student interests, talents, and needs; providing powerful feedback; and instilling a sense of belonging and connectedness that fosters innovation and risk-taking. One way that teachers get started is by increasing student choice about topics or providing optional ways for students to demonstrate their learning. Gradually, as the culture of trust is deepened, students begin to take more responsibility for self-monitoring and leading their own learning. Teachers are intentional in scaffolding learning so that students have the skills to collaborate, give feedback, and make wise decisions. The new roles of co-learners and co-designers increase meaningful student engagement and also push on the traditional role of teachers. Finding the right balance between structure and independence will be unique to each context.

## Learning Environments

The second element of learning design is the learning environment, which has two essential and interrelated aspects. The first involves the cultivation of a culture of learning that unleashes the potential of adults and students alike and the second addresses the design of physical and virtual space that optimizes the acquisition of the competencies.

# Cultures of Learning

If we want cultures of learning that cultivate energy, creativity, curiosity, imagination, and innovation, then we need to create learning spaces where students feel safe in taking risks. This begins when teachers intentionally create norms of belonging in which every voice matters, model empathy, deeply listen to student needs and interests, and structure tasks so that students feel competent as learners. Autonomy is cultivated when students have choice, and competence develops when they are challenged beyond their comfort level. The results are high levels of engagement and motivation. So, what does it look like in practice? While there is no recipe, we see some common characteristics in classroom cultures that are moving toward Deep Learning (see Figure 5.2).

FIGURE 5.2

## Characteristics of Cultures Moving Toward Deep Learning

| Students asking the questions. | They have skills and language to pursue inquiry and are not passively taking in the answers from teachers. |
|---|---|
| Questions valued above answers. | The process of learning, discovering, and conveying is as important as the end result. |
| Varied models for learning. | Selection of pedagogical models is matched to student needs and interests. Students are supported in reaching for the next challenge. |
| Explicit connections to real-world application. | Learning designs are not left to chance but are scaffolded and built on relevance and meaning. |
| Collaboration. | Students possess skills to collaborate within the classroom and beyond. |
| Assessment of learning that is embedded, transparent, and authentic. | Students define personal goals, monitor progress toward success criteria, and engage in feedback with peers and others. |

Source: Fullan & Quinn, 2016

Throughout this book, you will find practical suggestions to answer the question "How will we develop norms of respect, collaboration, a trusting community, a sense of risk-taking, time for curiosity and creativity, and student voice and agency?"

# Physical and Virtual Environments

If we want our students to be curious, connected collaborators, then we need to provide multidimensional spaces that offer flexibility for large- and small-group collaboration; quiet places for reflection and cognition; active areas for investigation, inquiry, communication, and documentation; and rich resources that are transparently accessible. Innovative learning spaces are emerging across the globe. One example is Derrimut School, where the learning spaces are organized into "caves" for students who need to think deeply about something, "watering holes" for students who need to share information and collaborate, and "campfires" for the students to share about the learning journey. To see innovative learning environments in action, view Video Derrimut Public School (www.deep-learning.global). Across our network of schools, it is not about the structures per se but the ways they are used to intentionally support learning. We see rigorous, innovative learning in the most traditional of spaces—it takes a bit of ingenuity and vision—while we also see expensive new structures that lack a pedagogical thoughtfulness that matches the digital richness.

Making the walls of the classroom transparent is not merely about redesigning space; it requires taking stock of the ways we can connect inside and outside the classroom. If we want students to seek out experts in the community and beyond and to build knowledge from multiple fields, then we need to help them identify ways to connect, skills to discern sources critically, and ways to build relationships in a diverse world. Our work has shown that when students are engaged, they begin to connect both inside and outside the school and make learning a 24/7 proposition.

Learning environments are changing rapidly both culturally as new partnerships emerge and physically as the walls of learning become transparent. One of the most powerful ways to make these new connections and open limitless possibilities is the third element of learning design—leveraging digital.

## Leveraging Digital

We use the term *digital* in place of *technology* to signal that we are not focused on the digital tools themselves—the devices, software, or apps of the day— but rather on the role that interaction with digital can play in enhancing Deep Learning. Effective use of digital facilitates Deep Learning partnerships with students, families, community members, and experts—regardless of geographic location—and supports students' capacity to take control of their own learning both within and outside the classroom walls.

The teacher's role becomes one of ensuring that students have the skills and competencies to discern, critically assess, discover, and create new knowledge in innovative ways. They can use digital ubiquitously to engage, motivate, and amplify learning. In the past, we mostly asked students to solve problems that had already been solved. As we move from asking our students to be consumers of knowledge to asking them to create and apply their solutions to real-world problems, the digital world gives us a mechanism to connect and collaborate locally and on a global scale.

This myriad of options generates crucial decision points for teachers regarding the thoughtful use of digital, including media and digital citizenship, as an integral part of the learning. In the learning design, teachers need to select the most appropriate digital choices from a vast array of options and ensure that students have the skills to not simply use these options but to be discriminating in how they employ these options in building knowledge, collaborating or producing knowledge, and sharing new learning. Leveraging digital is integral to the fourth element of learning design—pedagogical practices.

# Pedagogical Practices

This fourth element brings precision to the question "What is the best way for students to achieve these Deep Learning goals and success criteria?" When teachers want their students to experience deep collaborative learning that extends beyond the classroom walls, they must recognize that it means making changes to their own practice. When we started focusing on Deep Learning, the first question from teachers was "Does this mean that what I was doing was wrong?" The answer is a resounding *no*. It's not about throwing out what we already know; it's about putting a new lens of depth over many of the effective traditional pedagogies that remain essential for Deep Learning. It is about eliminating the outdated, ineffective ones. Teachers who embrace Deep Learning think in terms of creating Deep Learning experiences and richer units of learning, providing time to develop the competencies, and often utilizing teaching models such as inquiry, problem and project-based learning, and multidisciplinary learning. These models most often require the teacher to take on the role of activator and for students to have choice in and take responsibility for their learning. These longer learning experiences most often engage students in authentic, relevant problems or simulations where learning is applied in the real world. Most often, this combination of choice, more meaningful tasks, and increased student responsibility leads to increased engagement—the first attribute suggesting a deeper learning process. So how do teachers get started?

Teachers are faced with a tsunami of options. There is no one way to design Deep Learning, but the first step is to develop the skill and knowledge of both foundational and innovative pedagogical practices so that they can activate learning seamlessly as the learning experiences evolve. Teachers should start with what they know and then identify new practices they want to learn more about. Figure 5.3 captures a few of the proven pedagogical practices that are used widely in designing Deep Learning, along with innovative practices that are creating a fusion of what works. The graphic is in constant evolution as new practices are refined and shared collaboratively among our partners.

Teachers need to know how to scaffold experiences and challenges, finely tune them to the needs and interests of students, and maximize learning through relevance, authenticity, and real-world connections. They need a wide repertoire of strategies to meet diverse student needs and interests and a deep understanding of proven models (such as inquiry and problem-based learning). In addition to these foundational effective practices, teachers will develop expertise in innovative practices and uses of digital for both learning and assessment.

Today, bright spots of inquiry-based learning, problem-based learning, project-based learning, integrative thinking, knowledge building, and digital innovations can be found across schools and countries. There is no one cookie-cutter approach to facilitating Deep Learning. The four learning design elements combined with the six Global Competencies (6Cs) are helping thousands of teachers ask critical design questions and be more intentional in developing learning experiences that challenge and extend the learning to make it deep. The Learning Design Poster provides a visual organizer of how the Four Elements combine to foster Deep Learning experiences. It's a great anchor for collaborative design sessions. Explore mini-cases, learning design examples, and videos that bring the combination of these Four Elements to life throughout this book.

FIGURE 5.3

## Fusion of Effective Pedagogical Practices and Emerging Innovative Practices

### Proven Pedagogical Practices

**Models**
Inquiry • Problem Based
Experiential • Simulations

**Design Skills**
Universal Design • Scaffolding
Gradual Release of Responsibility
Learning Goals and Success
Criteria • Backward Design

**Strategies**
Cooperative Learning
Graphic Organizers
Reciprocal Teaching
Thinking Skills
Feedback
Interventions

**Assessment**
Formative
Summative

### FUSION

### Emerging Innovative Practices

**Models**
Learning Co-Design • Blended and Online
Learning • Design Thinking • STEAM
Computational Thinking • Student Agency

**Strategies and Tools**
Gamification • Virtual Simulations
Podcasts • Webinars • Sketch Noting
Robotics and Programming • Virtual Tours
Virtual Manipulatives • Digital Badging
Animation • Synchronous/Asynchronous
Cloud Communication and Collaboration
Translation and Language Learning Tools
Augmented/Virtual Reality/Mixed Reality
Social Media • Flexible Learning
Environments • Pedagogical
Documentation

**Assessment**
Self and Peer Assessment
Community (Local/Global) Feedback
Adaptive Learning/Learning Analytics

## Final Thoughts

Using the Global Competencies and the Four Elements of Learning Design provides a powerful foundation for learning. The collaborative processes that build capacity and accelerate the shift from current to future practices propel learning for all. This is the subject of Chapter 6.

## Protocols

### 7 The Four Elements of Learning Design

Engage learning partners or teams in building an understanding of the Four Elements of Deep Learning design through a jigsaw strategy and apply this understanding to classroom experiences through video observation.

### 8 The Four Elements in Practice

Use the organizer to analyze the ways you are using the four elements currently and to consider ways to amplify or expand their use.

## Resource

Four Elements of Learning Design Poster

## For more information:

Read Chapters 5 and 6 from *Deep Learning: Engage the World Change the World.*

CHAPTER 05

# 07 The Four Elements of Learning Design

Purpose: **Build understanding of the Four Elements of the Learning Design**

Process: **Applying the Four Elements Using a Jigsaw Strategy**

Time: **30–60 minutes**

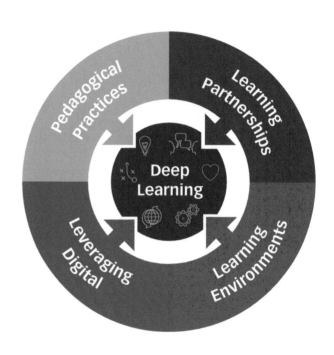

**1** **Form** groups of four and number 1 to 4.

**2** **Review** the descriptions of the Four Elements of Learning Design at the beginning of the chapter. Each person reads one of the four elements and makes notes in the four elements Organizer in the "What Is This?" section. Share key ideas with group members.

**3** **Select** a video from the resource list.

**4** **As you watch** the video, record observations of your element and make notes in the organizer.

**5** **Share** observations and evidence of your element.

**6** **Choose** another video clip and rotate assigned elements to observe and share.

**7** **Imagine** you want to convey these four elements to your school community on a poster. Create a visual representation of the four elements using colorful markers or digital.

## Resources:

Four Elements of Learning Design Poster

Videos at www.deep-learning.global:

• Kindergartners as Experts, USA
• Young Minds of the Future, Australia
• Eat Fit, Canada
• Project ROOT, USA
• Writing Conference: Peers, Canada
• Students Tackle Climate Change, Finland
• Learning Partnerships at the OCSB (Global Solutions Project), Canada

# The Four Elements Notetaker

What is this?

What is this?

What is this?

What is this?

Deep Learning — Pedagogical Practices, Learning Partnerships, Leveraging Digital, Learning Environments

CHAPTER 05

# The Four Elements Learning Design Organizer

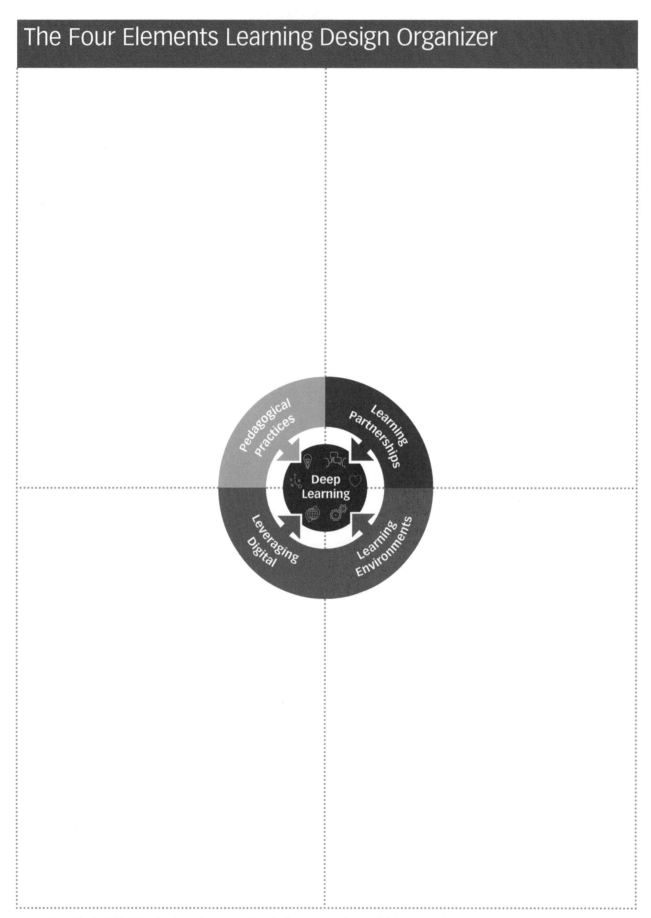

> **❝** Teachers don't need to start from scratch in selecting models but can draw from a rich history of Deep Learning approaches. **❞**
>
> *—DEEP LEARNING: ENGAGE THE WORLD CHANGE THE WORLD, P. 84*

# 08 The Four Elements in Practice

Purpose: **Examine current ways the four elements are used in Deep Learning and identify ways to increase their use**

Time: **20–40 minutes**

Process: **Currently We . . . In the Future We Could . . .**

**1** **Review** the Four Elements of Learning Design introduced in Protocol 7.

**2** **Consider** these questions and capture your thinking on the organizer:

- How do you currently use the four elements in your classroom or school?
- What could you do in the future to focus more deeply on each Element?

**3** **Review** your responses and select one or two actions you will take to improve the quality of Learning Design.

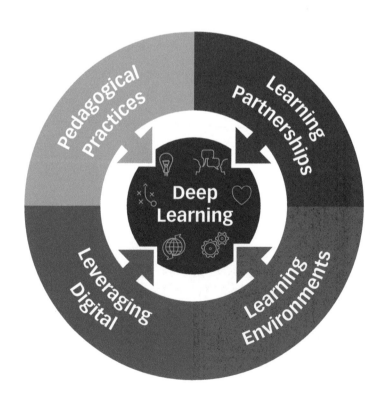

# Four Elements in Practice Organizer

| | Currently we . . . | In the future, we could . . . |
|---|---|---|
| **Pedagogical** Practices | | |
| **Learning** Partnerships | | |
| **Learning** Environments | | |
| **Leveraging** Digital | | |

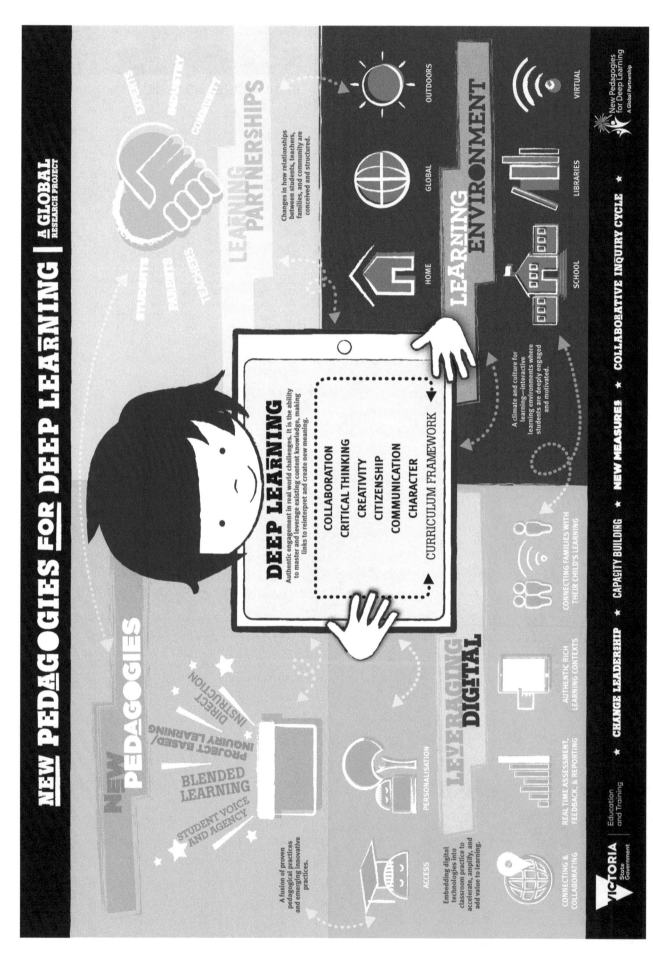

**NEW PEDAGOGIES FOR DEEP LEARNING** | A GLOBAL RESEARCH PROJECT

**LEARNING PARTNERSHIPS**

EXPERTS · INDUSTRY · COMMUNITY · STUDENTS · PARENTS · TEACHERS

Changes in how relationships between students, teachers, families, and community are conceived and structured.

OUTDOORS

GLOBAL

HOME

**LEARNING ENVIRONMENT**

VIRTUAL

LIBRARIES

SCHOOL

A climate and culture for learning—interactive learning environments where students are deeply engaged and motivated.

**DEEP LEARNING**

Authentic engagement in real world challenges. It is the ability to master and leverage existing content knowledge, making links to reinterpret and create new meaning.

COLLABORATION
CRITICAL THINKING
CREATIVITY
CITIZENSHIP
COMMUNICATION
CHARACTER

CURRICULUM FRAMEWORK

**NEW PEDAGOGIES**

DIRECT INSTRUCTION

PROJECT BASED/ INQUIRY LEARNING

BLENDED LEARNING

STUDENT VOICE AND AGENCY

A fusion of proven pedagogical practices and emerging innovative practices.

PERSONALISATION

ACCESS

Embedding digital technologies into classroom practice to accelerate, amplify, and add value to learning.

**LEVERAGING DIGITAL**

AUTHENTIC RICH LEARNING CONTEXTS

REAL TIME ASSESSMENT, FEEDBACK, & REPORTING

CONNECTING FAMILIES WITH THEIR CHILD'S LEARNING

CONNECTING & COLLABORATING

New Pedagogies for Deep Learning
A Global Partnership

VICTORIA State Government | Education and Training

CHANGE LEADERSHIP ★ CAPACITY BUILDING ★ NEW MEASURES ★ COLLABORATIVE INQUIRY CYCLE ★

" The crucial challenge at hand is to change the culture of schooling. Those running school systems will need to move away from notions of command, control, and ordered change from above and, instead, work to create emergent systems that support teachers and students owning their learning and taking it in new directions. Students, teachers, principals, parents, and districts must push from the bottom and the middle. "

—*DEEP LEARNING: ENGAGE THE WORLD CHANGE THE WORLD*, P. 84

" Collaborative work is a key driver in shifting behavior. It is the social glue that moves the organization toward coherence. "

—*COHERENCE: THE RIGHT DRIVERS IN ACTION FOR SCHOOLS, DISTRICTS, AND SYSTEMS*, P. 73

# Chapter 06
# The Collaborative Inquiry Process

Collaboration is at the heart of Deep Learning. Because Deep Learning involves innovation, and highly focused new practices, it needs mechanisms for developing and accessing powerful ideas. If teachers are to make a rapid shift into new practices, they need the support that comes from working with others to consolidate new thinking and innovative practices. Moving from pockets of innovation by a few teachers to having all teachers embrace Deep Learning and rethink their practices means we need a process that mobilizes the whole school or district to create conditions that support the new way.

In this chapter, we zero in on the collaborative inquiry process that permeates all aspects of Deep Learning. This compelling reflective process cultivates powerful conversations. It may be used by teachers to design Deep Learning experiences, by teams to collaboratively assess student work and progress, and by schools and districts to examine current models, practices, and assumptions for learning and design systems and plans to create the conditions needed for Deep Learning to flourish.

## What Is Collaborative Inquiry?

*Collaborative inquiry* is a process for examining existing practices and assumptions through engagement with colleagues or peers. It is a powerful strategy for change because it simultaneously promotes professional dialogue and contributes directly to improved student learning. It is not only a process for problem solving and refining individual practices but also a system approach for using evidence of student learning to build collaborative school teams and effective schools.

The modified collaborative inquiry process depicted in Figure 6.1 has four simple phases (adapted from the Deming Institute, n.d.).

Getting started in Deep Learning accelerates when teachers collaborate within and across schools and when they have protocols, examples, and a process for

FIGURE 6.1

## Collaborative Inquiry Cycle

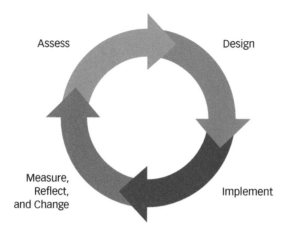

Assess

Design

Measure, Reflect, and Change

Implement

**Assess** current strengths and needs

**Design** a strategy for change

**Implement** the strategy using formative assessment data to monitor and adjust

**Measure, reflect, and change** by using evidence of progress to evaluate success and inform next steps

Source: New Pedagogies for Deep Learning™ (NPDL). Retrieved from www.deep-learning.global.

working together. Connecting face-to-face or virtually with those who share your goals helps with problem solving and with committing to stick to new behaviors. The mutual focus and intentional transparency of practices leads to shared understanding and a sense of common purpose. Next, we examine the four phases of the collaborative inquiry process as it is used in learning design.

# Collaborative Inquiry in Learning Design
## Phase I: Assess

The first phase begins with assessing where students are, considering the curriculum expectations, and building on student interests to establish learning goals and success criteria. Learning goals are established based on an assessment of student needs, strengths, and interests as well as proficiency in the six Global Competencies. Success criteria are identified to describe the evidence that would demonstrate that the learning goal has been achieved. Multiple methods of assessment are used to measure the degree of understanding and skill development.

## Phase II: Design

The second phase involves designing learning experiences that engage students in acquiring the competencies to meet the learning goals and success criteria. This step includes the selection of the most effective pedagogies, the consideration of the needed learning partnerships, the development of an environment that fosters a culture of learning, and the use of digital to leverage learning. Teachers use this iterative process of assessing where students are in their learning and scaffolding the next lesson to move them forward. Protocols 9 and 10 provide mini-case examples of teachers developing their "wonderings" that contribute to deeper learning designs. Working collaboratively on these learning designs increases innovation because teachers are stimulated by the ideas of other teachers and the students themselves. While initially time consuming, teachers find that the protocols help them focus their energies, and after the first few designs, they can build on one another's expertise, are more innovative, and actually save time as they share the design workload.

## Phase III: Implement

During the learning experience, the teacher monitors the learning, scaffolding as needed, and guides students into deeper discoveries by asking questions such as "How well are the students learning?" "What evidence do I/we have of the learning?" "What do students need next to deepen their learning?" During this phase, teachers may observe in each other's classes or share responsibility for students by grouping across classes for specific tasks or interests. Students develop skills in both peer and self-assessment. Students may even begin to lead the learning. As one teacher put it,

> **I used to think it was scary to let the students lead the learning, and now I think that it is one of the most valuable ways to create authentic learning for students as it allows them to take ownership and develop new ways to learn, express, share, and create their thoughts and ideas.**
>
> —*DEEP LEARNING: ENGAGE THE WORLD CHANGE THE WORLD*, P. 54

## Phase IV: Measure, Reflect, and Change

In the final phase of the process, teachers collaborate to document student learning. They consider a broad range of formal and informal assessment evidence from student work products and performances to measure growth in both academic content and the Global Competencies (6Cs). Student data then feeds into the next cycle of learning and provides rich input for the next learning design.

Skilled users of collaborative inquiry describe this process as an integrated way of thinking about the work rather than as a separate process. Sharing the learning designs across grade teams, departments, schools, and even globally provides vivid and powerful glimpses of what is possible. Teachers view these exemplars of learning experiences not as something to be replicated but as a catalyst for thinking about how to deepen the learning of their own students. Let's turn next to examining how this final phase of the collaborative inquiry process can be a powerful catalyst for change.

## Collaborative Assessment

The fourth phase of the collaborative inquiry process—measure, reflect, and change—can be very powerful, and yet it is often the most neglected in day-to-day practice. Time to collaborate is scarce; it can be more expedient to assign grades than to look deeply into the quality of learning, and meaningful professional dialogue takes skill and knowledge. However, we have seen that the process of collaborative assessment (what we call *moderation*) of learning designs and student work products and performances results in a deeper understanding of what the students have learned and builds professional reliability and validity for a more consistent determination of progress. The power of moderation lies in the professional discussion about the learning and the sharing of effective strategies in preparing for the next stage of learning. This professional discussion generates new knowledge and is a catalyst for refining practice. In short, moderation is a strategy to examine and improve pedagogical practice. As one principal recently shared,

> **This final step is so often overlooked but had the most power to actually change practice in the school as teachers really looked at the student learning and how their learning design had helped students achieve the learning goals.**
>
> —PERSONAL COMMUNICATION, FEBRUARY 2019

In New Pedagogies for Deep Learning (NPDL), we have used the process of moderation to engage teachers, school leaders, and NPDL leadership teams in professional dialogue centered on Deep Learning design, implementation, measurement, and outcomes. The intention is to develop a shared language and understanding about Deep Learning—its design, outcomes, and the new pedagogies that most effectively develop the 6Cs for all learners. The moderation process provides teachers and leaders with examples of Deep Learning that can be leveraged in their own local contexts. After teachers have designed, implemented, assessed, and reflected on a chosen Deep Learning experience, they have the opportunity to assemble and share examples. Deep Learning Exemplars are the examples of learning design, implementation, assessment, and outcomes that describe how Deep Learning develops and what it looks like in action. Chapter 9 provides protocols to build norms and steps to implement the collaborative assessment (moderation) process.

## Collaborative Assessment of School and District Conditions

This same four-phase process of collaborative inquiry is also beneficial for school or district leaders and leadership teams to examine current models, practices, and assumptions for learning and then to design systems and plans to create the conditions needed for Deep Learning to flourish. Chapters 11 and 12 provide protocols and explore a case study of how this process propels movement toward Deep Learning across whole schools and districts.

## Final Thoughts

The collaborative inquiry process is thus a way of thinking that facilitates reflective practice and continuous evolution for individual teachers as well as schools and districts. The process is a foundation for using the Global Competencies and the Four Elements of Learning Design. In the next chapters, we will examine ways to use these tools and concepts to design and assess Deep Learning.

## Protocols

**9** ## Examining the Phases of the Collaborative Inquiry Cycle

Build a shared understanding of the phases of the collaborative inquiry cycle and examine key practices.

**10** ## Making Meaning From Collaborative Inquiry

Use the case study to build a deeper understanding of collaborative inquiry and reflect on teacher practices.

**11** ## Reflective Practice: An Inquiry Cycle Case Study

Build an understanding of how a teacher uses reflective practice to design and modify learning in a Grade 9 math classroom.

### For more information:

Read Chapters 8 and 9 from *Deep Learning: Engage the World Change the World.*

# 09 Examining the Phases of the Collaborative Inquiry Cycle

Purpose: **Understand the Collaborative Inquiry Cycle**

Time: **15–30 minutes**

Process: **Say Something and Classify**

## Part One

**1** **Assemble a group** of four people. Locate the description of *Collaborative Inquiry* starting on page 74 and assign one phase to each person to read.

- Assess
- Design
- Implement
- Measure, Reflect, and Change

**2** **Each person summarizes** their assigned phase in their own words. Say something about your phase and add an ending to the following sentence stem:

❝ This phase leads to meaningful learning because . . .”

## Part Two

**1** **Photocopy** and cut up the Collaborative Inquiry Descriptions. Place the Collaborative Inquiry Cycle Template in the center of the table.

**2** **Read each description** that has been cut out and identify in which phase of the Collaborative Inquiry Cycle it belongs. Explain your thinking.

**3** **Write an instructional practice** in a blank square (provided). Invite others to classify where it would fit in the Collaborative Inquiry Cycle.

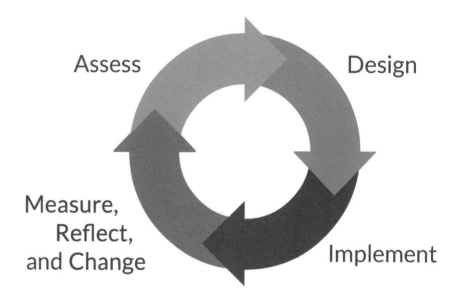

Assess

Design

Measure, Reflect, and Change

Implement

# Collaborative Inquiry Descriptions
## Cut into pieces before beginning.

| | | | |
|---|---|---|---|
| Meet with groups of students to monitor progress on their plans | Collaborate with a colleague to create a learning protocol | Consider what strategies worked and which need to be adapted in the future | Establish learning goals |
| Evaluate a student presentation | Engage students in co-creating success criteria | Provide feedback on a student-led debate | Identify key curriculum expectations to be addressed |
| Survey student interests | Have students self-assess using the collaboration learning progression | Prepare a Model UN experience | Scaffold experiences to build understanding |
| Ask students for feedback on a learning design | Review strengths and needs of students using a range of evidence | Compare student performance with previous examples of their work | Determine whether the intended learning goals were met by the design |
| Choose a jigsaw strategy to facilitate learning | Have a partner Skype into the classroom | Conduct a field trip | |

# 10 Making Meaning From Collaborative Inquiry

**Purpose: Build a shared understanding of Collaborative Inquiry**

**Time: 15–30 minutes**

**Process: Reflecting on Experiences**

**①  Reflect with a partner.**
What was your most profound professional learning experience? Explain why it was impactful. As this is being shared, the partner listens carefully and writes four different descriptive qualities on four different sticky notes (For example, one sticky might say "collaborative." Another might say "relevant").

**②  Switch roles** so that each shares their professional learning experience.

**③  Join another pair** so that you're in a group of four. Bring your 16 sticky notes together so that everyone can read them. Set your notes aside (for now).

**④  Read** the case study below.

**⑤  Discuss**

- What did the teachers learn?
- Why would this type of learning have an impact on teacher practice?
- What are three advantages to learning this way?
- How is Collaborative Inquiry different from conventional forms of professional learning?

**⑥  Make connections.** How do the sticky notes that you have written apply to the teachers' experience in the case study?

## INTRODUCTION TO COLLABORATIVE INQUIRY

## Case Study

It was the end of October. Sharma, Uta, and Gus were reflecting on their student progress in their three Grade 9 English classes. Many students were engaged in the discussions that were facilitated during class but only 41% of the students were submitting written assignments. This was unusual and detrimental to student success, and so the three teachers set off to better understand the problem and to come up with a solution.

The three teachers began by assessing. Gus identified six students in each class and reviewed their previous report cards. Uta wondered whether some of the students were having difficulty with the transition to high school. She networked with resource people and previous Grade 8 teachers to find out whether she was missing critical information. Sharma created a simple online survey that all three classes of students were asked to complete; the questions brought student voice to the problem and allowed each student to respond anonymously. Students were asked about their after-school workloads, extra unknown stresses, interests, and comprehension levels. All three teachers wrote notes home to students they were concerned about. They gathered up the information and learned that students were not submitting the work because they found it irrelevant.

The three teachers then set out to design a plan. They consulted the curriculum and the New Pedagogies for Deep Learning resource hub and discussed their vision for making the learning more interesting. Many of the students loved playing computer games and the three teachers didn't know anything about them, so they created an assignment that encouraged students to compose a persuasive piece. The students could choose various media, but the choice had to include writing. Students had to review a computer game and convince the three teachers (on a panel) how their computer games contributed to individual or societal improvement.

**Adaptations came as they implemented.**

Adaptations came as they implemented. For example, the three classes co-created the criteria and assembled into teams. Peer assessment was also incorporated into the lesson design. The teachers also realized that the "reflection" dimension of the Communication Learning Progression really addressed their main concern. So they encouraged students to reflect on their progress on this dimension once every three days, providing rationale and examples from their own experiences. As the lesson design unfolded, teachers used the criteria created by the students to monitor their progress, share thinking, and provide feedback. They also collected shorter pieces of reflective writing from students to ensure the groups were balancing the workloads mindfully. The three teachers met briefly but regularly to identify patterns, observations, and gaps. They adapted as they went and clarified misunderstandings along the way.

When it was time for the students to present their computer game reviews to the panel of teachers, every student was ready (and excited). Students also gathered their learning progression reflections and submitted final reflections. As the teachers reflected on the evidence, they were shocked that the work completion had improved from 41% to 100%. Sharma, Gus, and Uta learned three important lessons that could apply to their daily professional practice. First, student voice and student interest lead to increased engagement and commitment. Second, the deliberate and explicit reference to the learning progression clarified what learners were supposed to do. Third, most learners need regular touch points and an authentic opportunity to make face-to-face connections with the teacher.

# 11 Reflective Practice: An Inquiry Cycle Case Study

**Purpose:** Understand how the teacher's reflective practice aligns with the Inquiry Cycle

**Time:** 30–40 minutes

**Process:** Analyzing a Case Study

**1** **With a partner,** describe how you reflect on your daily practice.

**2** **Review** the Collaborative Inquiry diagram. Consider: How do these four phases apply to your own reflective practice?

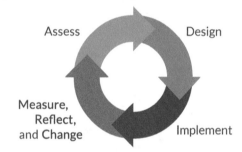

Assess — Design

Measure, Reflect, and Change — Implement

**3** **Read the Case Study:** A Grade 9 Classroom.

**4** **What do you notice** about Kim's reflective practice?

**5** **Discuss with a partner** and use the table below to capture your thoughts. Cite examples from the case study where Kim reflects using the four Inquiry phases in her reflection.

- How did the Inquiry Cycle help Kim to reflect on and improve her practice?
- How might she have used the Inquiry Cycle more effectively and intentionally?
- How is Inquiry similar to or different from the way(s) you currently plan and reflect on learning?
- How might you begin to use (or deepen your use of) Inquiry in your daily practice?

| | Examples where Kim uses the Inquiry Cycle to support her reflective practice |
|---|---|
| Assess | |
| Design | |
| Implement | |
| Measure, Reflect, and Change | |

## REFLECTIVE PRACTICE CASE STUDY

# A Grade 9 Classroom

"Is our planet changing?" Kim asked her Grade 9 students. They all nodded. "In what ways?" she probed. The students looked blankly at her. Kim was stuck. So she shifted gears and covered other material. At the end of the day, she connected with a colleague to help her think through a better plan.

The next day, Kim distributed pictures of environmental disasters from around the world; each picture had a location and date listed on the bottom. She asked her students to discuss their pictures with an elbow partner. Then the pair of students joined up with others and they examined multiple pictures, brainstorming what the pictures had in common. Students mentioned common weather issues but did not connect them to climate change as the cause. She then asked them what they noticed about the environment. She invited the students to pore over each picture and post a "wondering" on a sticky note. At the end of the lesson, she skimmed over the sticky notes and noticed that they began to wonder about case. Understanding climate change was a key expectation in the curriculum and was also a global competency, Citizenship (genuine interest in human and environmental sustainability), that these students needed to learn. She would need to design a strategy that built on the students' strengths and needs while also encouraging their voice and choice.

Kim returned with the wonderings the next day and students chose pictures that intrigued them. In small groups, they organized the wonderings to generate "burning questions" and set off to learn more about the pictures and the stories behind them. The students wanted to share their learning with another class, so together, Kim and the students articulated what would make a compelling PowerPoint presentation. As they did this, they looked over the Communication Learning Progression. Kim also incorporated some requirements of her own, drawing from the curriculum.

As the presentation planning unfolded, students shared their insights and progress with one another. On the last day of presentations, one of the students invited in a neighbor who rescued pets during Hurricane Irma, and the students were touched by his story. This led the students to question what more they could do to beat climate change. The student interest then shifted, and together the class extended the learning design by deciding to take action; they collectively determined what success would look like.

**She would need to design a strategy that built on the students' strengths and needs . . .**

Again, Kim drew students' attention back to the learning progressions; they continued to focus on communication and they also identified some collaboration, citizenship, creativity, and critical thinking dimensions that would be assessed throughout this next part of the learning journey. Students were also asked to choose one of the learning progression dimensions that they did not feel confident about and incorporate it into their take-action design. They used Y charts to identify what success in each competency would look like, sound like, and feel like. These were posted and referred to frequently. At midpoint, students were asked to stop and self-assess their place on the continuum, provide evidence, and consider how they could continue to develop. They chose peers to coach and assess the competencies using supportive norms and questioning techniques. Kim also met with the students regularly to hear about progress and their learning reflections and to nudge them on their next steps. When Kim noticed that multiple students were struggling with specific skills in the take-action design, she would pause the activity to clarify to small groups or with the entire class.

## Kim asked the question "What was most helpful to you?"

The take-action design had common criteria but took individual directions. For example, some students linked up with a local nursery and some elementary students to plant seedlings in an inner-city school yard. Others conducted an environmental sustainability audit of their own schools. Some students chose to research favorite coffee shops and retailers to learn more about their sustainability practices. There were classwide sub-tasks too. For example, the class began following reputable climate activists on Twitter and initiated their own Twitter campaign. The students also tracked and reflected on their own carbon footprints using an online calculator. Lastly, students wrote letters to environmental organizations and local politicians.

As this take-action design began to wrap up, students reflected on their learning and engaged in various co-designed assessment strategies. They assessed themselves along the global competency progression, Kim also asked the question "What was most helpful to you?" as a way of understanding what instructional strategies engaged her learners and helped them to develop deep understanding and competencies. She also asked, "If this were to continue, what would have been your next step?" to determine the depth of their reflections.

Kim discussed the learning journey with a teaching colleague and admitted that starting with that first question may not have been the best way to begin; she would do it differently next time. She admitted that it was difficult for her to give up complete control of the learning design; she needed to figure out a way of letting the student interest truly drive the learning. She

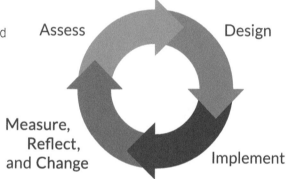

also recognized that she could have tapped richer partnerships through Skype. Students had demonstrated growth in conducting the research for the presentation and following their take-action plan. However, they still need to grow in the area of critical thinking, specifically in scrutinizing claims made online. This learning need would inform where she would take the class next when they started to look at cultural bias in the next Deep Learning experience.

> **Teachers gravitate toward greater transparency as they collaborate to assess starting points, design learning experiences, and reflect on student progress.**
>
> —*DEEP LEARNING: ENGAGE THE WORLD CHANGE THE WORLD*, P. 69

**“** Our global competencies, or the 6Cs as we often refer to them, differ from other 21st century lists in three crucial ways: comprehensiveness, precision, and measurability. **”**

—*DEEP LEARNING: ENGAGE THE WORLD CHANGE THE WORLD*, P. 18

# SECTION 03

## Learning Progressions

**"** The [learning] progressions serve as an anchor for professional dialogue in designing Deep Learning experiences and also as a monitoring and evaluation system during the learning process. **"**

# Chapter 07
# Using Learning Progressions

Before map apps were embedded onto our handheld devices, we lost our bearings from time to time. Today, satellite technology and GPS software make navigation so precise that they warn us to recalibrate the moment we take one wrong turn. What if the pathway for student learning afforded that level of precision and clarity? The learning progressions aim to take the guesswork out of Deep Learning so that all students can thrive. Let's examine how the learning progression tool is organized and how it can be used.

## Organization

Learning progressions are provided for each of the six Global Competencies to describe what learning looks like at each level of growth, provide a shared language and common understanding to design learning, and monitor and measure student progress in developing each of the six Competencies. On the left-hand side of the tool, the competency is broken down into four or five dimensions, which gives the competency depth (see Figure 7.1). As mentioned in Chapter 4, we want to have rich discussions that promote a common and substantial understanding of these Deep Learning Competencies, and that all begins with a comprehensive definition. Then, looking from left to right, each dimension has an articulated pathway describing what the learning looks like as it progresses across five levels from *limited evidence* to *emerging* to *developing* to *accelerating* to *proficient*. Notice the arrow that sits to the right of *proficient*, which serves as a nod to the commitment to continuous growth. Each cell provides a picture of the skills, capabilities, and attitudes that contribute to success in the competency. The learning progressions support all learners from kindergarten through high school and beyond, so teachers exercise their knowledge of the developmental level of their learners and the curriculum expectations as they use this tool.

## Designing Learning

Learning progressions are a robust tool for designing learning. When teachers understand the strengths and needs of the students as highlighted on the

FIGURE 7.1

# Collaboration Deep Learning Progression

## ORGANIZATION OF A LEARNING PROGRESSION

Learning Progression definition

## Collaboration Deep Learning Progression

Work interdependently and synergistically in teams with strong interpersonal and team-related skills, including effective management of team dynamics and challenges, making substantive decisions together, and contributing to learning from and having an impact on others.

New Pedagogies for **Deep Learning** A GLOBAL PARTNERSHIP

| Dimension | Limited Evidence | Emerging | Developing | Accelerating | Proficient |
|---|---|---|---|---|---|
| **Working inter-dependently as a team** | Learners either work individually on learning tasks or collaborate informally in pairs or groups but do not work as a team. Learners may discuss some issues or content together but may still be leaving the most important substantive decisions to one or two members. Group members' contributions may not be equitable. | Learners work together in pairs or groups and are responsible for completing a task in order for the group to achieve its task. Learners are starting to make some decisions together but may still be leaving the most important substantive decisions to one or two members. Group members' contributions may not be equitable. | Learners decide together how to match tasks to the individual strengths and expertise of team members and then work effectively together. Learners involve all members in making joint decisions about an important issue, problem, or process and in developing a team solution. | Learners can articulate how they work together to use each other's strengths to make substantive decisions and develop ideas and solutions. Teamwork is clearly evident in that learners' contributions are woven together to communicate an overarching idea and/or create a product. | Learners demonstrate a highly effective and synergistic approach to work in a way that not only leverages each member's strengths but provides opportunities. Each team member's strengths and perspectives are infused to come to the best possible decision that benefits all. |
| **Interpersonal and team-related skills** | Learners may help each other on tasks that contribute to a joint work product or outcome; interpersonal, and team-related skills are not yet evident. Learners do not yet demonstrate a genuine sense of empathy or a shared purpose for working together. | Learners report and demonstrate a sense of collective ownership for the work and are beginning to show interpersonal and team-related skills. Their focus is on achieving a common or joint outcome, product, design, response, or decision. Key decisions may be made or dominated by one or two members. | Strong interpersonal skills, collective ownership for the work, and an active sense of shared responsibility are evident. From beginning to end, learners listen effectively, negotiate and agree on the goals, content, process, design, and conclusions of their work. | Learners can clearly articulate how joint responsibility for the work and its product or outcome pervades the entire task. They show strong skills in listening, facilitation, and effective teamwork and ensure that all voices are heard and reflected in the work and work product. | Learners take active responsibility for ensuring that the collaborative process works. They ensure that each person's ideas and expertise are used to maximum advantage and that each work product or outcome is of the highest possible quality or value. |
| **Social, emotional, and intercultural skills** | Learners have a basic sense of awareness about themselves. Learners tend to see things only from their own perspective. In some cases, this may inhibit their ability to form positive relationships. | Learners are finding out about themselves, where they fit in the world, and how their behavior affects other people. This self-awareness is providing a base for better understanding about how others' viewpoints differ from their own. | Learners have an awareness of themselves and where their own perspective comes from. Self-awareness and listening skills allow learners to better understand and empathize with the emotions and viewpoints of others, moving beyond "tolerance" or "acceptance" to genuinely valuing perspectives quite different from their own. | Learners have a strong sense of self and understand where their own perspective comes from and how it differs from others'. Learners listen carefully, empathize with the emotions and viewpoints of others, and use these to enrich their own learning. As team members, they work effectively in ways that support, encourage, challenge, and progress themselves and others. | Learners have highly developed social and emotional skills grounded in a clear sense of their individual and cultural identities. Learners communicate well across cultures and disciplines, work effectively in teams, and form positive relationships. The skills they have developed in understanding the perspectives of others, empathy, and compassion impact team functioning. |

The Deep Learning Progressions have five levels: Limited Evidence, Emerging, Developing, Accelerating, and Proficient. The arrow placed to the right of *proficient* indicates that learning can go beyond proficient, as we discover and create new knowledge.

Each cell describes progress at each level of the competency.

Each Learning Progression is broken into four or five dimensions.

learning progressions, the teacher can design the next cycle of learning with great precision. The learning progressions provide common language and specificity that teacher teams need when they are co-planning learning. Be aware that the learning progressions are brimming with detail and can overwhelm even the most earnest learner if presented all at once; we encourage teachers to select the dimension(s) within the competencies that best align with the curriculum and learner needs and focus there first, then gradually consider additional dimensions and other competencies.

When students have understanding of and influence over learning design—what is expected and how to be successful—their engagement increases. So, too, it is with learning progressions; teachers can use Y charts to facilitate conversations with students about what the competencies look like, sound like, and feel like in order to make the learning more relevant and personalized. The learning progressions and an accompanying Student Self-Assessment Tool are available in student-friendly language so that even the youngest of learners can take an active role in design and assessment. You can find out how to use the Y chart and the student-friendly tools in Protocols 16 and 17.

## Assessing Learning

Learning progressions are also used for *assessment for, assessment as*, and *assessment of* learning. When students, teachers, and other partners use this tool to reflect on and assess learning, they can locate their precise position and anticipate practical next steps. The more they use this as a learning reference, the greater the growth of the understanding of the competency. Therefore, it's important to use the tool regularly in the learning design and provide varied opportunities to monitor progress over time. Imagine, too, how powerful it is when a student travels from one discipline/subject to the next and uses the same learning progression; he or she can not only fine-tune the competency but draw a greater understanding of how it is applied in different contexts. Now that's authentic learning! What's more, when the learning progression is actively used across grades, that metacognition sharpens and provides students with clarity about how to negotiate the challenges inherent in learning. It is a big boost to student efficacy when they can build on their learning from the previous year. And for the learners who struggle, this explicitness and familiarity softens the transition and gives them a boost of reassurance—"I got this!"— the sense of confidence and competence needed to tackle even the largest learning obstacles. We find that when students not only have opportunities to assess themselves using the progressions but also engage in regular reflective conversations and peer assessment, their learning abounds.

Assessing the competencies can be challenging because evidence of them is not always found in paper-and-pen tasks. How do you find hard evidence of students collaborating with each other or demonstrating Character? It's challenging to capture some of the competencies while there are many things happening in a classroom. Many of our Deep Learning teachers use varied forms of pedagogical documentation (which can include taking pictures and recordings) to capture student learning in the moment. In this way, they can observe students while they are engaged in the learning, then interpret the evidence and review the information again at another time. The bonus here is that teachers can also share that evidence with the student and engage in a rich self-assessment conversation. What is also rich about this approach is that it allows students to demonstrate their learning in diverse ways over time. Protocols 13 and 14 address assessment strategies for using the learning progression.

When teachers begin to dig into the learning progressions, they quickly learn that student work does not always neatly fall into a single cell of the progression. It is quite common for student learning to straddle two or more cells. How does one come up with a single rating, then? Drawing on multiple sources and types of student work taken over time provides a fuller picture of student proficiency. Synthesizing these evidence points allows the teacher to determine where students are on the progression. Also, collaboratively reflecting on the assessment and the thinking that informed it can help. Collaboratively assessing students using the learning progressions is a powerful capacity-building strategy; teachers gain greater insight into pedagogy and assessment while also sharpening their focus on what the students are learning. More powerful still is when teachers use multiple samples of student work from a range of students to check their inter-rater reliability. Many of us may be uncomfortable talking about student work because we assess students differently. It is common after examining the same student's work that teachers land on different parts of the learning progression. However, it is through these regular challenging and healthy conversations that we can establish a common understanding of learning—a benchmark, of sorts. We will explore collaborative assessment more in Chapter 9.

# Feedback

The learning progression clears the path for students and teachers. It serves a range of assessment and monitoring needs and supports design and reflection. When positioned as a reference tool for providing feedback, students can take charge of their learning. Much has been written about the power of providing feedback, and Protocol 17 provides some space for teachers to consider how to position feedback when using the learning progression.

Lastly, we have created a Conversation Guide in Figure 7.2 that has three basic questions. Throughout this chapter and in other parts of the book, you will see how this Conversation Guide supports learning conversations for students, adults, teams, or anyone using the Deep Learning tools.

Let's take a minute now to examine how a teacher could use the Conversation Guide and the learning progression with students. While using the learning progression as a reference for the learner, the Conversation Guide serves as a coaching tool.

FIGURE 7.2

## Conversation Guide

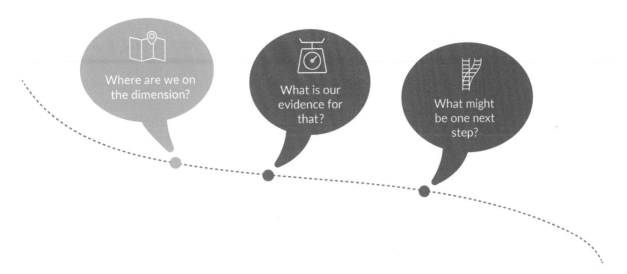

The first question asked is "Where are you on the continuum?" This question nudges the learner to reflect on his or her learning position. The next question is "What is your evidence to support that?" This question is part of a longer conversation as the learner draws upon multiple and varied contributions, experiences, and formal and informal assessments. Sometimes a teacher will need to probe the student to recall the learning and to make connections to the competency on the learning progression. Then, having considered all of the ways the student has demonstrated the learning, the last question is "What might be one next step?" Notice that the question doesn't ask for ten things, only one. One next step allows the learner to focus in and try this for a while; learning and growth are more likely to take hold when we focus on only one behavior change. Furthermore, the beauty of this question is that it puts the learner in the driver's seat. Reflecting on the learning progression, the student chooses one next move to support progress.

When this Conversation Guide is used the next time with the same learner, the teacher/coach might begin with the question "How did that next step go?" before engaging in the process again. If this process is used habitually and explicitly as a conferencing strategy, both with peers and adults, it takes the fear out of learning and enables the learner to construct deeper understanding and take greater ownership of learning. The Conversation Guide with helpful probing questions can be found in Protocol 44.

## Final Thoughts

The learning progressions are a strong foundation for both the design and assessment of Deep Learning. In the next chapter, we explore how the progressions are used in concert with the Four Elements of Learning Design to create Deep Learning experiences that inspire and transform learning.

Protocols

**12** Learning Progressions

Orient the reader to the components of the learning progression.

**13** Analyzing Student Work Using Learning Progressions

Use vignettes and videos to explore how to use the learning progression for assessment and providing feedback.

**14** Rating Students Using a Learning Progression

Examine a range of student work to synthesize into a single rating using two dimensions of the Citizenship learning progression.

**15** Providing Feedback to Students

Apply principles of effective feedback to the assessments completed in Protocol 14.

**16** Student-Friendly Learning Progressions

Acquaint the reader to the components of the student-friendly learning progression and encourage them to apply the learning progression in the school setting.

**17** Engaging Students With the Student-Friendly Learning Progressions

Introduce the use of a Y chart as a way of helping students better understand the Global Competencies.

**18** The Student Self-Assessment Tool

Examine the tool and consider how to optimize its use with students and other partners.

Tools

Deep Learning Progressions

Student-Friendly Deep Learning Progressions

Student Self-Assessment

For more information:

Read Chapters 2 and 9 from *Deep Learning: Engage the World Change the World*.

# Notes

# 12 Learning Progressions

**Purpose: Understand the dimensions and levels of a learning progression and use it to assess student proficiency**

Time: **20 minutes**

**Process: Understanding and Using Learning Progressions**

**1** **Distribute** the Collaboration Learning Progression to small groups or partners.

**2** **Examine** how the Learning Progression is organized with attention to

- the definition of the Competency,
- the dimensions,
- the five levels of growth, and
- the cells describing the continuum of growth across the dimension

**3** **Select** the Collaboration Deep Learning Progression and read across one dimension.

- What do you notice? Discuss your observation with a partner.
- How might a learning progression help learners in your classroom or school?

**4** **Focus** on the dimension "working interdependently as a team."

- Where would you place yourself on the dimension (from limited to proficient)?
- What is your evidence to support that?
- What might be a next step to move toward proficiency on that dimension?

**5** **Think of a student** that you observed recently:

- Where would you see the student on the dimension?
- What is your evidence to support that?
- What might be a next step to move that student toward proficiency on the dimension?

Where are we on the dimension?

What is our evidence for that?

What might be one next step?

# ORGANIZATION OF A LEARNING PROGRESSION

Learning Progression definition

## Collaboration Deep Learning Progression

Work interdependently and synergistically in teams with strong interpersonal and team-related skills, including effective management of team dynamics and challenges, making substantive decisions together, and contributing to learning from and having an impact on others.

New Pedagogies for **Deep Learning**
A GLOBAL PARTNERSHIP

| Dimension | Limited Evidence | Emerging | Developing | Accelerating | Proficient |
|---|---|---|---|---|---|
| **Working interdependently as a team** | Learners either work individually on learning tasks or collaborate informally in pairs or groups but do not work as a team. Learners may discuss some issues or content together but skip over important substantive decisions (such as how the process will be managed), which has significant adverse impacts on how well the collaboration works. | Learners work together in pairs or groups and are responsible for completing a task in order for the group to achieve its task. Learners are starting to make some decisions together but may still be leaving the most important substantive decisions to one or two members. Group members' contributions may not be equitable. | Learners decide together how to match tasks to the individual strengths and expertise of team members and then work effectively together. Learners involve all members in making joint decisions about an important issue, problem, or process and in developing a team solution. | Learners can articulate how they work together to use each other's strengths to make substantive decisions and develop ideas and solutions. Teamwork is clearly evident in that learners' contributions are woven together to communicate an overarching idea and/or create a product. | Learners demonstrate a highly effective and synergistic approach to work in a way that not only leverages each member's strengths but provides opportunities. Each team member's strengths and perspectives are infused to come to the best possible decision that benefits all. |
| **Interpersonal and team-related skills** | Learners may help each other on tasks that contribute to a joint work product or outcome; interpersonal, and team-related skills are not yet evident. Learners do not yet demonstrate a genuine sense of empathy or a shared purpose for working together. | Learners report and demonstrate a sense of collective ownership for the work and are beginning to show interpersonal and team-related skills. Their focus is on achieving a common or joint outcome, product, design, response, or decision. Key decisions may be made or dominated by one or two members. | Strong interpersonal skills, collective ownership for the work, and an active sense of shared responsibility are evident. From beginning to end, learners listen effectively, negotiate and agree on the goals, content, process, design, and conclusions of their work. | Learners can clearly articulate how joint responsibility for the work and its product or outcome pervades the entire task. They show strong skills in listening, facilitation, and effective teamwork and ensure that all voices are heard and reflected in the work and work product. | Learners take active responsibility for ensuring that the collaborative process works. They ensure that each person's ideas and expertise are used to maximum advantage and that each work product or outcome is of the highest possible quality or value. |
| **Social, emotional, and intercultural skills** | Learners have a basic sense of awareness about themselves. Learners tend to see things only from their own perspective. In some cases, this may inhibit their ability to form positive relationships. | Learners are finding out about themselves, where they fit in the world, and how their behavior affects other people. This self-awareness is providing a base for better understanding about how others' viewpoints differ from their own. | Learners have an awareness of themselves and where their own perspective comes from. Self-awareness and listening skills allow learners to better understand and empathize with the emotions and viewpoints of others, moving beyond "tolerance" or "acceptance" to genuinely valuing perspectives quite different from their own. | Learners have a strong sense of self and understand where their own perspective comes from and how it differs from others'. Learners listen carefully, empathize with the emotions and viewpoints of others, and use these to enrich their own learning. As team members, they work effectively in ways that support, encourage, challenge, and progress themselves and others. | Learners have highly developed social and emotional skills grounded in a clear sense of their individual and cultural identities. Learners communicate well across cultures and disciplines, work effectively in teams, and form positive relationships. The skills they have developed in understanding the perspectives of others, empathy, and compassion impact team functioning. |

Each cell describes progress at each level of the competency.

Each Learning Progression is broken into four or five dimensions.

The Deep Learning Progressions have five levels: Limited Evidence, Emerging, Developing, Accelerating, and Proficient. The arrow placed to the right of *proficient* indicates that learning can go beyond proficient, as we discover and create new knowledge.

# 13 Analyzing Student Work Using Learning Progressions

Purpose: **Use a Learning Progression to analyze student work and provide feedback**

Process: **Assessing Students Using Three Video Examples**

Time: **30–60 minutes**

> Resources:
> Tools:
> • Collaboration Learning Progression
> • Communication Learning Progression
> Vignettes:
> • Daily Deep Learning:
>   Fitness for the Mind
> • Student-Friendly Language:
>   Meet Them Where They're At
> Videos at www.deep-learning.global:
> • Team Dynamics
> • Peer Conferencing

## Part One: The Vignette

**1** **Read** Daily Deep Learning: Fitness for the Mind or Student-Friendly Language: Meet Them Where They're At.

**2** **Discuss** the advantages of explicitly sharing learning progressions with students.

## Part Two: Video One: Collaboration—Managing Team Dynamics

Note—This clip has two parts. Pause the video clip where indicated.

**3** **Watch the first part** of the Team Dynamics video clip. Focus on the behavior of the student facilitator (standing up). Jot notes about his behaviors. What feedback would you give to the boy? Write your feedback on a piece of paper and set it aside.

**4** **Locate** the **Collaboration Learning Progression** and read the dimension: Managing Team Dynamics. Summarize in your own words what proficiency looks like.

**5** **Watch again** the first part of the Team Dynamics video, focusing only on the behavior of the student facilitator (standing up). As you observe, jot any additional notes about his behavior.

**6** **Discuss**

- Where might you place this boy on the Managing Team Dynamics dimension?
- What is your evidence for that?
- What might be a next step for him?
- What feedback might you give him?

**7** **Watch the second part** of the video which includes a new group of students. Focus on the student facilitator (standing up). Jot notes about the behaviors you observe.

- Where might you place this boy on the Managing Team Dynamics dimension?
- What is your evidence for that?
- What might be a next step for him?
- What feedback might you give him?

# COLLABORATION LEARNING PROGRESSION

Where might you place this boy on the Managing Team Dynamics dimension?

What is your evidence for that?

What might be a next step for him?

What feedback might you give him?

| Dimension | Limited Evidence | Emerging | Developing | Accelerating | Proficient |
|---|---|---|---|---|---|
| Managing team dynamics and challenges | Learners are deeply invested in their own viewpoints, lack the empathy to hear or learn from others, and have difficulty suspending judgment to genuinely listen to others' views.<br><br>They avoid conflict by deferring to others' views or change views quickly in the face of peer pressure. Teams may get stuck in conflict or move forward in the wrong team direction. | Learners still need guidance to forge and maintain positive working relationships and to resist inappropriate peer pressure.<br><br>Learners take a more thoughtful approach to dealing with disagreements, asking each member to share their perspective and discussing any differences.<br><br>They begin to dig beneath those differences to identify what underpins them. | Learners generally work quite effectively in a team, although they are likely to need help with conflict resolution, inappropriate peer pressure, and other challenging issues.<br><br>Learners are developing the ability to identify what underpins their own and others' points of view.<br><br>They are getting better at expressing their viewpoints and listening to and learning from others. | Learners are skilled at identifying what underpins their own and others' points of view. They can pick their battles in deciding what to debate.<br><br>They are building both courage and clarity to express their own viewpoints and listen to and learn from others.<br><br>Learners are becoming skilled at exploring different opinions in ways that contribute to the learning of others without holding up team progress. | Learners have a deep understanding of what underpins their own and others' points of view, the courage and clarity to effectively express their own viewpoints, and the empathy to hear and learn from others.<br><br>Learners respectfully explore different opinions in ways that enrich their own and others' learning and thinking.<br><br>Learners leverage a range of strategies to propose solutions and minimize tensions. |

## 1 Discuss

- What are some of your observations about assessing collaboration?
- What were some differences in the quality of your feedback when you used the learning progression?
- Were your observations straddled over multiple cells on the dimension? If so, how might that inform your feedback?

## Part Three: Video Two: Communication—Reflection to further develop and improve communication

### 2 Locate the Communication
Deep Learning Progression and refer specifically to the dimension Reflection to further develop and improve communication. Summarize in your own words what proficiency would look like in your classroom.

### 3 Watch the Peer Conferencing
video clip and focus on both boys. Jot notes about their behavior.

### 4 Discuss

- Where might you place these boys on this Communication dimension?
- What is your evidence for that?
- What might be a next step for them?
- What feedback might you give them?

### 5 Think about something
you will teach soon. Which progressions might you use to assess student work?

## COMMUNICATION LEARNING PROGRESSION

| Dimension | Limited Evidence | Emerging | Developing | Accelerating | Proficient |
|---|---|---|---|---|---|
| Reflection to further develop and improve communication | Learners seek feedback from others when directed. | Learners seek feedback from others using checklists or other teacher-directed rubrics and protocols | Learners seek feedback from others and are beginning to reflect on their communication processes. Learners are developing the ability to monitor, manage, and improve their communication throughout each task. | Learners participate in continuous cycles of feedback and self-reflection to improve upon and refine messages. Learners understand multiple perspectives and can adapt messages. | Learners proactively reflect, revise, and refine communication to be sure their messages will be understood as intended. They seek multiple perspectives and check for personal bias. |

" Getting started in Deep Learning design accelerates when teachers collaborate within and across schools and when they have protocols, examples, and a process for working together. "

—*DEEP LEARNING: ENGAGE THE WORLD CHANGE THE WORLD*, PP. 101–102

# 14 Rating Students Using a Learning Progression

Purpose: **Review a range of evidence and synthesize into a single rating using the Learning Progression**

Process: **Simulation: Using Multiple Sources of Evidence**

**1** **Read** through Learning Design Example: A Sustainable Approach, Grade 6, at the end of this chapter.

**2** **Note the focus** on Citizenship, in particular, the dimensions:

- A global perspective
- Empathy and compassion for diverse values and worldviews

**3** **Review** collaboratively three samples of the work generated by a student.

    A. Student Work: Student Conferencing
    B. Business Plan PowerPoint
    C. Journal Entry

Time: **30–40 minutes**

> Resources:
> Tools:
> - Learning Design Example: Exploring Poverty: A Sustainable Approach, Grade 6
> - Citizenship Learning Progression

**4** **Consider:**

- Where would you place Student A on these two dimensions?
- What is your evidence to support that?
- What would be one next step for Student A?

# SAMPLES OF STUDENT ARTIFACTS

## A. Student Work: Student Conferencing

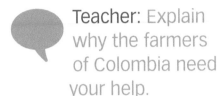 **Teacher:** Explain why the farmers of Colombia need your help.

 **Student:** The farmers can't make much money selling bananas because it costs too much to get the bananas transported. As well, a lot of the banana crops have been ruined by awful hurricanes. Farmers like Juan can't just go out and get another job because his whole village relies on farming and in his village, most people are very poor, so they can't lend him the money.

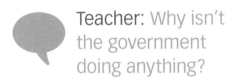 **Teacher:** What else is happening in his community?

**Student:** As well, there are more people coming to his village all the time because there is violence and gang wars happening in other places of the country. That puts more pressure on his village, which isn't really fair for the people in that village.

There seems to be a lot of violence and a drug war going on with cocaine and I think the farmers get bullied by the drug lords. I think he feels pressured to grow cocaine but doesn't want to, even though it would get him more money.

**Teacher:** Why isn't the government doing anything?

**Student:** Unfortunately, the government isn't helping either because they are fighting the drug lords but I don't really understand why they can't help the farmers more.

So, I feel bad for Juan because he has seven children and he is having a hard time feeding them all. . . . But to be honest, I don't know why he just doesn't pack up his family and leave Colombia, like my grandfather did.

Obviously, it's a tough place to live and raise a family.

## B. Business Plan PowerPoint

### What is Kiva?

- Kiva is a website that lets you see people who need help with education, jobs and other areas of life.
- You can raise money for them and invest it like a loan.
- They pay back your loan and you can then reinvest in someone else.

We envision a world where all people hold the power to create opportunity for themselves and others.

### Why I chose Kiva

- There are 2 main reasons I chose to use Kiva
- I could go into the site and look at many people who needed help. I could really find out a lot of information about their needs and make a decision based on that.
- Helping one person doesn't just stop there because when you help one person you can also influence a community.

### Who I chose to fund and why

I chose to fund Juan Carlos Alfonso because:

- My loan helps him buy farm supplies such as fertilizer and pesticides, as well as wood and wire. These will help him become more sustainable as a farmer, and then give back to his community.
- I also chose him because my Grandfather was from Columbia and he tells me stories about how hard he had to work on his farm, and about the sharing that communities do to help each other out.
- It is important to me that I can understand this and do something to make a difference fast.
- He was almost at his loan target, and my loan would help make a

### How I raised money

I did 2 things to raise money for Juan Carlos:

- I put aside $10 weeks - $25
- I mowed my neighbors lawn for $5 five times (and I am still doing this so earning more money to loan to another person on Kiva). I liked connecting that I was mowing a lawn to raising money for a farmer who also works on the land!
- So I raised $50 in 10 weeks
- 2.50 per week from my allowance ($5) over

### My reflections on what I learned

- I really like the fact that you can lend to multiple people with the same $50. It's a sustainable approach.
- Learning to really be more empathetic is important because when you are empathetic, you can actually connect to other people, no matter where they are in the world, using technology. Once you connect to them and understand their community, you can focus your thinking to take actions that can help them and their community.
- I hope that my example proves that anyone can contribute to solving global issues and challenges, even elementary school students!

### My donation jar that I put at my Dad's store.

- The logo and a picture

KIVA
loans that change lives

help someone

My poster that went with the donation jar at my Dad's store.

There are thousands of people all over the world who are doing their best to provide food and shelter for their families and communities.

My class is working to help some of them by providing micro loans. These loans will be paid back and then reinvested again using KIVA, a well-respected micro loan company.

I chose to fund Juan Carlos because of several reasons.

My loan will help him buy farm supplies such as fertilizer and pesticides, as well as wood and wire. These will help him become more sustainable as a farmer, and then give back to his community.

Every dollar you give will be sustainably invested and reinvested. My aim is to raise $50.

help someone
help themselves

thanks, Jose

## C. Journal Entry

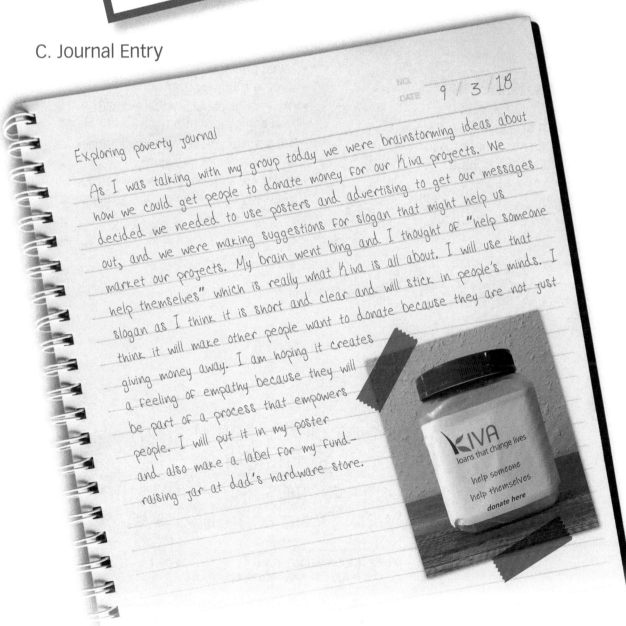

NO.
DATE   9 / 3 /18

Exploring poverty journal

As I was talking with my group today we were brainstorming ideas about how we could get people to donate money for our Kiva projects. We decided we needed to use posters and advertising to get our messages out, and we were making suggestions for slogan that might help us market our projects. My brain went bing and I thought of "help someone help themselves" which is really what Kiva is all about. I will use that slogan as I think it is short and clear and will stick in people's minds. I think it will make other people want to donate because they are not just giving money away. I am hoping it creates a feeling of empathy because they will be part of a process that empowers people. I will put it in my poster and also make a label for my fund-raising jar at dad's hardware store.

# 15 Providing Feedback to Students

**Purpose: Provide effective feedback to a student engaged in Deep Learning**

**Process: Thought Bubbles**

**Time: 20–30 minutes**

Resource:
• Student A's Work, Protocol 14

**1** **Refer** to the three examples of Student A's work in Protocol 14.

**2** **Read** the principles of effective feedback.

**3** **Construct** feedback for Student A while keeping the principles in mind. Write out what you would say to Student A in the white dialogue bubble.

**4** **Share** what you have written with a partner.

**5** **Reflect** together:

- What principle of feedback do you routinely use?
- What principle of feedback could you apply more often?
- How might you provide the feedback in the form of a question?
- What are some of the challenges you regularly face when providing feedback?

" Building clarity and shared understanding of the Competencies is the first step toward Deep Learning. "

*—DEEP LEARNING: ENGAGE THE WORLD CHANGE THE WORLD, P. 56*

# THOUGHT BUBBLES

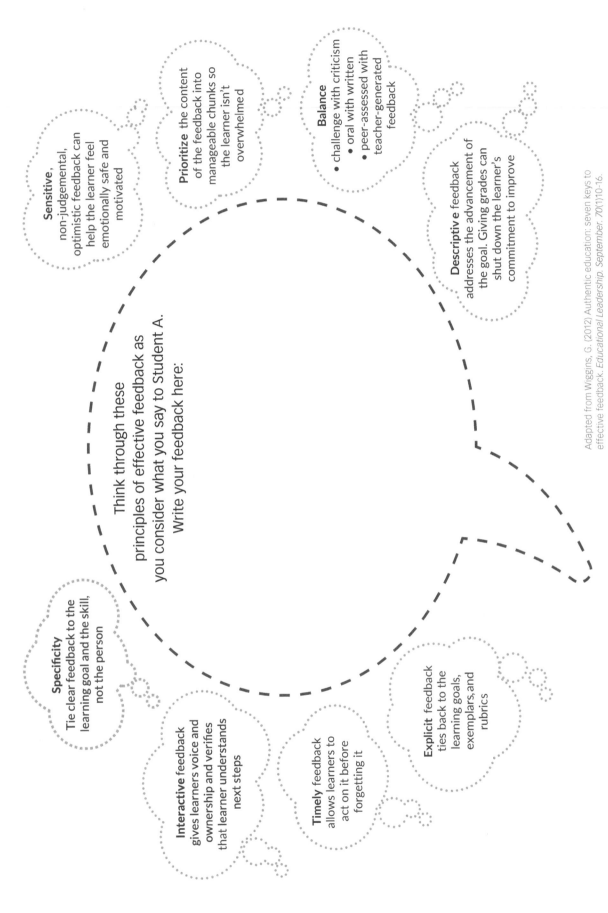

Think through these principles of effective feedback as you consider what you say to Student A. Write your feedback here:

**Sensitive,** non-judgemental, optimistic feedback can help the learner feel emotionally safe and motivated

**Prioritize** the content of the feedback into manageable chunks so the learner isn't overwhelmed

**Balance**
• challenge with criticism
• oral with written
• peer-assessed with teacher-generated feedback

**Descriptive** feedback addresses the advancement of the goal. Giving grades can shut down the learner's commitment to improve

**Specificity** Tie clear feedback to the learning goal and the skill, not the person

**Interactive** feedback gives learners voice and ownership and verifies that learner understands next steps

**Timely** feedback allows learners to act on it before forgetting it

**Explicit** feedback ties back to the learning goals, exemplars, and rubrics

Adapted from Wiggins, G. (2012) Authentic education: seven keys to effective feedback. *Educational Leadership. 70*(1)10-16.

# 16 Student-Friendly Learning Progressions

**Purpose: Understanding the Student-Friendly Learning Progressions**

**Time: 10–30 minutes**

**Process: Discussing**

**Resources:**
Tools:
- Collaboration Learning Progression
- Collaboration Student-Friendly Learning Progression

Vignettes:
- Student-Friendly Language: Meet Them Where They're At

**1** **View** the Student-Friendly Learning Progressions.

**2** **Discuss**

- What are some similarities to and differences from the **Collaboration Learning Progression** in Protocol 12?
- What added value does a **Student-Friendly Learning Progression** bring to the learning?
- How might you use this tool to help your students become self-directed learners?
- How might you adapt this tool to support learners with diverse needs?
- How might this **Student-Friendly Learning Progression** be used within your school?

**3** **Form a group of three** and read the vignette **Student Friendly Language: Meet Them Where They're At**. Share the insights in your small group and consider how the Student-Friendly Learning Progressions can be used in your classroom or school.

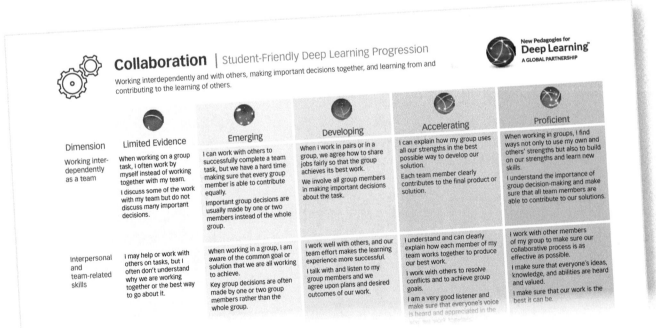

" Students need to take responsibility for their learning and to understand the process of learning, if it is to be maximized. This requires students to develop skills in *metacognition*, giving and receiving *feedback*, and enacting *student agency*. "

—*DEEP LEARNING: ENGAGE THE WORLD CHANGE THE WORLD*, P. 62

# 17 Engaging Students With the Student-Friendly Learning Progressions

**Purpose: Use a Y chart to understand how to engage students with Student-Friendly Learning Progressions**

**Process: Using a Y Chart**

**Time: 30 minutes**

**Resources:**

Tools:
- Collaboration Learning Progression
- Collaboration Student-Friendly Learning Progression

**1** **Form small groups.**

**2** **Review**

- Collaboration Learning Progression and the dimension: Managing Team Dynamics
- Student-Friendly Learning Progression; Collaboration

**3** **Identify key concepts** that are evident in both.

**4** **Using a Y chart**, identify what those key concepts would look like, sound like, and feel like in your classroom using student-friendly language.

**5** **Discuss**

- In what ways do Y Charts help us make sense of our observations?
- What are some ways you could use the Student-Friendly Learning Progression in your classroom? In your school? With your parent community?

**6** **Repeat** the process with other dimensions or progressions to build familiarity.

**7** **Read the quote.** Each person takes turns responding to the whole quote (or a part of it), by beginning with the sentence stem: "This makes me think . . ."

> What we see happening is that a collective understanding of the 6Cs emerges as a living part of the culture. Students begin to act more ethically and with greater empathy in their interactions with peers and the world. But it's not just about feeling good—a depth of intentionality begins to emerge both in the way the teacher designs and codesigns learning using the progressions as an anchor and on the part of students to develop themselves and to see that growth in others.

*—DEEP LEARNING: ENGAGE THE WORLD CHANGE THE WORLD, P. 55*

# Y Chart Organizer
What might this look, sound, and feel like in your classroom?

sound like?

look like?

feel like?

# 18 The Student Self-Assessment Tool

Purpose: **Understand the structure and purpose of the Student Self-Assessment Tool**

Process: **Discussion**

Time: **15–30 minutes**

Resources:
Tools:
• Collaboration Student Friendly Learning Progression
• Student Self-Assessment Tool

**1** **Review** the Student Friendly Learning Progression.

• Notice how a learner has highlighted areas of his or her competence.

**2** **Review** the Student Self-Assessment Tool and note:

• the descriptors of the five dimensions of the Collaboration Progression on the left
• how the student has transferred the highlighted descriptors into ratings
• the ratings scale from Limited to Proficient
• that this tool asks learners to provide evidence that supports their self-assessments
• the prompts that ask students to consider future focus and action

**3** **Discuss**

• How does the Student Self-Assessment Tool help learners to reflect and commit to action?
• At what point(s) in Learning Design would this be most helpful to students?
• How might you introduce this tool to students?
• How might you use this tool with parents?

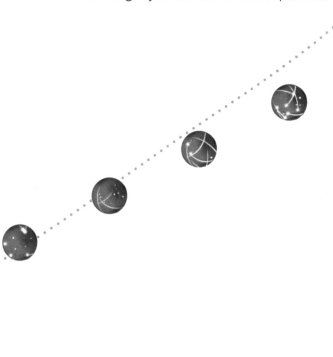

# SAMPLE STUDENT-FRIENDLY LEARNING PROGRESSION

## Collaboration | Student-Friendly Deep Learning Progression

 New Pedagogies for **Deep Learning**™ A GLOBAL PARTNERSHIP

Working interdependently and with others, making important decisions together, and learning from and contributing to the learning of others.

| Dimension |  Limited Evidence |  Emerging |  Developing |  Accelerating | Proficient |
|---|---|---|---|---|---|
| **Working interdependently as a team** | When working on a group task, I often work by myself instead of working together with my team. I discuss some of the work with my team but do not discuss many important decisions. | I can work with others to successfully complete a team task, but we have a hard time making sure that every group member is able to contribute equally. Important group decisions are usually made by one or two members instead of the whole group. | When I work in pairs or in a group, we agree how to share jobs fairly so that the group achieves its best work. We involve all group members in making important decisions about the task. | I can explain how my group uses all our strengths in the best possible way to develop our solution. Each team member clearly contributes to the final product or solution. | When working in groups, I find ways not only to use my own and others' strengths but also to build on our strengths and learn new skills. I understand the importance of group decision-making and make sure that all team members are able to contribute to our solutions. |
| **Interpersonal and team-related skills** | I may help or work with others on tasks, but I often don't understand why we are working together or the best way to go about it. | When working in a group, I am aware of the common goal or solution that we are all working to achieve. Key group decisions are often made by one or two group members rather than the whole group. | I work well with others, and our team effort makes the learning experience more successful. I talk with and listen to my group members and we agree upon plans and desired outcomes of our work. | I understand and can clearly explain how each member of my team works together to produce our best work. I work with others to resolve conflicts and to achieve group goals. I am a very good listener and make sure that everyone's voice is heard and appreciated in the way we work together. | I work with other members of my group to make sure our collaborative process is as effective as possible. I make sure that everyone's ideas, knowledge, and abilities are heard and valued. I make sure that our work is the best it can be. |
| **Social, emotional, and intercultural skills** | I am beginning to see that my behavior has an impact on others but still have trouble seeing things from other people's perspectives. I sometimes struggle to form positive relationships with my group members. | I am developing a better understanding of who I am and what I am interested in. I see how my behavior affects others and know that people may have different feelings and opinions than my own. | I understand who I am as a person and why I have my perspectives. I listen to and understand other people's viewpoints, and I value their perspectives even if they differ from my own. | I have a strong sense of who I am. I fully understand my own perspectives and know how and why they differ from others'. I listen to the emotions and viewpoints of others and use them to improve my own learning. In teams, I work in ways that help me grow as a person and that help my team members grow as well. | My social and emotional skills show that I have a strong sense of myself and my culture. I communicate respectfully with everyone and form positive relationships with team members. I understand other people's perspectives and am able to change my behavior after listening to others. |

 New Pedagogies for **Deep Learning**™ A GLOBAL PARTNERSHIP

## Collaboration (Cont'd) | Student-Friendly Deep Learning Progression

Working interdependently and with others, making important decisions together, and learning from and contributing to the learning of others.

| Dimension |  Limited Evidence |  Emerging |  Developing | Accelerating | Proficient |
|---|---|---|---|---|---|
| **Managing team dynamics and challenges** | When working in groups, I have trouble listening to or accepting viewpoints that are different from my own, or I avoid conflict by not sharing my own ideas. This negatively impacts my team and our work. | I need help forming positive relationships with my group members. I am learning to handle disagreements by listening to the perspectives of others, but we have trouble working through our differences. | I most often work well as a team member but sometimes need help solving problems and challenges. I respectfully share my viewpoints and learn from the viewpoints of others. I am beginning to understand why people view things the way they do. | I understand my own and others' points of view and know what goes into our beliefs. I share my own views and listen to and learn from the views of others without holding up our team's progress. | I firmly understand my own and others' points of view, clearly express my own viewpoints, and consistently learn from others. I respect group members' opinions in ways that help us grow and achieve our common goal. |
| **Using technology for learning (leveraging digital)** | I can use some technologies to collaborate with others. | I can use technology to work with others and monitor our group effectiveness. | I use technology to work independently and collaboratively. Technology allows me to understand and appreciate others' points of view. | I can clearly describe how technology improves how we work together, how we share responsibilities, and how we make decisions about important aspects of our work. | I effortlessly use technology to collaborate effectively, working and thinking in new and deeper ways. Technology allows me to work in ways that suit my needs. Technology allows all our team members to make significant contributions to the task. |

# Character Deep Learning Progression

New Pedagogies for **Deep Learning**™
A GLOBAL PARTNERSHIP

Learning to deep learn, armed with the essential social and emotional character traits of self-directed learning, grit, tenacity, perseverance, and resilience, the ability to make learning an integral part of living; and to proactively change outcomes for themselves and others.

| Dimension | Limited Evidence | Emerging | Developing | Accelerating | Proficient |
|---|---|---|---|---|---|
| **Self-directed learners with a proactive stance toward life and learning to learn** | When given a Deep Learning experience, learners need a lot of direction and structure. They expect to be given rather than to create a plan. Learners do not yet demonstrate an openness to learning. | With guidance, learners are starting to build their skills in planning and making choices and decisions about their learning. Learners can work with teachers to choose a topic and find or create an opportunity to learn what they need. Learners are beginning to view errors and feedback as opportunities to learn. Learners are beginning to demonstrate a positive view toward learning; they are developing a sense of self-efficacy and interest in achievement. | Learners are increasingly taking responsibility for their own learning, both as individuals and within groups. They can plan their approach to tasks, monitor their own progress, and reflect on and improve the quality of their work as they do it. They welcome feedback as an opportunity to learn and improve. Learners show a positive view toward learning and understand that this willingness to learn leads to achievement. | Learners have strong capabilities in self-regulation, self-reflection, and taking responsibility for their own learning. They can think effectively, make decisions for themselves, and take ownership of their learning. Learners seek feedback as needed and either adjust the current learning experience or improve the next learning task. Learners regularly show a positive learning stance that is open to learning. They are eager to bring their best to each learning and achievement opportunity. They are learning to balance the drive to succeed with other important aspects of life. | Learners are highly efficient at finding and creating their own learning opportunities in ways that help them build the knowledge and skills they will need to succeed in life and to create worthwhile solutions. Learners are self-directed, self-regulated co-learners and co-designers of the learning. Learners actively seek out feedback and use it to better understand their approaches to learning. They see learning as an integral part of life. Learners share their positive outlook with others and have a drive to do their best, even in challenging circumstances. They balance their drive to succeed with other important aspects of life. |
| **Grit, tenacity, perseverance, and resilience** | Learners become discouraged or give up when faced with challenges, unexpected problems, or negative feedback when trying to complete a task, experience, or action. This seriously impacts their ability to work through the challenge and find a solution. | Learners require support and encouragement to deal with setbacks, negative feedback, and difficult challenges. They are starting to show some grit and resilience but tend to lose momentum unless supported. | Grit, tenacity, perseverance, and resilience are developing in the way learners approach and complete their Deep Learning or experience and deal with challenges. Major setbacks or negative feedback may challenge them They deal well with small to moderate challenges, pausing and reflecting to think of new solutions and persisting until they find a breakthrough. | Grit, tenacity, and perseverance are clearly evident in the way learners approach and complete their Deep Learning tasks. In the face of major setbacks or negative feedback, they pause, reflect, adapt as necessary, and approach the issue with determination until they find a breakthrough. Learners are able to articulate how and why these character qualities are essential for life and work. | Learners have highly developed grit, tenacity, perseverance, and resilience. This allows them to be flexible and work through and support others through challenges. Feedback and challenges are sought out and used as an opportunity to learn. They understand the importance of these character qualities as essential for creating meaningful change in life, work, and the world. |

Source: McEachen, J., & Quinn, J. Copyright © 2019 by Education in Motion (New Pedagogies for Deep Learning™). All rights reserved. Reproduction authorized for educational use by educators, local school sites, and/or noncommercial or nonprofit entities that have purchased the book.

## Character Deep Learning Progression (Cont'd)

Learning to deep learn, armed with the essential social and emotional character traits of self-directed learning, grit, tenacity, perseverance, and resilience; the ability to make learning an integral part of living; and to proactively change outcomes for themselves and others.

New Pedagogies for
**Deep Learning**™
A GLOBAL PARTNERSHIP

| Dimension | Limited Evidence | Emerging | Developing | Accelerating | Proficient |
|---|---|---|---|---|---|
| **Empathy, compassion, and integrity in action** | Learners have yet to understand how empathy, compassion, and integrity impact learning interactions and broader contexts. | Learners are beginning to understand how empathy, compassion, and integrity impact learning interactions and broader contexts. | Learners understand from personal experience how empathy, compassion, and integrity impact learning interactions and broader contexts. They show genuine commitment to developing these virtues. | Learners self-reflect and are striving regularly to demonstrate empathy, compassion, and integrity in all aspects of learning and life. | Learners demonstrate a high degree of compassion, empathy, and integrity. They hold a high standard for themselves even when it is unnoticed by others. They model sincerity, trustworthiness, fairness, and bravery for others, even when it is inconvenient. They take action when they encounter injustices. |
| **Leveraging digital** | Learners use some digital elements during the learning process, but they do not recognize how digital can support their learning and attitude toward learning. | Learners use digital elements to assist with their learning. They are beginning to use digital to develop empathy, compassion, and grit. | Learners regularly use digital elements to advance their learning. They use digital to develop traits like empathy, compassion, and grit. | Learners can articulate how using digital elements enhances their ability to learn from and reflect on their learning and development of traits like empathy, compassion, and grit. | Learners choose and use appropriate digital platforms, tools, and technologies to define and monitor the success of their learning goals and strategies. They use digital elements to support the empathy, compassion, and grit in others. |

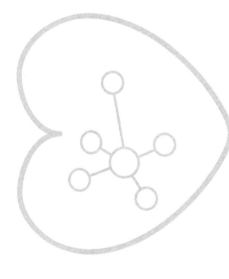

# Citizenship Deep Learning Progression

Thinking like global citizens, considering individual and societal well-being, and global issues based on a deep understanding of diverse values and worldviews, with genuine interest, empathy, compassion, and ability to solve ambiguous and complex real-world problems that impact equity and human and environmental sustainability.

| Dimension | Limited Evidence | Emerging | Developing | Accelerating | Proficient |
|---|---|---|---|---|---|
| **A global perspective** | Learners have an inward view of the world and show little interest in or understanding of issues and perspectives of people beyond their immediate world. | Learners explore or show interest in local or global issues, considering different viewpoints as they try to understand causes and consequences. | Learners show an understanding of local and global issues. They have a clearer sense of concepts such as peace and conflict, global interdependence, and the inequities and injustices that exist in the world. | Learners actively engage in thinking about and take action in response to global issues both individually and collectively. They are beginning to recognize their own agency and respect that they and everyone can contribute in a global society. | Learners think and act as global citizens. They seek out issues of global importance and have a belief that people can make a difference in the world, and they actively engage in making this happen. |
| **Commitment to human equity and well-being through empathy and compassion for diverse values and worldviews** | Learners have difficulty understanding, accepting, and appreciating the perspectives of people in cultures different from their own. | Learners are starting to show some awareness of their own identities and cultures and understand a few of the differences from cultures other than their own. Learners still need significant guidance to understand and accept other ways of thinking. | Learners are developing a sense of their individual and cultural identities and know how this affects the way they see the world. With guidance, they are learning to have empathy for and compassion toward other worldviews. | Learners have an open-minded curiosity about different cultures and worldviews that is rooted in a strong awareness of their own. Learners genuinely care about equity, showing empathy and compassion for others. | Learners use their understanding of their own and others' cultures to take action to alleviate inequities. They consider global issues in relation to diverse values and worldviews. They model empathy and compassion as they proactively engage with others to enhance equity and well-being in the world. |
| **Genuine interest in human and environmental sustainability** | Learners have a low level of awareness and caring about environmental issues. | Learners recognize how each person's actions impact the human and local environment. With guidance, they are able to build these concepts into their inquiries. | Learners have appreciation of the importance of human and environmental sustainability in the local and/or wider world. They are beginning to build these concepts into their inquiries. | Learners can generate environmentally sustainable solutions that affect the planet and its inhabitants. They are independently applying these concepts into their inquiries. | Learners have a compelling view of human and environmental issues and their importance. They infuse this perspective into their work and actively improve outcomes for human and environmental sustainability. |

New Pedagogies for
**Deep Learning**™
A GLOBAL PARTNERSHIP

## Citizenship Deep Learning Progression (Cont'd)

Thinking like global citizens, considering individual and societal well-being, and global issues based on a deep understanding of diverse values and worldviews, with genuine interest, empathy, compassion, and ability to solve ambiguous and complex real-world problems that impact equity and human and environmental sustainability.

| Dimension | Limited Evidence | Emerging | Developing | Accelerating | Proficient |
|---|---|---|---|---|---|
| **Solving ambiguous and complex problems in the real world to benefit citizens** | Learners have a low level of comfort working with real-world challenges and problems. They need tasks identified, framed, or structured for them. | Learners are starting to develop some familiarity with open-ended real-world challenges and problems. They still need some guidance to work out where to start, but a level of comfort with ambiguity is emerging. | Learners have developed interest in open-ended real-world challenges and problems. Learners require only broad parameters to get started on the task and have a developing ability to work with ambiguity. | Learners are motivated to learn more and address real-world challenges and problems that affect local and global citizens. Learners have skill in exploring complex real-world problems that have high levels of ambiguity and no pre-determined solution. | Learners tackle real-world challenges and problems. They can create a perspective or way of looking at the issue rather than needing to have one identified for them. |
| **Leveraging digital** | Learners do not yet use digital elements to generate questions and explore global issues. | Learners are beginning to use digital elements to begin to understand issues in their community. They connect with community members through technology and are beginning to understand that digital citizenship means communicating and using technology respectfully. | Learners effectively use digital elements to amplify their connections locally and globally. Learners use digital to connect and understand issues. They are learning that digital citizenship means communicating and engaging with technology in respectful, empathetic, legal, and appropriate ways. | Digital is used to connect and create empathetic global, culturally relevant, equitable, just, and environmentally sustainable solutions. Learners connect digitally with people from a variety of cultures and backgrounds and demonstrate consistently strong digital citizenship behaviors. They can articulate how infusing a digital element has enhanced the global, cultural, and environmental elements of the learning process. | Learners choose and use appropriate digital platforms, tools, and technologies to deepen and enrich their perspectives. Digital technologies enable collaborative examination of complex problems from multiple perspectives. Learners are able to articulate and model digital citizenship in ways that contribute to enhancing equity, justice, and sustainability in different cultures and environments. |

# Collaboration Deep Learning Progression

Work interdependently and synergistically in teams with strong interpersonal and team-related skills, including effective management of team dynamics and challenges, making substantive decisions together, and contributing to learning from and having an impact on others.

| Dimension | Limited Evidence | Emerging | Developing | Accelerating | Proficient |
|---|---|---|---|---|---|
| **Working interdependently as a team** | Learners either work individually on learning tasks or collaborate informally in pairs or groups but do not work as a team. Learners may discuss some issues or content together but skip over important substantive decisions (such as how the process will be managed), which has significant adverse impacts on how well the collaboration works. | Learners work together in pairs or groups and are responsible for completing a task in order for the group to achieve its task. Learners are starting to make some decisions together but may still be leaving the most important substantive decisions to one or two members. Group members' contributions may not be equitable. | Learners decide together how to match tasks to the individual strengths and expertise of team members and then work effectively together. Learners involve all members in making joint decisions about an important issue, problem, or process and in developing a team solution. | Learners can articulate how they work together to use each other's strengths to make substantive decisions and develop ideas and solutions. Teamwork is clearly evident in that learners' contributions are woven together to communicate an overarching idea and/or create a product. | Learners demonstrate a highly effective and synergistic approach to work in a way that not only leverages each member's strengths but provides opportunities. Each team member's strengths and perspectives are infused to come to the best possible decision that benefits all. |
| **Interpersonal and team-related skills** | Learners may help each other on tasks that contribute to a joint work product or outcome; interpersonal, and team-related skills are not yet evident. Learners do not yet demonstrate a genuine sense of empathy or a shared purpose for working together. | Learners report and demonstrate a sense of collective ownership for the work and are beginning to show interpersonal and team-related skills. Their focus is on achieving a common or joint outcome, product, design, response, or decision. Key decisions may be made or dominated by one or two members. | Strong interpersonal skills, collective ownership for the work, and an active sense of shared responsibility are evident. From beginning to end, learners listen effectively, negotiate and agree on the goals, content, process, design, and conclusions of their work. | Learners can clearly articulate how joint responsibility for the work and its product or outcome pervades the entire task. They show strong skills in listening, facilitation, and effective teamwork and ensure that all voices are heard and reflected in the work and work product. | Learners take active responsibility for ensuring that the collaborative process works. They ensure that each person's ideas and expertise are used to maximum advantage and that each work product or outcome is of the highest possible quality or value. |
| **Social, emotional, and intercultural skills** | Learners have a basic sense of awareness about themselves. Learners tend to see things only from their own perspective. In some cases, this may inhibit their ability to form positive relationships. | Learners are finding out about themselves, where they fit in the world, and how their behavior affects other people. This self-awareness is providing a base for better understanding about how others' viewpoints differ from their own. | Learners have an awareness of themselves and where their own perspective comes from. Self-awareness and listening skills allow learners to better understand and empathize with the emotions and viewpoints of others, moving beyond "tolerance" or "acceptance" to genuinely valuing perspectives quite different from their own. | Learners have a strong sense of self and understand where their own perspective comes from and how it differs from others'. Learners listen carefully, empathize with the emotions and viewpoints of others, and use these to enrich their own learning. As team members, they work effectively in ways that support, encourage, challenge, and progress themselves and others. | Learners have highly developed social and emotional skills grounded in a clear sense of their individual and cultural identities. Learners communicate well across cultures and disciplines, work effectively in teams, and form positive relationships. The skills they have developed in understanding the perspectives of others, empathy, and compassion impact team functioning. |

New Pedagogies for
**Deep Learning**™
A GLOBAL PARTNERSHIP

## Collaboration Deep Learning Progression (Cont'd)

Work interdependently and synergistically in teams with strong interpersonal and team-related skills, including effective management of team dynamics and challenges, making substantive decisions together, and contributing to learning from and having an impact on others.

| Dimension | Limited Evidence | Emerging | Developing | Accelerating | Proficient |
|---|---|---|---|---|---|
| **Managing team dynamics and challenges** | Learners are deeply invested in their own viewpoints, lack the empathy to hear or learn from others, and have difficulty suspending judgment to genuinely listen to others' views.<br><br>They avoid conflict by deferring to others' views or change views quickly in the face of peer pressure. Teams may get stuck in conflict or move forward in the wrong team direction. | Learners still need guidance to forge and maintain positive working relationships and to resist inappropriate peer pressure.<br><br>Learners take a more thoughtful approach to dealing with disagreements, asking each member to share their perspective and discussing any differences.<br><br>They begin to dig beneath those differences to identify what underpins them. | Learners generally work quite effectively in a team, although they are likely to need help with conflict resolution, inappropriate peer pressure, and other challenging issues.<br><br>Learners are developing the ability to identify what underpins their own and others' points of view.<br><br>They are getting better at expressing their viewpoints and listening to and learning from others. | Learners are skilled at identifying what underpins their own and others' points of view. They can pick their battles in deciding what to debate.<br><br>They are building both courage and clarity to express their own viewpoints and listen to and learn from others.<br><br>Learners are becoming skilled at exploring different opinions in ways that contribute to the learning of others without holding up team progress. | Learners have a deep understanding of what underpins their own and others' points of view, the courage and clarity to effectively express their own viewpoints, and the empathy to hear and learn from others.<br><br>Learners respectfully explore different opinions in ways that enrich their own and others' learning and thinking.<br><br>Learners leverage a range of strategies to propose solutions and minimize tensions. |
| **Leveraging digital** | Learners use some digital elements to connect and collaborate. | Learners use digital elements to facilitate shared ways of working, learning, and reflecting on group progress. | Learners effectively use digital elements to build interdependence and understand other points of view. | Learners can articulate how using digital elements facilitates interdependence, deepens the nature of collaboration, builds a better sense of shared responsibility, and improves the learning or product. | Learners choose and use appropriate digital platforms, tools, and technologies to enrich their learning and the learning of others.<br><br>Learners use digital technologies to enable them to work highly effectively and efficiently, regardless of physical location. |

# Communication Deep Learning Progression

Communicating effectively with a purpose and voice in a variety of modes and tools (including digital) and tailored to impact a range of audiences and learning outcomes.

| Dimension | Limited Evidence | Emerging | Developing | Accelerating | Proficient |
|---|---|---|---|---|---|
| **Communication designed for audience and impact** | Learners follow a prescribed format for communicating and may restrict their communication to one particular mode (e.g., written, texting, verbal, visual). | Learners choose from a range of communication modes to convey their message but still need guidance. | Learners are becoming skilled at choosing a range of communication modes and tools to convey their message. | Learners can analyze advantages of using different communication modes and tools. They are beginning to consider how their message will be received by a range of audiences. | Learners are selective about when and how to communicate with a range of specific audiences. They can clearly articulate how and why they make choices about communication modes and tools to convey their impactful message. |
| **Message advocates a purpose and makes impact** | The learner's message is unclear. Learners do not yet use communication techniques with intentionality. | The learner's message is coherent. Learners are becoming aware, through trial and error, of ways in which communication techniques (language, tone, timing, organizational patterns, and representational features) can advance credibility. | The learner's message is coherent but the call to action is unclear. Learners are aware of communication techniques (language, tone, timing, organizational patterns, and representational features) but do not use them to their full advantage. | The learner's message is thought provoking but may not inspire change. Learners use communication techniques (language, tone, timing, organizational patterns, and representational features) to communicate effectively but the message may lack impact. | The learner's message is compelling and may challenge thinking or call for action. They skillfully use subtle and overt communication techniques (language, tone, timing, organizational patterns, and representational features) to communicate convincingly. |
| **Reflection to further develop and improve communication** | Learners seek feedback from others when directed. | Learners seek feedback from others using checklists or other teacher-directed rubrics and protocols. | Learners seek feedback from others and are beginning to reflect on their communication processes. Learners are developing the ability to monitor, manage, and improve their communication throughout each task. | Learners participate in continuous cycles of feedback and self-reflection to improve upon and refine messages. Learners understand multiple perspectives and can adapt messages. | Learners proactively reflect, revise, and refine communication to be sure their messages will be understood as intended. They seek multiple perspectives and check for personal bias. |

## Communication Deep Learning Progression (Cont'd)

Communicating effectively with a purpose and voice in a variety of modes and tools (including digital) and tailored to impact a range of audiences and learning outcomes.

| Dimension | Limited Evidence | Emerging | Developing | Accelerating | Proficient |
|---|---|---|---|---|---|
| **Voice and Identity expressed to advance humanity** | Learners are unaware of their own voice and identity or the connections to experience, value, culture, and interests. | Learners are exploring their own experiences, values, culture, and interests and are working to articulate their voice and identity.<br><br>They are beginning to recognize diverse voices and identities of others. | Learners are reflecting on their own experiences, values, culture, and interests and are working to understand how their unique voice and identity can impact others.<br><br>They are beginning to include diverse voices and identities in their communication. | Learners express themselves authentically and communicate with the intention of improving a condition greater than themselves.<br><br>Their communication authentically incorporates the voices and identities of those who may not be heard. | Learners express themselves authentically and the impact of this has the transformational power of improving a condition greater than themselves or enriching the understanding of others.<br><br>They champion for those whose voices and identities may not be heard. |
| **Leveraging digital** | Learners occasionally use digital elements for communication or to present findings.<br><br>Learners use technology but it does not yet contribute to the quality, reach, or speed of communication either within the team or with the audience.<br><br>Learners have difficulty explaining how digital enhances communication. | Learners use digital elements for communication during the learning process and/or to deliver the key messages to intended audiences.<br><br>Communication may be more efficient, broader, or faster, but may not significantly enhance the quality of communication.<br><br>They can articulate how familiar digital tools can enhance communication. | Learners use digital elements effectively to improve both the efficiency and quality of communication during the learning process.<br><br>Learners use technology to tailor communication of key concepts to different audiences in ways that enhance their understanding and retention of key ideas and concepts.<br><br>Learners are beginning to explore and reflect upon the effectiveness of new technologies for communication. | Learners can use familiar and newly discovered technologies to clearly articulate how infusing digital elements has enhanced communication aspects.<br><br>Learners use tools to create messages likely to stick in the minds of the audience and lead them to take action.<br><br>They regularly consider and reflect on how digital tools enhance the effectiveness and reach of their communication. | Learners choose and use appropriate multi-model digital platforms, tools, and technologies to meet the needs of both the task and their audience.<br><br>Learners use tools to deepen the efficiency, reach, quality, and value of communication within the team and across audiences.<br><br>Learners can articulate in detail how each digital element has enhanced communication. |

# Creativity Deep Learning Progression

Having an "entrepreneurial eye" for economic and social opportunities, expressing oneself in unique ways, asking the right inquiry questions to generate novel ideas, and leadership to pursue those ideas and turn them into action.

| Dimension | Limited Evidence | Emerging | Developing | Accelerating | Proficient |
|---|---|---|---|---|---|
| **Economic and social entrepreneurialism** | Learners have not yet developed an "entrepreneurial eye" for spotting opportunities to create value or meet needs, whether social or economic. | With guidance, learners are beginning to develop an entrepreneurial way of looking for a need, problem, or opportunity in the world that they might be able to solve in a way that generates economic and/or social benefits. | With practice, learners have developed a keen eye to identify opportunities to solve real problems in ways that deliver both social and economic benefits. Learners can identify the resources needed to bring their ideas to life. | Learners have a strong drive to find worthwhile solutions that are economically viable. Learners can visualize what the future could be like and are finding ways to optimize resources to create impactful solutions. Their entrepreneurial spirit embodies innovation, risk taking, vision, and a can-do attitude. | Learners have developed a talent for implementing change that solves real-world problems. Learners can review talents and resources to bring together those needed to make the change happen. They display a relentless drive to question and imagine new futures and take action to improve lives and make change. |
| **Asking the right inquiry questions** | Learners struggle to generate significant questions that would inspire deep exploration of issues or problems. They may be able to design an inquiry process if questions are defined for them but are not yet creating questions independently. | Learners can brainstorm inquiry questions to identify authentic needs and opportunities, define real-world problems, and design ways for inquiring into them. They may need guidance (co-constructing questions with a teacher), but the skills are clearly emerging. | Learners have skills in identifying authentic issues and problems and can compose and refine good questions that will advance their inquiry. They can follow a structured process. | The inquiry skills and the process for pursuing understanding are well established; learners can identify authentic, challenging issues and can select an inquiry process to help them understand the issue in a real-world context. | Learners can select and frame complex problems, questions, and wonderings that open up more questions, thinking, and possibilities. They actively grapple to understand "big ideas" and draw from a range of important thinking processes and skills to support their inquiry. They have a genuine curiosity to define and explore issues. |
| **Pursuing and expressing novel ideas and solutions** | Learners are in the mindset of looking for a pre-determined or existing solution rather than coming up with original approaches or designs and testing them out to see what works. | Learners' thinking is grounded in knowledge of existing solutions. Students can build improvements by tweaking and adapting with guidance and prompting. Learners use a limited range of thinking and creativity strategies (such as brainstorming) to generate thinking that is new to them. | Learners challenge their own mindsets by identifying and evaluating promising ideas. They are developing skills in using thinking and creativity strategies. Their expressions and solutions contribute to improvement of what currently exists. | Learners exhibit divergent thinking that questions the status quo. They are skilled in a wide range of thinking and creativity strategies, which they use to generate new possibilities. They actively pursue ideas that are innovative and are not hindered by constraints. Their expressions and solutions bring value and originality. | Learners are highly observant and can identify novel ideas and solutions to real problems. Learners draw new connections to their innovative thinking. This leads to fresh applications across diverse disciplines. They confidently express and share their unique perspectives about how to act on their ideas. |

New Pedagogies for
**Deep Learning**™
A GLOBAL PARTNERSHIP

## Creativity Deep Learning Progression (Cont'd)

Having an "entrepreneurial eye" for economic and social opportunities, expressing oneself in unique ways, asking the right inquiry questions to generate novel ideas and leadership to pursue those ideas and leadership to pursue those ideas and turn them into action.

| Dimension | Limited Evidence | Emerging | Developing | Accelerating | Proficient |
|---|---|---|---|---|---|
| **Leadership to turn ideas into action** | Learners at this level are unlikely to have the skills or confidence to bring together other people to make a vision into a reality. | Learners are developing some leadership skills and can take responsibility for particular parts of a task or experience. | Learners are developing skills in action-oriented leadership and how best to manage their roles so as to balance out competing interests. They are able to see the vision of what success will look like, and they know what it will take to make it happen. | Learners have skills in leadership for action and a can-do attitude that others respond to positively. They organize a plan that leverages their strengths and interests while building the skills. | Learners are skilled at challenging the status quo and bringing people with them to create deep change. They have action-oriented leadership skills and genuine courage to pursue a task. Learners have the perseverance and vision to lead their learning through to outcomes, negotiating any obstacles along the way. |
| **Leveraging digital** | Learners use some digital elements during the creative process or to present findings. These elements do not substantially contribute to the efficiency of the process or the quality of the creative products produced. | Learners use digital opportunities to identify and pursue creative ideas. Digital elements make the creative process faster or more efficient but are unlikely to have significantly enhanced the value of what was created. | Learners effectively use digital elements in creative ways and to create new artifacts. They can refine their questions, inquiries, and thinking through the use of digital elements. Learners can explore local opportunities to create new knowledge through the use of digital elements. | Learners can use digital elements to design, identify, and solve challenges in new ways. Learners use technology to enhance and understand the questions they are asking and being asked. They are beginning to broaden their perspectives and explore possibilities for real-world application of their ideas. | Learners choose and use appropriate digital platforms, tools, and technologies to create original works or repurpose existing resources into new or novel artifacts. Learners use technology to inquire, define, and refine questions and realize the full potential of an idea. Learners use technologies to tap new opportunities, partners, or environments. |

**CHAPTER 07 | Using Learning Progressions**   123

Source: McEachen, J., & Quinn, J. Copyright © 2019 by Education in Motion (New Pedagogies for Deep Learning™). All rights reserved. Reproduction authorized for educational use by educators, local school sites, and/or noncommercial or nonprofit entities that have purchased the book.

# Critical Thinking Deep Learning Progression

Critically evaluating information and arguments, seeing patterns and connections, constructing meaningful knowledge, and applying and assessing it in the real world.

| Dimension | Limited Evidence | Emerging | Developing | Accelerating | Proficient |
|---|---|---|---|---|---|
| **Evaluating information and arguments** | Learners can find information on any topic, but they have difficulty discerning flaws in the premises, reasoning, assumptions, and/or conclusions of given arguments. | Learners are beginning to evaluate assumptions, premises, reasoning, and conclusions using effective information search skills. | Learners can source and evaluate trustworthy, relevant information. They can intuitively identify strengths and weaknesses but may struggle to articulate their reasoning. | Learners are skilled at determining whether information is trustworthy, relevant, and useful. They can evaluate strengths and weaknesses in an argument and can explain their rationale. They are able to understand opposing viewpoints. | Learners are skilled at determining, both logically and intuitively, whether information is trustworthy, relevant, and useful. They are skilled evaluators of logical arguments and can identify and articulate strengths and weaknesses with clarity and insight. They can defend their position with relevant references to information or data. |
| **Making connections and identifying patterns** | Learners are able to see relatively simple patterns and connections when they are pointed out. They are unlikely to realize interdisciplinary connections, (that a concept, a learning process, or one curriculum area is connected to another). | Learners are developing their ability to seek, access, explore, and learn from multiple sources and diverse perspectives and viewpoints to expand thinking toward greater understanding, coherence, and appreciation. They are starting to see patterns and make connections, seeing the whole, not just the parts. | Learners can make connections between significant ideas, topics, questions, issues, and thinking and learning processes they are working with. They are also making some connections across artificial boundaries, such as classes, communities, and cultures; time: past, present, and future; and key learning areas or disciplines. | Learners are able to articulate the importance of identifying patterns and connection-making across artificial boundaries, especially across disciplines. They know that this reflects and strengthens their understanding of the interconnected nature of learning and of the world and how it works. | Learners are skilled in anticipating and analyzing connections, patterns, and relationships. Learners are well equipped to draw from diverse sources to construct deep understanding in an interconnected global world. |
| **Meaningful knowledge construction** | Learners can consume and recall information and repeat information in their own words. They are able to respond to direct questions but need guidance to explain their thinking. | Learners begin each experience by exploring what they already know and believe about a topic and use this as the starting point to create new knowledge. Knowledge construction is still "surface level" (limited to interpretation, with minimal use of analysis, synthesis, or evaluation). | Learners are able to find pathways into learning that activate, assess, and build on their existing knowledge and beliefs. They are able to interpret and analyze information and use it to construct meaningful new knowledge but usually only within one discipline at a time. | Learners are able to articulate how they actively create knowledge that is new and usable to them. They are able to interpret, analyze, synthesize, and evaluate information from two or more disciplines or perspectives and make meaningful connections between new ideas and their prior knowledge. | Learners have strong critical thinking and reasoning skills, including interpretation, analysis, synthesis, and evaluation. Knowledge construction is deep, insightful, interdisciplinary or connected across multiple perspectives, and characterized by sound practical thinking. |

## Critical Thinking Deep Learning Progression (Cont'd)

Critically evaluating information and arguments, seeing patterns and connections, constructing meaningful knowledge, and applying and assessing it in the real world.

| Dimension | Limited Evidence | Emerging | Developing | Accelerating | Proficient |
|---|---|---|---|---|---|
| **Experimenting, reflecting, and taking action on ideas in the real world** | Learners tend to see the task and solutions within their own world and struggle to see any wider implications for their learning. They need significant guidance to help them think through how to test out ideas in the real world. | Learners are starting to develop basic skills for experimenting with different ideas and learning what works. They are also learning to think about real-world applications for what they have learned, supported by a teacher who actively scaffolds their thinking. Learners are beginning to apply their learning in different contexts. | Learners are developing the ability to apply logic and reasoning, draw conclusions and design a course of action, and evaluate procedures and outcomes. They are able to adapt, extend, or customize their new knowledge for new, specific situations/contexts, and they apply what they have learned to real-world challenges or situations. | Learners can engage in a process of experimentation to develop rough plans and prototypes and test them out in real-world settings. They can articulate the importance of applying their new knowledge appropriately to new and authentic situations and settings and can explain how they conduct analyses to identify where else this could be applied and how. | Learners routinely apply learning in new and practical ways. They reflect on their own processes, adapt as necessary, and work out how to transfer knowledge into new contexts and take action that makes some difference, based on what they discovered. They have likely identified processes that are effective for identifying and evaluating ideas for creative applications of the knowledge in new contexts. |
| **Leveraging digital** | Learners do not yet use digital elements to contribute to the generation of significant questions, the construction of new knowledge, the making of connections, developing ways of thinking together, or the application of learning to new contexts. | Learners are beginning to use digital elements to generate questions and find patterns, and as a tool for developing thinking together. They are beginning to make connections between concepts and deepen their critical thinking skills. | Learners use digital elements to generate questions and find patterns and as a tool for developing thinking together. They make connections between concepts and are beginning to deepen their critical thinking skills. | Learners effectively use digital elements to generate significant lines of inquiry, explore the topic across multiple disciplines, identify patterns and connections, and deepen their critical thinking skills.<br><br>They use digital elements as tools to enable thinking together and find new contexts for the application of new knowledge. | Learners choose and use appropriate digital platforms, tools, and technologies to deepen the quality and value of their evaluative thinking. They can locate and curate digital information and resources.<br><br>Learners use digital tools to identify patterns and make connections across multiple contexts.<br><br>Learners articulate in detail about how each digital element has enhanced their ability to think critically and apply that understanding to new and different real-world contexts. |

# Character | Student-Friendly Deep Learning Progression

Learning to deep learn, to keep trying, to have integrity, empathy, and compassion, and to always be a learner.

| Dimension | Limited Evidence | Emerging | Developing | Accelerating | Proficient |
|---|---|---|---|---|---|
| | | |  |  |  |
| Proactive stance toward life and learning to deep learn | I am not clear about what I need to learn and why I need to learn it. I can complete tasks my teacher prepares for me, but I need help to reflect on and understand how I am doing with a task. Learning is not a positive experience for me yet. | With help, I can identify what I know, what I need to learn, and why. With help, I can choose a topic and find the information I need. I am learning to see peer and teacher feedback as opportunities to learn and improve. I think I can learn and achieve. | I can describe what I am interested in, what I know, what I need to learn, and why I need to learn it. I can choose a topic and create/design a project to help my learning. I listen to peer and teacher feedback and use it to improve the way I learn. Learning is a positive experience and it leads to a feeling of accomplishment and achievement. | I understand what I need to learn and am skilled at working out how to learn it. As I learn, I reflect on my progress and seek feedback to improve my learning. I use what I learn to help improve current and future projects. I enjoy learning and see it as a way to improve my life. I try to balance work with play. | I have the skills to find and create my own learning opportunities. I am continually building the knowledge and skills that help me succeed in life. I create meaningful solutions that impact my life and the world. I actively seek out feedback and use it to better understand how I learn and what helps me grow. I look for any opportunity to learn something new, even when it's challenging. I balance work with play. |
| Grit, tenacity, perseverance, and resilience | I usually give up when I face an unexpected challenge or receive negative feedback. When a task or experience is too hard, I am unable to work through the challenge to find a solution. | I need a lot of support to deal with setbacks, negative feedback, and difficult challenges. I am starting to work through challenges but still need to be supported and encouraged not to give up. | I am learning to persevere and to not give up even when tasks are challenging. Major setbacks or difficulties may throw me off track sometimes, but I can deal with small or medium challenges by pausing, reflecting, adapting, and finding new solutions. | I persevere and never give up, even when working on the most challenging tasks. When faced with major setbacks or negative feedback, I pause, reflect, adapt, and work through the challenge to find a solution. I understand and can talk about why the character qualities are important for my life. | My grit, tenacity, perseverance, adaptability, and resilience allow me to work through any challenge or setback and to help others do the same. I seek out feedback and use it to help my learning. I understand that the character qualities are essential for creating meaningful change in my life and the world. |

New Pedagogies for **Deep Learning**™ A GLOBAL PARTNERSHIP

New Pedagogies for
**Deep Learning**™
A GLOBAL PARTNERSHIP

## Character (Cont'd) | Student-Friendly Deep Learning Progression

Learning to deep learn, to keep trying, to have integrity, empathy, and compassion, and to always be a learner.

| Dimension | Limited Evidence | Emerging | Developing | Accelerating | Proficient |
|---|---|---|---|---|---|
| | 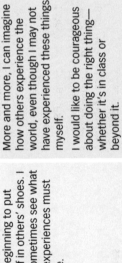 | | 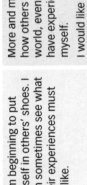 | | |
| Empathy, compassion, and integrity | I am not sure about what other people might feel like when I am interacting with them or when I hear about issues happening in the world. | I am beginning to put myself in others' shoes. I can sometimes see what their experiences must be like. | More and more, I can imagine how others experience the world, even though I may not have experienced these things myself.<br><br>I would like to be courageous about doing the right thing—whether it's in class or beyond it.<br><br>I want to develop empathy, compassion, and integrity in order to be a better person. | I regularly reflect about how I can feel more empathy and show more compassion for others. This is an authentic goal for me.<br><br>I strive to be courageous within the class and beyond it. | I regularly show and model compassion, empathy, and integrity, even when no one notices or when it is inconvenient to do so.<br><br>Virtues such as sincerity, fairness, trustworthiness, and bravery matter to me and it's how I wish others to describe me and the work I do. |
| Using technology for learning (leveraging digital) | I use some digital during the learning process, but I don't see how it supports my learning. | I use digital to assist with my learning occasionally. I am beginning to use digital to develop empathy, compassion, and grit. | I regularly use digital to support my learning and I understand how digital can deepen traits like empathy, compassion, and grit. | I know and can explain how digital helps me to learn and reflect and develop traits like empathy, compassion, and grit. | I effortlessly use technology to help me throughout my learning experience.<br><br>I use digital to support others with their learning by encouraging them and providing feedback. |

# Citizenship | Student-Friendly Deep Learning Progression

Thinking like global citizens and considering global issues with empathy and compassion.

| Dimension | Limited Evidence | Emerging | Developing | Accelerating | Proficient |
|---|---|---|---|---|---|
| A global perspective | I care about my own life and I am not interested in what happens in my own neighbourhood or country. | I am starting to explore and develop interest in local and global issues. I consider these issues from different viewpoints and try to understand why people view issues differently and why these differences are important. | I am actively engaged with the world and interested in its problems and challenges. I am beginning to understand that what happens in one part of the world affects other parts as well. I know that injustices exist, and I want to help make a difference in others' lives and the world. | Individually and with others, I think about and take action on issues affecting our world. I understand that I live in a global, connected world and that this perspective is important in the way I live my life every day. I see that everyone has a role to making the world better. | I think and act as a global citizen. I believe that people can make a difference in the world, and I work hard to make change happen in my community and beyond. |
| Commitment to human equity and well-being through empathy and compassion for diverse values and worldviews | I see the world from my own perspective and don't understand or appreciate the perspectives of people in different cultures. | With help, I am beginning to understand my own culture and some differences of other cultures. | I am beginning to understand that who I am and how I see the world is influenced by where I was born and how I was raised. With guidance, I am learning to understand what the experiences of others might be like and respect other cultures' values and worldviews. | I really care about the world and everyone who lives in it. I am curious about different cultures and worldviews and have a strong understanding of my own. I care about the welfare of people from across the world, even though I don't know them. | I use my strong understanding of my culture and other cultures to better understand global issues from different points of view. When I speak up for others (who can't speak up for themselves), I am helping to make the world better. It is this wider view that allows me to take action to improve the human condition in small and big ways. |
| Genuine interest in human and environmental sustainability | I am not very aware of or concerned about issues relating to the environment. | I recognize that everybody's actions have an impact on the environment. With help, I can think of ideas that benefit the earth and its people. I am starting to see change opportunities in my local environment. | I understand that caring for the environment is important for our survival as human beings. The solutions I create take into account the environment and the threats it is facing. | I understand and appreciate the importance of the environment for human life and survival. I care about environmental issues and can generate sustainable solutions that affect the planet and its inhabitants. | I have a strong understanding of environmental issues and their importance. My understanding of the issues and care for the environment allow me to act in ways that create positive, lasting change. |

## Citizenship (Cont'd) | Student-Friendly Deep Learning Progression

Thinking like global citizens and considering global issues with empathy and compassion.

| Dimension | Limited Evidence  | Emerging  | Developing  | Accelerating  | Proficient  |
|---|---|---|---|---|---|
| Solving ambiguous and complex problems to benefit citizens | I am not comfortable working with the world's issues, challenges, or opportunities. I prefer to work on tasks that have clear solutions and steps for finding them. | With guidance, I am starting to feel comfortable working on real-world challenges that do not have set solutions. | I need a little help getting started on a task, but I feel comfortable working on open-ended, real-world challenges. | I am interested in and comfortable working on real-world challenges that affect people in my community and the world. I feel comfortable with tasks that do not have set solutions. | I am skilled and interested in working on real-world tasks that are open-ended and unstructured. I am comfortable creating new ways of looking at complex issues and do not need an approach framed for me. |
| Using technology for learning | I do not yet use technology to learn about issues. | I can use technology to connect to others and understand their context. I am learning about digital citizenship and usually communicate respectfully when using technology. | I use technology to improve my understanding of local, global, cultural, and environmental issues. Technology allows me to create solutions for a multicultural audience and contribute to sustainability and social justice. When I communicate using technology I respect laws, digital etiquette, and the feelings of other people, even if I don't know them. | I can describe how technology improves my global, environmental, and cultural understandings. Technology allows me to create relevant, equitable, fair, and sustainable solutions to benefit humankind and our planet. I model digital citizenship skills. | I effortlessly use technology to improve my global, environmental, and cultural understandings. I am able to transfer and apply these understandings to new challenges or contexts. I can clearly describe how technology enhances my products or solutions to global challenges of equity, justice, and sustainability. I encourage others to be good digital citizens. |

# Collaboration | Student-Friendly Deep Learning Progression

Working interdependently and with others, making important decisions together, and learning from and contributing to the learning of others.

New Pedagogies for **Deep Learning™** A GLOBAL PARTNERSHIP

| Dimension | Limited Evidence  | Emerging | Developing  | Accelerating | Proficient |
|---|---|---|---|---|---|
| Working inter-dependently as a team | When working on a group task, I often work by myself instead of working together with my team.<br><br>I discuss some of the work with my team but do not discuss many important decisions. | I can work with others to successfully complete a team task, but we have a hard time making sure that every group member is able to contribute equally.<br><br>Important group decisions are usually made by one or two members instead of the whole group. | When I work in pairs or in a group, we agree how to share jobs fairly so that the group achieves its best work.<br><br>We involve all group members in making important decisions about the task. | I can explain how my group uses all our strengths in the best possible way to develop our solution.<br><br>Each team member clearly contributes to the final product or solution. | When working in groups, I find ways not only to use my own and others' strengths but also to build on our strengths and learn new skills.<br><br>I understand the importance of group decision-making and make sure that all team members are able to contribute to our solutions. |
| Interpersonal and team-related skills | I may help or work with others on tasks, but I often don't understand why we are working together or the best way to go about it. | When working in a group, I am aware of the common goal or solution that we are all working to achieve.<br><br>Key group decisions are often made by one or two group members rather than the whole group. | I work well with others, and our team effort makes more successful.<br><br>I talk with and listen to my group members and we agree upon plans and desired outcomes of our work. | I understand and can clearly explain how each member of my team works together to produce our best work.<br><br>I work with others to resolve conflicts and to achieve group goals.<br><br>I am a very good listener and make sure that everyone's voice is heard and appreciated in the way we work together. | I work with other members of my group to make sure our collaborative process is as effective as possible.<br><br>I make sure that everyone's ideas, knowledge, and abilities are heard and valued.<br><br>I make sure that our work is the best it can be. |
| Social, emotional, and intercultural skills | I am beginning to see that my behavior has an impact on others but still have trouble seeing things from other people's perspectives.<br><br>I sometimes struggle to form positive relationships with my group members. | I am developing a better understanding of who I am and what I am interested in.<br><br>I see how my behavior affects others and know that people may have different feelings and opinions than my own. | I understand who I am as a person and why I have my perspectives.<br><br>I listen to and understand other people's viewpoints, and I value their perspectives even if they differ from my own. | I have a strong sense of who I am.<br><br>I fully understand my own perspectives and know how and why they differ from others'. I listen to the emotions and viewpoints of others and use them to improve my own learning.<br><br>In teams, I work in ways that help me grow as a person and that help my team members grow as well. | My social and emotional skills show that I have a strong sense of myself and my culture.<br><br>I communicate respectfully with everyone and form positive relationships with team members.<br><br>I understand other people's perspectives and am able to change my behavior after listening to others. |

**New Pedagogies for**
# Deep Learning™
A GLOBAL PARTNERSHIP

## Collaboration (Cont'd) | Student-Friendly Deep Learning Progression

Working interdependently and with others, making important decisions together, and learning from and contributing to the learning of others.

| Dimension | Limited Evidence | Emerging | Developing | Accelerating | Proficient |
|---|---|---|---|---|---|
| Managing team dynamics and challenges | When working in groups, I have trouble listening to or accepting viewpoints that are different from my own, or I avoid conflict by not sharing my own ideas. This negatively impacts my team and our work. | I need help forming positive relationships with my group members. I am learning to handle disagreements by listening to the perspectives of others, but we have trouble working through our differences. | I most often work well as a team member but sometimes need help solving problems and challenges. I respectfully share my viewpoints and learn from the viewpoints of others. I am beginning to understand why people view things the way they do. | I understand my own and others' points of view and know what goes into our beliefs. I share my own views and listen to and learn from the views of others without holding up our team's progress. | I firmly understand my own and others' points of view, clearly express my own viewpoints, and consistently learn from others. I respect group members' opinions in ways that help us grow and achieve our common goal. |
| Using technology for learning (leveraging digital) | I can use some technologies to collaborate with others. | I can use technology to work with others and monitor our group effectiveness. | I use technology to work independently and collaboratively. Technology allows me to understand and appreciate others' points of view. | I can clearly describe how technology improves how we work together, how we share responsibilities, and how we make decisions about important aspects of our work. | I effortlessly use technology to collaborate effectively, working and thinking in new and deeper ways. Technology allows me to work in ways that suit my needs. Technology allows all our team members to make significant contributions to the task. |

## Communication | Student-Friendly Deep Learning Progression

Communicating clearly, in a variety of ways, and for specific audiences.

| Dimension | Limited Evidence | Emerging | Developing | Accelerating | Proficient |
|---|---|---|---|---|---|
| Communication designed for audience and impact | I find it difficult to express myself clearly through talking or writing. I rely on the teacher's direction and examples/models. | I am starting to understand different ways to communicate. I need help to present my thoughts in a way others can understand. | I can make myself clear to others when sharing my thoughts. I make choices on what format to use to get my message across. I can connect and communicate more than a single idea and in more ways than one. | I know the qualities of different formats and what are the advantages of using some rather than others. I can use different tools and processes to express myself clearly in multiple ways. The way I choose to communicate makes sense to others. | I can express myself in different ways, depending on the situation, and can clearly communicate why I chose to express myself in that way. My communication is clear and connected and makes it easy for audiences to understand what I am trying to express. |
| Message advocates a purpose and makes an impact | I communicate in ways that I am comfortable with but don't always make sense to my audience. | I am starting to consider who needs to understand my message. I need some help to make sure my communication choices are suitable and helpful. I am becoming aware of different ways I can express myself. | I understand that the way I communicate should depend on the type of audience I am hoping to reach. I know some effective ways of communicating with specific audiences. My communication is relevant to my audience and allows them to understand my points. My message does not yet encourage my audience to take action. | I think about and research my audiences' needs before designing my communication. I understand that messages are "heard differently," depending on audience members' life experiences. I know how to design communication that is relevant and adds value for my audience. My message is clear, but it doesn't inspire others to take action. | I can excite and motivate my audience in ways that make them care about my message. I use my knowledge and intuition to challenge audiences beyond what they already think, know, or feel. I know how to create messages that will stick in the minds of my audience and change the way they think and act. |

## Communication (Cont'd) | Student-Friendly Deep Learning Progression

Communicating clearly, in a variety of ways, and for specific audiences.

| Dimension | Limited Evidence | Emerging | Developing | Accelerating | Proficient |
|---|---|---|---|---|---|
| **Reflection to further develop and improve communication** | I communicate with others without thinking much about how well I am getting my message across. I consider the suggestions I get but I don't ask others for feedback. | I am beginning to understand that the way I communicate matters and that clear communication helps me work better with others. With some help, I am starting to think about how to improve my communication based on my experiences. I use checklists and rubrics to support my reflection. | I am beginning to monitor, manage, and improve my communication throughout each task. I see that this has resulted in better communication and outcomes. | I regularly seek out feedback. I also reflect on my own in order to improve. I use many different perspectives to adapt, revise, and improve, even if it means making substantial changes to my original work. | I am aware of how I communicate and take initiative to review and change how I communicate from moment to moment. I seek out opportunities to continuously improve my communication and interpret feedback as an opportunity for growth. I also check my own personal bias or other barriers that may limit my ability. I can reach my intended audiences. |
| **Voice and Identity expressed to advance humanity** | I am not sure how I connect the way I communicate with who I am. | I am beginning to understand that I am unique. My culture and background make me who I am and how I communicate. I am beginning to see that in others as well. | I attempt to communicate using my own unique voice, which is informed by my own culture, background, and interests. I am beginning to include voices and identities of others as I communicate. | I can usually express myself honestly and communicate to influence change. When I communicate, I also consider the voices and identities of those who may not be heard. | I can express my true self. When I communicate, it has impact on others and generates positive change. I am a champion for those whose voices and identities may not be heard. |
| **Using technology for learning (leveraging digital)** | I sometimes use technology to communicate with my team but I do not understand how it can make communication better. | I can use technology as a tool to communicate what I am learning or to give key messages. Technology allows me to reach new audiences. | I use technology to communicate efficiently. Technology allows me to create high-quality products with clear messages. I can use technology to adapt my presentations for different audiences so that they can each understand and remember my key ideas. | I can describe how technology improves the way I communicate and helps me learn. Technology allows me to communicate with others in ways that are memorable and stimulate them to take action. | I effortlessly use technology to work efficiently, create high-quality products, and communicate effectively with others. I can clearly describe how technology enhances my ability to communicate and how it influences others to take action. I am comfortable using technologies that are new to me to communicate with others and can do so effectively. |

# Creativity | Student-Friendly Deep Learning Progression

Being able to see and take opportunities, creating new ideas or products, leading others.

| Dimension | Limited Evidence | Emerging | Developing | Accelerating | Proficient |
|---|---|---|---|---|---|
| Economic and social entrepreneurialism | I have trouble noticing when there is an opportunity to create something that is needed by other people. | With some help, I am learning to see that a problem or need is an opportunity to challenge myself and create something valuable. | I am able to find opportunities to solve real-world problems in ways that can help others. I can share my ideas with others and gather a team to put my ideas into action. | I enjoy seeking out and solving real-world problems. My solutions are realistic and practical. I clearly see how I can change things for the better. I am good at working with others to create solutions. I am innovative, a risk taker, and have a can-do attitude. | I can find opportunities where others cannot. I can create solutions for real-world problems and can imagine and describe new futures where lives are better and the world is changed. I can share my ideas with others and invite them to join my team to make our vision come true. We make things happen. |
| Asking the right inquiry questions | I may be interested in a topic, but I am not sure about how to really explore it. I need help to know how to find further information and what to look for. | With help, I am learning to ask relevant questions about topics that interest me. | I can identify real-life issues or challenges and come up with good inquiry questions to address them. I still need some help to design an inquiry or problem-solving process. | I can identify real-world and controversial issues and define what the challenge is. I understand the issue from different perspectives and come up with important questions to help design a solution. | I am good at framing problems and can pose questions in ways that open up thinking and possibilities. I can generate and work with "big ideas" using reliable thinking processes. I am curious and believe that things are not "carved in stone." I can challenge what exists and make it better. |
| Pursuing and expressing novel ideas and situations | When I face a challenge, I look for what others did or the tools they used to solve it. If a solution looks like a good one, I will use it without considering others' ideas. | When facing a challenge, I look for different solutions that may have been tried. With some help, I try to adapt these to suit my goals. I know and can use some strategies that help me work or think in new ways. | When facing a challenge, I can imagine and create new solutions or ideas. I can organize my creative thoughts in a way that helps me come up with promising ideas. I often use "what if" thinking to create or add value to what already exists. | When facing a challenge, I think about how and why previous solutions worked and what I can do to make them even better. I encourage and consider other people's ideas, looking for opportunities in the different points of view. I am happy to take risks in creating solutions. I ensure that my solution addresses the issues and adds something of real value. | When facing a challenge, I not only come up with "game-changing" solutions but know how to build a plan and use the right resources to make it happen. I can change problems into opportunities and develop solutions based on multiple perspectives. I think outside the box and my solutions make a real difference in people's lives. |

New Pedagogies for **Deep Learning**™ A GLOBAL PARTNERSHIP

## Creativity (Cont'd) | Student-Friendly Deep Learning Progression

Being able to see and take opportunities, creating new ideas or products, leading others.

| Dimension | Limited Evidence | Emerging | Developing | Accelerating | Proficient |
|---|---|---|---|---|---|
| **Leadership to turn ideas into action** | I have ideas, but I am not ready to share these ideas or bring people together to make them a reality. | I am becoming more confident as a leader. I am willing to share some of my ideas with others. I am beginning to take responsibility for parts of certain tasks. | I recognize my own strengths and the strengths of others and can see how different strengths fit together to achieve certain results. I know that to be successful I need to promote collaboration and compromise to meet goals. | I recognize and use the skills and interests of team members to meet our goals. I can motivate others to take on an active role in our creative process. I build skills and understanding in others. My teammates respect the way I work with them. | As a leader, I persevere and share my positive attitude with others. I can work out problems and inspire others to do the same. I understand what I need to do to create successful change and how to communicate this to my team. |
| **Using technology for learning** (leveraging digital) | I can use some technologies to create products or demonstrate my ideas. | Technology allows me to efficiently and effectively identify, investigate, and pursue my ideas. | I can use technology to create, support, and improve new ideas or products. I can use technology to refine my questions, inquiries, and thinking as well as create new knowledge or products. | I use technology to design, identify, and solve challenges in new ways. I also use it to enhance and understand the questions I am asking and being asked. I use technology to consider how I might apply my ideas in the real world. | I effortlessly use technology to develop new and creative ideas into products or processes that can impact the real world. I tap new opportunities and find new partners and discover new places that can broaden my learning. |

# Critical Thinking | Student-Friendly Deep Learning Progression

Evaluating information and arguments, seeing patterns and connections, constructing meaningful knowledge, and applying it in the real world.

| Dimension | Limited Evidence | Emerging | Developing | Accelerating | Proficient |
|---|---|---|---|---|---|
| Evaluating information and arguments | I can find information on a topic using my computer or by asking an adult, but I have trouble knowing how trustworthy or useful the information is. I copy and share what I have found or heard without thinking about and trying to improve it. | I can usually find the information I need. I am starting to be able to decide if that information is true, relevant, and useful. There are some arguments that I disagree with or that don't make sense, but I have trouble explaining why I feel this way. | I can find and evaluate information easily. I can distinguish between good and bad arguments and am beginning to be able to explain why an argument does or does not make sense. | I am highly skilled at finding and evaluating information. I can explain how I evaluate information but may not always demonstrate the correct understanding of the information or argument. | I can analyze different sources of information and comment on why I am using the data I have selected. I have a clear understanding of whether information is trustworthy, relevant, and useful, and can explain my thinking to others. I only select information I know is right, clear, and adds value to what I am trying to prove, say, or do. |
| Making connections and identifying patterns | I understand that when learning about something, information and ideas connect (relate) to each other. I have trouble making these connections by myself. | I am beginning to understand that I can seek, access, and explore information in many different ways. I am beginning to connect what I am learning with what I already know. With help, I am able to make connections and expand my understanding. | I can connect what I know with what I learn and expand my understanding of a topic. I am able to make some difficult connections, such as across classes, cultures, periods of time, or multiple key learning areas. | I understand that looking at a topic or task from different points of view is an important part of learning. I am able to make connections between and across subject areas. | I am skilled at making connections, identifying patterns, and seeing relationships. I can use the connections I see to understand topics or themes deeply. I understand that the world is full of conflicting information and am able to decide which information is most relevant and useful. |
| Meaningful knowledge construction | I can find information on a topic but have trouble engaging with the information in a meaningful way. I understand what I see or hear but don't think about how to improve it. | I am beginning to be able to explore what I already know and use this as a starting point for new learning. I try to improve the information I see or hear but don't use evidence to back up my thinking. | I can use a number of strategies to find and create new knowledge and beliefs. I can evaluate information and use it to answer questions in class but usually don't make connections between subject areas. | I am able to think about topics in new and exciting ways and can explain why my new knowledge is useful. I make meaningful connections and clearly understand why they are important in my life. | I can analyze, interpret, synthesize, and evaluate information. I am skilled at looking at topics from different points of view and then creating my own opinion about them. I reflect on and evaluate how and what I learn and improve my own learning outcomes. |

## Critical Thinking (Cont'd) | Student-Friendly Deep Learning Progression

Evaluating information and arguments, seeing patterns and connections, constructing meaningful knowledge, and applying it in the real world.

| Dimension | Limited Evidence | Emerging | Developing | Accelerating | Proficient |
|---|---|---|---|---|---|
| Experimenting, reflecting, and taking action on ideas in the real world | I can understand the task but often don't see how it fits in with who I am and what is important to me. Sometimes, with help, I can test my ideas out in different and relevant ways. | I am beginning to learn how to experiment with different ideas and figure out what works best for a particular task. With some help, I can see how I can use what I have learned in a different subject or class or even outside school. | I can think about the impact of my ideas and design new courses of action to improve outcomes. I use what I have learned in one task to solve new or different tasks. I use techniques I learn in class to solve problems in my life and the world. | I can test and evaluate my solutions in diverse settings to find out which are most effective. I reflect on my work and can explain why it is successful and how I could apply what I learn in different situations. | I can regularly apply what I learn in different contexts, adapting and transferring my knowledge as needed. I understand how to evaluate ideas and their potential for success in new contexts. |
| Using technology for learning (leveraging digital) | I have difficulty in using technology to help me learn, to connect my ideas and with others. | I can use technology as a tool to produce questions, to connect, and to develop my thoughts. | I use technology to generate and explore important ideas. I can use technology to connect with others and explore ways to apply new knowledge. | I can use a variety of technologies to evaluate, generate, and explore both new and unfamiliar concepts and arguments. | I effortlessly use technology to help me think critically about issues and share and develop this thinking with others. I can clearly describe how technology enhances my ability to think critically. In new contexts, I can use technology as a tool to think and work effectively. |

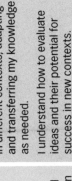

New Pedagogies for **Deep Learning™**
A GLOBAL PARTNERSHIP

# Student Self-Assessment Tool

**Name:** _____  **Grade:** _____  **Date:** _____

| Global competency name | *Competency definition* |
| --- | --- |

**dimension**

☐ Limited
☐ Emerging
☐ Developing
☐ Accelerating
☐ Proficient

What evidence shows you are at this stage of development?

_____

**dimension**

☐ Limited
☐ Emerging
☐ Developing
☐ Accelerating
☐ Proficient

What evidence shows you are at this stage of development?

_____

**dimension**

☐ Limited
☐ Emerging
☐ Developing
☐ Accelerating
☐ Proficient

What evidence shows you are at this stage of development?

_____

**dimension**

☐ Limited
☐ Emerging
☐ Developing
☐ Accelerating
☐ Proficient

What evidence shows you are at this stage of development?

_____

**dimension**

☐ Limited
☐ Emerging
☐ Developing
☐ Accelerating
☐ Proficient

What evidence shows you are at this stage of development?

_____

**Future Focus**

This assessment suggests that I should now focus my attention on

_____

I could do this by

_____

# Student Self-Assessment Exemplar

| Name: | Jose Malsten | Grade: | 6 | Date: | 7/24/18 |
|---|---|---|---|---|---|

## Collaboration

Working interdependently and with others. Making important decisions together and learning from and contributing to the learning of others.

**Working with each other as a team**
(work interdependently as a team)

☐ Limited
☒ Emerging
☐ Developing
☐ Accelerating
☐ Proficient

What evidence shows you are at this stage of development?

Most of the decisions about our project were made by me and ****. This was because we needed to get the work done on time and some of our group did not know where to focus.

**Interpersonal and team-related skills**

☐ Limited
☒ Emerging
☐ Developing
☐ Accelerating
☐ Proficient

What evidence shows you are at this stage of development?

We did care about the quality of our work together and helped each other to work effectively but me and **** had to direct the others to do their parts. So we did not really have an active sense of shared responsibility.

**Social, emotional, and intercultural skills**

☐ Limited
☒ Emerging
☐ Developing
☐ Accelerating
☐ Proficient

What evidence shows you are at this stage of development?

Being able to let other people speak. Waiting my turn and thinking about what I would say to them. Knowing that my words and actions can make other people comfortable or uncomfortable.

**Using technology for learning**
(leveraging digital)

☐ Limited
☐ Emerging
☐ Developing
☐ Accelerating
☐ Proficient

What evidence shows you are at this stage of development?

**Understanding my team and solving problems**
(Managing team dynamics and challenges)

☐ Limited
☐ Emerging
☒ Developing
☐ Accelerating
☐ Proficient

What evidence shows you are at this stage of development?

I was thinking about the language and actions as I worked with others on my team, but I did not always listen to others. I could stop being myself being judgemental but could not always use appropriate language to help others and the team.

### Future Focus

This assessment suggests that I should now focus my attention on

Becoming better at listening effectively, negotiating and agreeing on the goals, content, process, design, and conclusions of our work. Also making sure everyone in our group is allowed to contribute and can contribute to the end project.

I could do this by

Stopping everything I am doing when other people are talking or discussing our project. Making a list of jobs for each team member and making sure we all have something important to contribute. We could start using an online document to check our progress as individuals and as a team.

**"** The journey to Deep Learning is just that—a journey. There is no one pathway. **"**

SECTION 04

# Designing Deep Learning

" The elements lead to intentionality in building new relationships between and among teachers, students, and families and using digital to facilitate and amplify learning. "

—*DEEP LEARNING: ENGAGE THE WORLD CHANGE THE WORLD*, P. 36

# Chapter 08
# Deep Learning Design

In Chapter 5, we introduced the Four Elements of Learning Design: learning partnerships, learning environments, pedagogical practices, and leveraging digital. We examined how they integrate to propel powerful conversations and provide an organizer for designing learning experiences that foster development of the Global Competencies. The Four Elements have real horsepower and give disengagement a swift kick—but how do we saddle up? In this chapter, we will focus on learning design: its key components, how to begin, and how to develop an adaptive, responsive plan. We will also look at the Learning Design Rubric and how it can deepen our understanding of good design. Before we head over to the corral, there is some horse sense we need to address up front and it's this: Teachers learn best from the examples, insights, and input of other teachers.

In this chapter, there are opportunities for teachers to reflect on other teachers' work (through vignettes, videos, case studies, and learning templates). These examples provide concrete clarity that can be inspiring, instructive, and confidence building. Most importantly, teachers see themselves in these examples. When teachers realize that they are already on the Deep Learning pathway, it is reassuring and it nudges them to continue learning.

## Learning Design: The Key Components

The students who are in front of us deserve our undivided attention. As professionals, we need to know them well. What are their interests, strengths, and learning needs? How do they collaborate with others? What are they curious about? How do they approach learning, failure, and challenge? What patterns are emerging? How do students respond to prompts, assessments, and strategies? How well we know them informs how we teach them. Students know when we know them; they feel supported, efficacious, and engaged in the learning process. When we know students well, our stance shifts. We begin to see students' true potential. To borrow a line from Stuart Shanker, "See a child differently and see a different child."

Sadly, some teachers begin the year in September by cracking open the textbook and beginning at page one; the students in front of them are merely a revolving audience. Racing through the term, teachers like this lean heavily on that textbook, hoping to reach the back cover in time for report card grading. We encourage teachers to turn this thinking on its head with backward design.

## Backward Design

There are three key steps to backward design, as depicted in Figure 8.1.

FIGURE 8.1
Backward Design

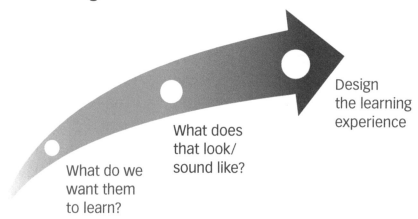

Design the learning experience

What does that look/ sound like?

What do we want them to learn?

## Phase One

This means that you begin with students in mind. Know who your students are and what it is they need to be able to do by the end of the year/term. This encourages us to take a good look at the curriculum (the textbook is not the curriculum) and its stated expectations for student learning and achievement. Also look to the Global Competencies. Some people initially worry that addressing the overall curriculum expectations in addition to the Global Competencies is doubling the workload. It's not. The Global Competencies normally dovetail with the curriculum in play. It may be helpful to do some cross-referencing here. We encourage teams of teachers to take out highlighters and identify the verbs articulated in the curriculum and compare them with the Deep Learning outcomes; it is likely that the Global Competencies are hidden in there. (And while you're examining that curriculum, look for words such as *regurgitate* and *recall*. You probably won't find these low-order verbs anywhere, even though they have dominated our instructional practice for far too long.) Those two big questions—*Who are our students?* and *What do we want students to learn?*—represent the starting place for Deep Learning design.

At this point, the combined curriculum expectations and Global Competencies are still not ready for the classroom. They will need to be unpacked (ideally by a team of teachers) by clustering and scaffolding them into manageable chunks. Often, the curriculum expectations are not written in language that students understand. Enter learning goals and success criteria. **Learning goals** clarify, in student-friendly language, what students should know, understand, and be able to do by the end of a learning period. **Success criteria** further drills this down more precisely to what it looks like when it's in action. This clarity helps students target their learning focus and monitor their progress. What's even better? When students have the opportunity to contribute to the co-creation of success criteria, their motivation and quality of learning increases. The student-friendly learning progressions (addressed in Chapter 7) are integral to increasing student understanding to this end.

## Phase Two

Now that you have identified what you want the students to learn, you need to ask yourself, "What does that look like/sound like? What would serve as proof that they have learned it?" If the curriculum expectations speak to the Global Competencies, then we are certain that tests alone will not satisfy you as evidence. Students learn in different ways and at varied rates. This is a great time for teams of teachers to consider the alternative and rich ways students would be able to demonstrate their learning. Have some fun with this and give yourself license to be creative with Deep Learning products and experiences—think cooperative group learning, role plays, blogs, webpages, experiments, debates, campaigns, letters, simulations, social causes, presentations, conferences—the possibilities are endless.

## Phase Three

Only after you know what students will learn and what will serve as evidence do we design the learning experience. This is when we consider how to optimize those Four Elements and how the learning will be sequenced. Part of the challenge here is that when you include student voice, choice, and interest, your best-laid learning plan may not go as planned. Having agility goes a long way. Plot out the big picture—that is, how the learning will unfold—and allow for adaptations. Listening to students' thoughts and observing student contributions and behaviors inform your strategic moves within the learning space. The teacher shifts from being the command and control center of teaching to a flexible, responsive activator who is regularly assessing student learning. Kelly Brownrigg, a teacher on the Ottawa Catholic School Board, describes this important shift:

> " Every day, we're assessing for learning. We're looking at where are the students? Where do we need to go tomorrow? Where do we need to go in the next three minutes, sometimes. . . . I reflect on thirty years ago when we planned for

two weeks at a time and it's just not like that anymore. The students are vehicles. They take you where they need you to take them. **"**

—NPDL DEEP LEARNING IN GRADE 3 MATH VIDEO

The Learning Design Planning Template provides a structure that can support teachers as they navigate through this approach to learning. The prompts in each box support the thinking (see Figure 8.2). Protocols 20, 21, and 22 also support teachers in designing this way.

## The Learning Design Rubric

To add richness to the planning, use the Learning Design Rubric. This tool is the jewel in the crown. If there is anything you want to laminate in this day and age, it's this. The Learning Design Rubric gets at the substance of Deep Learning by articulating in precise and explicit language what those Four Elements look like in a learning setting, whether it's kindergarten or Grade 12 physics. Just like the Learning Progressions Tool, the Learning Design Rubric provides four levels of proficiency conveyed as four different levels of development: limited evidence, emerging, accelerating, and advanced. This enables teachers to self-assess the degree to which their learning design meets the intended learning outcomes. (See Figure 8.3.)

The Learning Design Rubric serves many purposes, and like the Learning Progressions, the more it is used, the more meaningful it becomes. Here are some of the ways the Learning Design Rubric is used:

- Build shared precise understanding of Deep Learning design.

- Assess current practice.

- Clarify and guide how learning might be deepened.

- Anchor self-reflection.

- Collaboratively support, coach, and analyze shared practice.

- Encourage us to pause and recalibrate when we are feeling stuck.

Notice that this list of uses for the Learning Design Rubric does not include teacher evaluation. Here is the thing: When we are trying to shift our practice and do something new amid the frantic pace of school life, it's important that we feel supported about doing things differently and employ a high tolerance for fumbling. For many teachers, wading into Deep Learning territory seems uncertain and they need to know that we have each other's backs. In Chapter 9, we will delve into the kinds of norms that live in Deep Learning cultures. For now, it's worth underlining the importance of reserving judgment when examining teacher practice.

FIGURE 8.2
# The Learning Design Planning Template

| | |
|---|---|
| **Assess** | **Assess:** What do you already know about your students? (strengths, needs, interests) |
| | What are the students' knowledge, skills, interest, and needs?<br>How might you capture this? |
| | **Learning Outcomes:** What do we want students to learn? |
| | **Curriculum Standards** — Review your local curriculum standards. List those you will focus on in this learning opportunity. **Deep Learning Competencies** — Which of the Global Competencies (6Cs) might you focus on? |
| | **Success Criteria Evidence of Outcomes:** How will we know they have learned it? |
| | List your success criteria in simple, explicit language. Will the learners have the opportunity to co-construct the success criteria? |

| | |
|---|---|
| **Design** | **Learning Design Overview** |
| | Provide an overview of the learning design. |
| | • What activities will learners engage in? |
| | • What are some critical points, both instructionally and for the learners? |
| | • What products will come out of the learning? |
| | • What processes will support the outcomes? |

**Four Elements of Learning Design**

| | |
|---|---|
| **Pedagogical Practices** | List some of the pedagogical strategies you will use in this task.<br>Consider how to meet the needs of all learners in your class. |
| **Learning Partnerships** | How might partnerships strengthen the task and deepen the learning?<br>Consider partnership possibilities that involve other learners, adults in the school environment and those outside the school and in the community. |
| **Learning Environments** | Where will the learning physically occur?<br>How will you support learners to take risks and try new ways of thinking, learning, presenting, and reflecting. |
| **Leveraging Digital** | How might technology amplify, accelerate, and connect learners and learning? |

| | |
|---|---|
| **Implement** | **Implement the Learning Design:**<br>Note any adaptations, observations, and insights as you go. |

| | |
|---|---|
| **Measure, Reflect, and Change** | **Measure:** What assessments will you use? |
| | How will you and others assess learning?<br>How will you use a variety of assessment modes, both formative and summative? |
| | **Reflect and Change:** Assessing learning<br>How well did the learning design meet the intended learning outcomes? |
| | After: Consider how the evidence collected met your learning goals and design expectations. |
| | **Reflect and Change:** Assessing learning design<br>What parts of the learning design worked well, and what can be improved? |
| | After: Talk with colleagues. What worked well? What might you improve? How might you do that? |

FIGURE 8.3
## Learning Design Rubric

| | Limited Evidence | Emerging | Accelerating | Advanced |
|---|---|---|---|---|
| Learning Partnerships | The learning design does not yet actively promote students and teachers working in a learning partnership. The teacher may assume a directing role. Student voice, choice, and agency are limited and this may impact students' sense of belonging. There is limited demonstration of equity between students, teachers, and others; there is no clear shared goal(s) across the learning partners and the learning outcomes are not transparent to all; the measures for success are not explicit to students. | The learning design includes elements of students, teachers, and others working in a learning partnership to ensure Deep Learning outcomes. Teachers are starting to facilitate student voice, choice, and agency. There are shared goal(s) for the learning that students support; there is growing equity in the learning partnership relationships; learning outcomes are transparent to students with an increasing understanding of how it will be measured. | The learning design has a clear strategy for students, teachers, and other partners to achieve Deep Learning outcomes for all students. Students have a sense of belonging. Student voice, choice, and agency and contribution to learning design have been integral; there is equity in the relationships between students and teachers, learning outcomes, processes, and expectations are transparent; and there is consensus about what success looks like and how it will be measured. | The learning design is a collaborative partnership among students and teachers and others, with a clear focus on achieving Deep Learning outcomes for all students. Student voice, choice, agency, and contribution have been critical to improving the learning design.<br><br>All students have a genuine sense of belonging. The learning partnership is driven by high levels of partner equity, transparency, and mutual benefit/accountability. There are clear collaborative processes and measures to enable students to persevere and encounter success. |
| Learning Environments | The learning design does not yet take advantage of interaction or student voice. It is unclear how students can contribute to the learning. Opportunities to optimize the physical or virtual environment have not yet been employed. | The learning design states how an interactive learning environment establishes a climate and culture for learning. In doing so, the learning design includes strategies to engage *most* students but does not yet have clear approaches to ensure equity or to generate student influence. The physical and virtual environments provide new contexts for learning. | The learning design includes an interactive and equitable learning environment to enable Deep Learning for all students. It includes strategies to develop collaborative processes with and between students and incorporates student voice to influence the ways we work together. Physical and virtual environments provide diverse contexts for learning. | An equitable and interactive learning environment permeates the learning design; all students are deeply engaged and committed to collaborative processes. Their voice drives learning and improvement.<br><br>The physical and virtual environments within and beyond the classroom provide rich, authentic contexts for learning. |

| | Limited Evidence | Emerging | Accelerating | Advanced |
|---|---|---|---|---|
| **Pedagogical Practices: Learning and Teaching Strategies** | The learning design includes a traditional range of pedagogical practices that may be more teacher directed without taking into account the needs, interests, or voices of students in the learning process. | The learning design includes research-proven pedagogical practices to advance Deep Learning goals.<br><br>The design includes opportunities for active engagement but may not be based on the needs, interests, and abilities of all students or informed by research-proven models.<br><br>Assessment practices are more teacher directed with limited opportunities for peer/ self-assessment. They may not represent a broad range of assessment approaches. | The learning design addresses students' strengths, interests, and needs and invites student voice and agency. It includes pedagogical practices that best match the learning goals and needs of the students.<br><br>The learning design uses research-proven models, scaffolds thinking and levels of complexity, and personalizes learning.<br><br>The learning design engages students through choice and authentic tasks to ensure appropriate challenge and maximization of learning potential. Students see themselves as emerging partners in the learning design process.<br><br>The design engages students in a range of assessment approaches with rapid cycles of self and peer feedback to promote metacognition and self regulation. | The learning design reaches each student's strengths, interests, and needs and ensures that each student's voice and agency is activated. Through its design, students fulfil a purpose beyond the learning.<br><br>The most appropriate research-proven pedagogy is facilitated at the right time to respond to learners' needs. It scaffolds thinking and levels of complexity to enable the Deep Learning outcomes to be realized by all students. A broad repertoire of strategies generates authentic experiences, personalized learning, and increased engagement.<br><br>Continuous rapid cycles of self and peer feedback as well as a variety of learning and assessment strategies accelerate metacognition and self-direction. |
| **Leveraging Digital** | Learning design includes limited student access and use of digital and is focused on low-level or shallow use. Digital is often a substitution for traditional learning approaches.<br><br>Use of digital does not yet enable students to interact with each other and does not advance Deep Learning outcomes.<br><br>Digital citizenship and personal safety have not been addressed in the learning design. | The learning design provides access to digital to encourage student motivation, engagement, and connection to local and global sources.<br><br>Digital provides new opportunities for students to reflect, share, communicate, and further develop Deep Learning outcomes.<br><br>The learning design addresses digital citizenship and personal safety. | The learning design includes digital to encourage student motivation, engagement, and connection to local and global sources at any time.<br><br>Digital provides explicit and flexible opportunities for students to reflect, share, communicate, and further develop Deep Learning outcomes.<br><br>The learning design is clear about digital citizenship and personal safety and monitors this effectively. | The learning design includes digital seamlessly and authentically to encourage student motivation, engagement, and connection locally and globally.<br><br>Digital amplifies innovation, enabling students to achieve something that was otherwise not possible. Digital normalizes channels for reflection, sharing, communication, and knowledge building in the learning design.<br><br>The learning design incorporates processes to ensure that students exercise a high degree of digital citizenship and personal safety for themselves and others. |

Earlier in the book, we introduced collaborative inquiry. This stance of openness to cyclical learning and improvement is also incorporated into learning design. By way of quick summary, the process has four phases and applies to learning design in this way (see Figure 8.4).

FIGURE 8.4

## Four Phases of Collaborative Inquiry

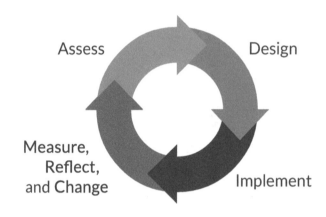

**Assess** (student strengths, interests and needs)

**Design** (a learning strategy that is informed by the curriculum, the Global Competencies, and the Four Elements of Learning Design)

**Implement the learning strategy** (and allow for adaptations along the way)

**Measure, reflect, and change** (use the Learning Design Rubric, learning progressions, evidence of student learning, and other information to determine how well the learning design met the intended outcomes)

# Final Thoughts

As you begin designing for Deep Learning, consider drawing on existing examples. Look at some of the teacher examples available in this book or the more detailed exemplars on our Deep Learning hub (www.deep-learning.global). Use an evidence-based strategy that is already working and tweak it by incorporating the Four Elements. Think back to the fusion graphic in Chapter 5 (Figure 5.3). It acknowledges that we don't throw out existing effective practice when we innovate; we build from a position of strength.

We encourage teachers to "go slow to go fast" with learning design: Take small steps when you're starting out. Our Deep Learning teachers tell us that the first time they design for Deep Learning, it can feel a little unfamiliar. When they pause to assess and reflect on it, they revise their thinking and improve upon the design. Then the second attempt goes much smoother. We recommend that you dedicate as much time to self-assessment, reflection, and measurement as you do to the initial planning. Consider what went well and what you would revise for next time. In the next chapter, we will build on learning design as we consider collaborative assessment.

## Protocols

### 19 Investigating Deep Learning Vignettes

Use the vignettes to capture observations about the Global Competencies and the Four Elements of Learning Design.

### 20 The Learning Design Planning Template

This introduces the Learning Design Planning Template with prompts and invites discussion to compare the Template with those being used.

### 21 Backward Mapping Using the Learning Design Planning Template

Explore lesson design using a case study.

### 22 Fostering the Global Competencies Through Learning Design

Five learning design examples allow groups to explore and analyze how Global Competencies are developed.

### 23 Comparing Learning Designs

Examine two of the five learning design examples in more detail and compare similarities and differences.

### 24 Using the Learning Design Planning Template

Begin co-creating a lesson using the Template.

### 25 The Learning Design Rubric

This introduces the Learning Design Rubric—its organization and language and how it can be used.

### 26 Applying the Learning Design Rubric

A video example is provided to focus on and analyze two of the Four Elements using the Learning Design Rubric.

**27** Deepening the Analysis of the Learning Design Rubric

Use a video example to challenge deeper observation and analysis of pedagogical practices.

**28** Enhancing the Learning Design

Draw on the first attempt at designing learning (from Protocol 24) to analyze evidence of student learning and to guide next steps.

## Tools

Learning Design Planning Template

Learning Design Planning Template: Working Copy

Learning Design Rubric

## Deep Learning Design Examples

Learning About Landmarks, Grade 2

Exploring World Peace, Grade 4

Exploring Poverty: A Sustainable Approach, Grade 6

Speed Dating: Critical Thinking and Writing, Grade 10 English

Vulnerable Populations and Economic Activity, Grade 12 Economics

## For more information:

Read Chapters 5 and 6 from *Deep Learning: Engage the World Change the World.*

# Notes

# 19 Investigating Deep Learning Vignettes

Purpose: **Uncover components of the Deep Learning Framework**

Process: **What Do You Notice?**

Time: **20–30 minutes**

Resources:

Vignettes:
- Bee the Change
- Ask Yourself: So What?
- Learning to Juggle Life's Demands
- No Planet B
- Daily Deep Learning: Fitness for the Mind

**1** **Assemble** a group of four and use the Deep Learning Framework Placemat to review the Global Competencies and Four Elements of Learning Design.

**2** **Select** a vignette to read from the resource list.

**3** **Use** the Deep Learning Framework Placemat to capture your observations about the Global Competencies and the Four Elements of Learning Design.

**4** **Take** turns identifying how the vignette used the 6Cs and Four Elements to deepen learning. Record your notes using the Deep Learning Framework Placemat.

**5** **Discuss**

- Were there any components of the Deep Learning Framework missing (or not evident) in this vignette? If so, how could you adapt this example in order to include all of the components of the Deep Learning Framework?
- In your opinion, is this Deep Learning? Why or why not?

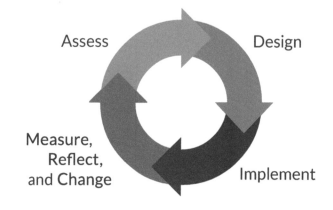

# DEEP LEARNING FRAMEWORK PLACEMAT

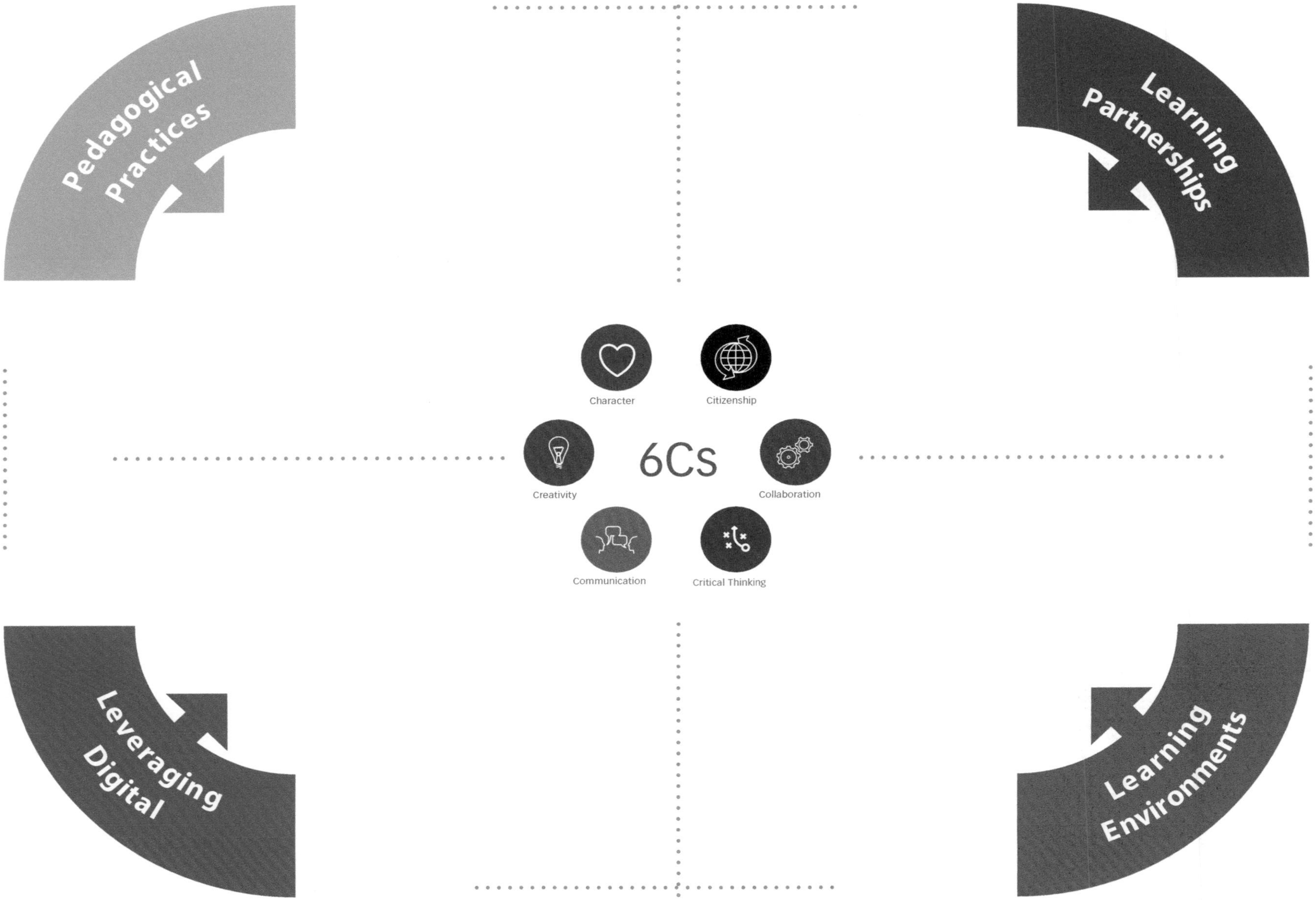

Learning Partnerships

Learning Environments

Pedagogical Practices

Leveraging Digital

6Cs

Collaboration

Critical Thinking

Citizenship

Communication

Character

Creativity

# 20 The Learning Design Planning Template

**Purpose: Understand the components of the Learning Design Planning Template**

**Process: Compare the Learning Design Planning Template to Your Own**

**Time: 20–30 minutes**

**Resource:**

- Tool: Learning Design Planning Template

**1** **Review** the Learning Design Planning Template.

**2** **Compare** this to your existing learning design plan. Is it similar or different?

**3** **Consider** would you add any components to yours? Would you remove any?

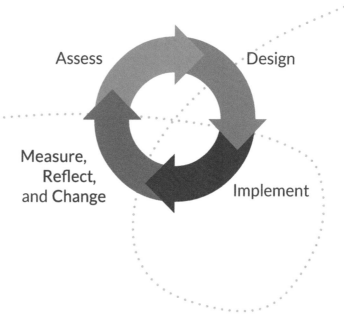

Assess

Design

Measure, Reflect, and Change

Implement

# THE LEARNING DESIGN PLANNING TEMPLATE

## Assess

### Assess: What do you already know about your students? (strengths, needs, interests)

What are the students' knowledge, skills, interest, and needs?
How might you capture this?

### Learning Outcomes: What do we want students to learn?

| Curriculum Standards | Deep Learning Competencies |
| --- | --- |
| Review your local curriculum standards. List those you will focus on in this learning opportunity. | Which of the Global Competencies (6Cs) might you focus on? |

### Success Criteria Evidence of Outcomes: How will we know they have learned it?

List your success criteria in simple, explicit language. Will the learners have the opportunity to co-construct the success criteria?

## Design

### Learning Design Overview

Provide an overview of the learning design.

- What activities will learners engage in?
- What are some critical points, both instructionally and for the learners?
- What products will come out of the learning?
- What processes will support the outcomes?

### Four Elements of Learning Design

| Pedagogical Practices | List some of the pedagogical strategies you will use in this task. Consider how to meet the needs of all learners in your class. |
| --- | --- |
| Learning Partnerships | How might partnerships strengthen the task and deepen the learning? Consider partnership possibilities that involve other learners, adults in the school environment and those outside the school and in the community. |
| Learning Environments | Where will the learning physically occur? How will you support learners to take risks and try new ways of thinking, learning, presenting, and reflecting. |
| Leveraging Digital | How might technology amplify, accelerate, and connect learners and learning? |

## Implement

### Implement the Learning Design:
Note any adaptations, observations, and insights as you go.

## Measure, Reflect, and Change

### Measure: What assessments will you use?

How will you and others assess learning?
How will you use a variety of assessment modes, both formative and summative?

### Reflect and Change: Assessing learning
How well did the learning design meet the intended learning outcomes?

After: Consider how the evidence collected met your learning goals and design expectations.

### Reflect and Change: Assessing learning design
What parts of the learning design worked well, and what can be improved?

After: Talk with colleagues. What worked well? What might you improve? How might you do that?

# 21 Backward Mapping Using the Learning Design Planning Template

Purpose: **Understand and use the Learning Design Planning Template**

Process: **Backward Mapping**

Time: **30–45 minutes**

Resource:

• Tool: Learning Design Planning Template

**1** **Read** through the mini-case study "Who's Afraid of Algebra?"

**2** **With a partner,** identify relevant information from the case study and record it in the appropriate sections of the Learning Design Planning Template

**3** **What information was missing?** What information do you need to infer?

**4** **What** would you like to have more information about?

**5** **Reflect** on one of your recent lessons. How might the template help you deepen learning?

## MINI-CASE STUDY
## Who's Afraid of Algebra?

Tom teaches seventh-grade math and he knows from experience that many are afraid of algebra!

As Tom looked through the Learning Design Planning Template, he hypothesized that using the ***Making connections and identifying patterns*** dimension of Critical Thinking might actually help his students to become more comfortable with, and engaged in, learning algebra.

He handed out copies of the dimension from the student-friendly rubric, talked through it with students, and discussed what each cell might look like in math.

His pedagogical practice focus was to engage his students in pattern-finding activities using technology. In their first two lessons together, Tom used a number of online resources to introduce the idea of patterning. Students were asked to give an example of their own practice at each of the five levels—each example was related to how they used patterning in the online resources. This really positioned the idea that algebra was just about finding patterns.

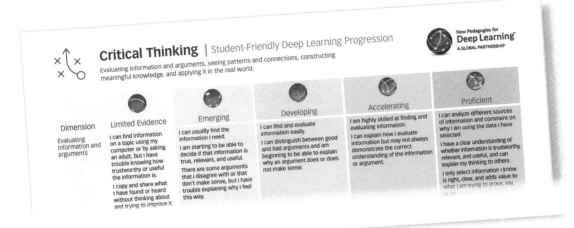

**Critical Thinking** | Student-Friendly Deep Learning Progression

Evaluating information and arguments, seeing patterns and connections, constructing meaningful knowledge, and applying it in the real world.

New Pedagogies for **Deep Learning** A GLOBAL PARTNERSHIP

| Dimension | Limited Evidence | Emerging | Developing | Accelerating | Proficient |
|---|---|---|---|---|---|
| Evaluating information and arguments | I can find information on a topic using my computer or by asking an adult, but I have trouble knowing how trustworthy or useful the information is. I copy and share what I have found or heard without thinking about and trying to improve it. | I can usually find the information I need. I am starting to be able to decide if that information is true, relevant, and useful. There are some arguments that I disagree with or that don't make sense, but I have trouble explaining why I feel this way. | I can find and evaluate information easily. I can distinguish between good and bad arguments and am beginning to be able to explain why an argument does or does not make sense. | I am highly skilled at finding and evaluating information. I can explain how I evaluate information but may not always demonstrate the correct understanding of the information or argument. | I can analyze different sources of information and comment on why I am using the data I have selected. I have a clear understanding of whether information is trustworthy, relevant, and useful, and can explain my thinking to others. I only select information I know is right, clear, and adds value to what I am trying to prove, say, or do. |

Tom could then move on to more algebra-specific instruction, using the text and teaching for mastery. Over the next 10 lessons, he also directed students back to conversations that used the language of the **Making connections and identifying patterns** dimension. He asked them to reflect with peers (incorporating Learning Partnerships) on their capacity to look at a topic or task from different points of view; how they made connections, identified patterns, and saw relationships; and how they were able to connect new learning with what they already knew. Many students mentioned that, in particular, thinking about what worked for them previously helped them navigate *the process* of learning algebra.

Tom observed that the language of the dimension allowed students to make the intangible nature of algebra much more concrete. It provided strategic touch points for students to focus on the process of learning rather than just the learning outcomes. Compared to previous years, Tom observed that his students were more engaged, open to algebra, and able to grasp the core concepts more rapidly. His formative and summative tests also showed an overall improvement in student success, with students achieving higher average grades than in previous years.

> Many students mentioned that, in particular, thinking about what worked for them previously helped . . .

# 22 Fostering the Global Competencies Through Learning Design

Purpose: **Investigate the Learning Design Planning Template example**

Time: **40–60 minutes**

Process: **Building on Thinking**

## Part One

**1** **Form** a group of four and review the list "Learning Experiences That Foster the Global Competencies."

**2** **Share** examples from your own practice that demonstrate these characteristics.

**3** **What is it** about these characteristics that fosters Deep Learning?

## Part Two

**4** **Choose** one Learning Design Example to review as a group:

- Learning about Landmarks, Grade 2
- Exploring World Peace, Grade 4
- A Sustainable Approach, Grade 6
- Speed Dating—Critical Thinking and Writing, Grade 10
- Vulnerable Populations and Economic Activity, Grade 12 Economics

**5** **Read** the example individually.

**6** **Consider** the focus question:

- Which characteristics from the list are evident in the learning example?

**7** **Share** responses to the focus question.

**8** **In what ways** could the learning experience be enhanced to further develop the Global Competencies?

# LEARNING EXPERIENCES THAT FOSTER THE
# Global Competencies

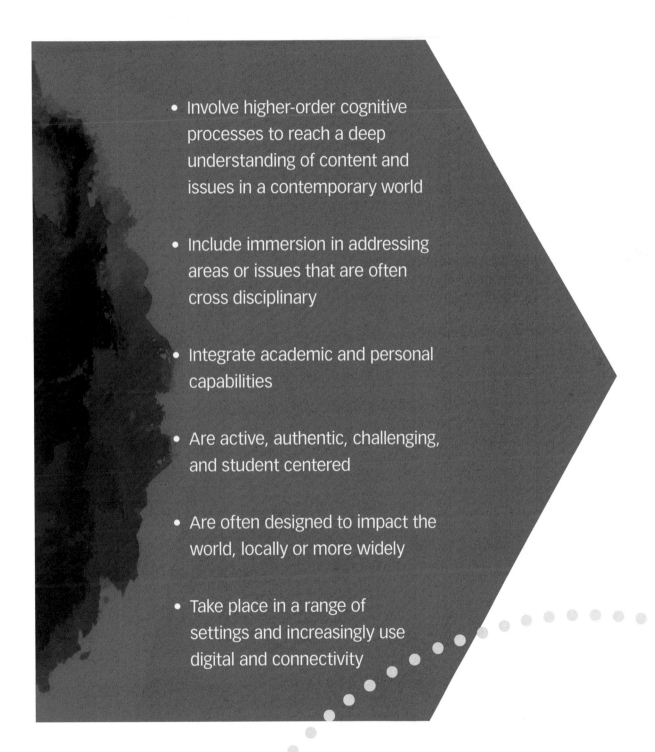

- Involve higher-order cognitive processes to reach a deep understanding of content and issues in a contemporary world

- Include immersion in addressing areas or issues that are often cross disciplinary

- Integrate academic and personal capabilities

- Are active, authentic, challenging, and student centered

- Are often designed to impact the world, locally or more widely

- Take place in a range of settings and increasingly use digital and connectivity

Source: *Deep Learning: Engage the World Change the World*, p. 21

# 23 Comparing Learning Designs

**Purpose: Compare Learning Design Examples**

**Time: 30–45 minutes**

**Process: Venn Diagram**

Resources:
• Learning Design Examples

**1** **Choose** two Learning Design Examples.

**2** **Read** them, using the Four Elements and the six Global Competencies as a lens for discussion.

**3** **Identify** what the two examples have in common. In the middle part of the Venn diagram, record those similarities.

**4** **Identify** what is different for each Learning Design and make notes in the corresponding sections of the Venn diagram.

**5** **Share** your thinking with others and discuss the questions below.

## DISCUSSION QUESTIONS

? What might you change?

? How might you build on these designs?

? What are you curious about? What information is missing for you?

In what ways are these examples of Deep Learning? How are these experiences different than traditional lesson design?

When you reflect on one of these designs, what might work with your students?

# VENN DIAGRAM

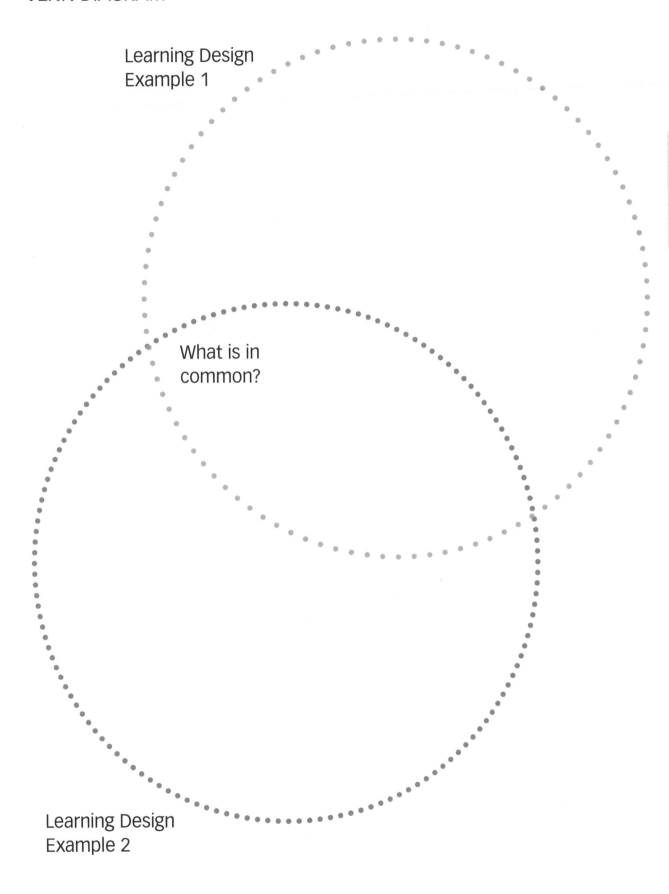

Learning Design
Example 1

What is in
common?

Learning Design
Example 2

# 24 Using the Learning Design Planning Template

Purpose: **Co-create a lesson using the Learning Design Planning Template**

Process: **Co-Planning**

Time: **30–60 minutes**

Resources:

Tools:

- Learning Design Planning Template
- Learning Design Planning Template: Working Copy

**1** **Look** at the graphic with a partner. Discuss how this approach to learning design may be different from your current practice.

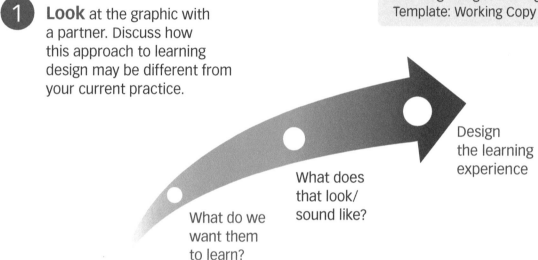

What do we want them to learn?

What does that look/ sound like?

Design the learning experience

**2** **Use the questions** from the Learning Design Planning Template in Protocol 20 to guide your thinking and record your plan on the Working Copy.

**3** **Think** about your students and identify their

- strengths
- needs
- interests

**4** **Identify 2–3 curriculum outcomes** that you will be addressing in your class soon.

**5** **What are some Global Competencies** that would deepen the learning?

**6** **Brainstorm** ways you could design a Deep Learning task using the Four Elements of Learning Design as a reference.

**7** **Consider** assessments (both formative and summative).

**8** **Implement** the design.

**9** **Use** Protocol 28 to support your reflection after implementation.

# 25 The Learning Design Rubric

**Purpose: Understand the Learning Design Rubric and how it is used**

**Time: 20–30 minutes**

Process: **Read–Pair–Share**

Resource:
• Learning Design Rubric

**1** **Form groups** of four.

**2** **Each person selects** one of the Four Elements and reads the description across the rubric. Highlight the most important ideas.

**3** **Describe** in your own words the main ideas within the Element and how it becomes more advanced.

**4** **Discuss** the following questions, as a group:

- What Elements of the rubric do you tend to focus on when you design a lesson?
- What Element would you like to further develop?
- In what ways could you use this tool as an individual and with groups?

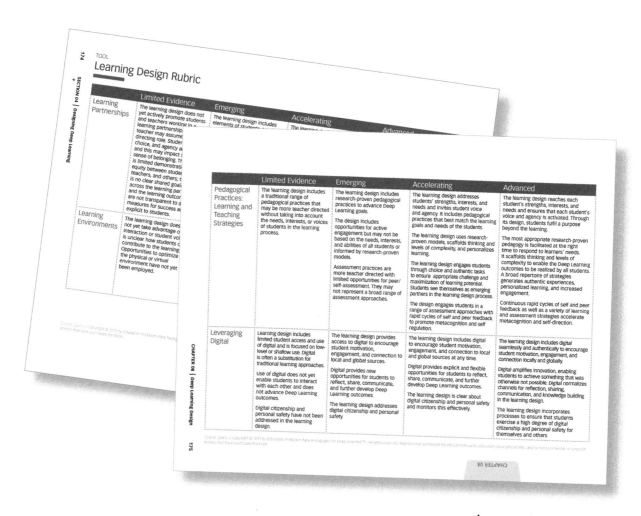

# 26 Applying the Learning Design Rubric

**Purpose: Apply the Learning Design Rubric to a video example**

**Time: 45 minutes**

**Process: Video Analysis**

**Resources:**
- Tool: Learning Design Rubric
- Video at www.deep-learning.global: Innovative Learning at St. Louis School

**1** **Form groups** of four.

**2** **Review** the Learning Design Rubric. One pair reviews the Leveraging Digital Element and the other pair reviews the Pedagogical Practices Element.

**3** **Watch the video:** Innovative Learning at St. Louis School, looking for evidence of your assigned Element.

**4** **Highlight** the descriptors that best capture the evidence you observed. Make a rating for each dimension.

**5** **Share your ratings** and discuss in your pairs:

- Where would you place this learning design on the rubric?
- What is your evidence?
- What would be one next step toward improvement in Pedagogical Practices/ Leveraging Digital?

**6** **Share your ratings** in groups of four.

**7** **Reflect** on the video and consider the other two Elements of Learning Design:

- What inferences did you need to make?
- What did you notice about the Learning Environment?
- What might be one way to amplify Learning Partnerships?

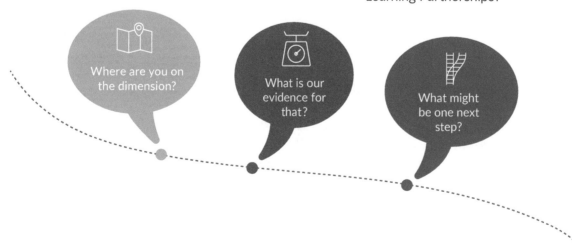

Where are you on the dimension?

What is our evidence for that?

What might be one next step?

# Learning Design Rubric Organizer

| Pedagogical Practices | Rating on the Rubric:<br><br>Evidence: |
|---|---|
| Leveraging Digital | Rating on the Rubric:<br><br>Evidence: |

# 27 Deepening the Analysis Using the Learning Design Rubric

**Purpose: Deepen the understanding of Pedagogical Practices**

**Process: Video Analysis and Discussion**

**Time: 45–60 minutes**

**1** **Work** with a partner and review the following:

- Looking for Evidence of Pedagogical Practices: Organizer
- Learning Design Rubric (Pedagogical Practices dimension)

**2** **Prepare** to find evidence of Pedagogical Practices as you watch the video.

- Person A watches the students' behavior and looks for evidence
- Person B watches the teacher's behavior and looks for evidence

**3** **Watch** the video Activate the Learning, Deep Learning in Grade 3—Flourishing in a Complex World.

**4** **Share** the evidence found in the video.

**5** **Return** to the Pedagogical Practices dimension of the Learning Design Rubric and discuss the following:

- Where would you place this learning experience on the Pedagogical Practices dimension of the rubric?
- What is your evidence?
- What might be one next step?

| | Limited Evidence | Emerging | Accelerating | Advanced |
|---|---|---|---|---|
| Pedagogical Practices: Learning and Teaching Strategies | The learning design includes a traditional range of pedagogical practices that may be more teacher directed without taking into account the needs, interests, or voices of students in the learning process. | The learning design includes research-proven pedagogical practices to advance Deep Learning goals.<br><br>The design includes opportunities for active engagement but may not be based on the needs, interests, and abilities of all students or informed by research-proven models.<br><br>Assessment practices are more teacher directed with limited opportunities for peer/ self-assessment. They may not represent a broad range of assessment approaches. | The learning design addresses students' strengths, interests, and needs and invites student voice and agency. It includes pedagogical practices that best match the learning goals and needs of the students.<br><br>The learning design uses research-proven models, scaffolds thinking and levels of complexity, and personalizes learning.<br><br>The learning design engages students through choice and authentic tasks to ensure appropriate challenge and maximization of learning potential. Students see themselves as emerging partners in the learning design process.<br><br>The design engages students in a range of assessment approaches with rapid cycles of self and peer feedback to promote metacognition and self regulation | The learning design reaches each student's strengths, interests, and needs and ensures that each student's voice and agency is activated. Through its design, students fulfil a purpose beyond the learning.<br><br>The most appropriate research-proven pedagogy is facilitated at the right time to respond to learners' needs. It scaffolds thinking and levels of complexity to enable the Deep Learning outcomes to be realized by all students. A broad repertoire of strategies generates authentic experiences, personalized learning, and increased engagement.<br><br>Continuous rapid cycles of self and peer feedback as well as a variety of learning and assessment strategies accelerate metacognition and self-direction. |

## Looking for Evidence of Pedagogical Practices

| Look for . . . | Evidence |
|---|---|
| **Person A**<br>(watches students)<br><br>• Learning goals and needs of students are matched with design<br><br>• Active engagement<br><br>• Student choice<br><br>• Student agency<br><br>• Authentic focus<br><br>• Appropriate challenge<br><br>• Students are partners in the learning process<br><br>• Self and peer feedback to promote metacognition | |
| **Person B**<br>(watches teacher)<br><br>• Learning goals are explicit<br><br>• Success criteria are explicit<br><br>• Uses research-proven Pedagogical Practices<br><br>• Uses strategies to deepen the global competencies<br><br>• Innovative pedagogies used<br><br>• Engages students in rapid cycles of feedback<br><br>• Digital is leveraged to deepen the learning<br><br>• Scaffolds thinking and levels of complexity<br><br>• A range of assessment approaches used | |

# 28 Enhancing the Learning Design

**Purpose: Reflect on and improve a Deep Learning Design**

**Process: Reflect, Assess, and Enhance**

**Time: 45–60 minutes**

> **Resources:**
> - Tool: Learning Design Rubric
> - Video at www.deep-learning.global: Activate the Learning—Deep Learning in Grade 3—Flourishing in a Complex World

**1** **Connect** with your teaching partner and reflect on your completed Learning Design Planning Template from Protocol 24, before teaching the lesson.

**2** **Identify** three students that you will focus on to assess progress. These students should be representative of varied levels of performance.

**3** **Activate** the learning using the Learning Design Planning Template as a guide.

**4** **Come together,** following the lesson with the following artifacts:

- Completed Learning Design Planning Template
- Learning Design Rubric
- Learning Progressions that were used
- Range of student work from three students

**5** **Complete** the Reflecting on Student Performance Organizer.

**6** **Reflect.**

- How effectively did it support students to meet the learning outcomes?
- How well did the learning design support the intended outcome?

**7** **Based on the analysis** of evidence:

- Redesign to ensure that the intended learning outcomes are met

- Design the next phase of learning

# Reflecting on Student Performance Organizer

| Evidence of Student Work | How well did students meet the stated curriculum standards? Where do they need more support? | How well did students develop the Global Competencies? Where were they placed on the Learning Progression? Where do they need more support? | What do you notice generally about the student performance? What patterns are emerging? Were there any surprises? |
|---|---|---|---|
| A | | | |
| B | | | |
| C | | | |

# LEARNING DESIGN PLANNING TEMPLATE

**Assess**

**Assess: What do you already know about your students? (strengths, needs, interests)**

What are the students' knowledge, skills, interests, and needs?
How might you capture this?

**Learning Outcomes: What do we want students to learn?**

## Curriculum Standards

Review your local curriculum standards. List those you will focus on in this learning opportunity.

## Deep Learning Competencies

Which of the Global Competencies (6Cs) might you focus on?

**Success Criteria Evidence of Outcomes: How will we know they have learned it?**

List your success criteria in simple, explicit language. Will the learners have the opportunity to co-construct the success criteria?

**Design**

**Learning Design Overview**

Provide an overview of the learning design.

- What activities will learners engage in?
- What are some critical points, both instructionally and for the learners?
- What products will come out of the learning?
- What processes will support the outcomes?

**Four Elements of Learning Design**

| | |
|---|---|
| Pedagogical Practices | List some of the pedagogical strategies you will use in this task. Consider how to meet the needs of all learners in your class. |
| Learning Partnerships | How might partnerships strengthen the task and deepen the learning? Consider partnership possibilities that involve other learners, adults in the school environment, and those outside the school and in the community. |
| Learning Environments | Where will the learning physically occur? How will you support learners to take risks and try new ways of thinking, learning, presenting, and reflecting. |
| Leveraging Digital | How might technology amplify, accelerate, and connect learners and learning? |

**Implement**

**Implement the Learning Design:**
Note any adaptations, observations, and insights as you go.

**Measure, Reflect, and Change**

**Measure: What assessments will you use?**

How will you and others assess learning?
How will you use a variety of assessment modes, both formative and summative?

**Reflect and Change: Assessing learning**
How well did the learning design meet the intended learning outcomes?

After: Consider how the evidence collected met your learning goals and design expectations.

**Reflect and Change: Assessing learning design**
What parts of the learning design worked well, and what can be improved?

After: Talk with colleagues. What worked well, What might you improve? How might you do that?

# LEARNING DESIGN PLANNING TEMPLATE: WORKING COPY

| | |
|---|---|
| **Assess** | **Assess:** What do you already know about your students? (strengths, needs, interests) |
| | **Learning Outcomes:** What do we want students to learn? |
| | **Curriculum Standards**        **Deep Learning Competencies** |
| | •                  • |
| | **Success Criteria Evidence of Outcomes:** How will we know they have learned it? |
| | • |

| | |
|---|---|
| **Design** | **Learning Design Overview** |
| | **Four Elements of Learning Design** |
| | Pedagogical Practices |
| | Learning Partnerships |
| | Learning Environments |
| | Leveraging Digital |

| | |
|---|---|
| **Implement** | **Implement the Learning Design:** Note any adaptations, observations, and insights as you go. |

| | |
|---|---|
| **Measure, Reflect, and Change** | **Measure:** What assessments will you use? |
| | • |
| | **Reflect and Change: Assessing learning** How well did the learning design meet the intended learning outcomes? |
| | • |
| | **Reflect and Change: Assessing learning design** What parts of the learning design worked well, and what can be improved? |

# Learning Design Rubric

| | Limited Evidence | Emerging | Accelerating | Advanced |
|---|---|---|---|---|
| Learning Partnerships | The learning design does not yet actively promote students and teachers working in a learning partnership. The teacher may assume a directing role. Student voice, choice, and agency are limited and this may impact students' sense of belonging. There is limited demonstration of equity between students, teachers, and others; there is no clear shared goal(s) across the learning partners and the learning outcomes are not transparent to all; the measures for success are not explicit to students. | The learning design includes elements of students, teachers, and others working in a learning partnership to ensure Deep Learning outcomes. Teachers are starting to facilitate student voice, choice, and agency. There are shared goal(s) for the learning that students support; there is growing equity in the learning partnership relationships; learning outcomes are transparent to students with an increasing understanding of how it will be measured. | The learning design has a clear strategy for students, teachers, and other partners to achieve Deep Learning outcomes for all students. Students have a sense of belonging. Student voice, choice, and agency and contribution to learning design has been integral; there is equity in the relationships between students and teachers, learning outcomes, processes, and expectations are transparent; and there is consensus about what success looks like and how it will be measured. | The learning design is a collaborative partnership among students and teachers and others, with a clear focus on achieving Deep Learning outcomes for all students. Student voice, choice, agency, and contribution have been critical to improving the learning design.<br><br>All students have a genuine sense of belonging. The learning partnership is driven by high levels of partner equity, transparency, and mutual benefit/accountability. There are clear collaborative processes and measures to enable students to persevere and encounter success. |
| Learning Environments | The learning design does not yet take advantage of interaction or student voice. It is unclear how students can contribute to the learning. Opportunities to optimize the physical or virtual environment have not yet been employed. | The learning design states how an interactive learning environment establishes a climate and culture for learning. In doing so, the learning design includes strategies to engage *most* students but does not yet have clear approaches to ensure equity or to generate student influence. The physical and virtual environments provide new contexts for learning. | The learning design includes an interactive and equitable learning environment to enable Deep Learning for all students. It includes strategies to develop collaborative processes with and between students and incorporates student voice to influence the ways we work together. Physical and virtual environments provide diverse contexts for learning. | An equitable and interactive learning environment permeates the learning design; all students are deeply engaged and committed to collaborative processes. Their voice drives learning and improvement.<br><br>The physical and virtual environments within and beyond the classroom provide rich, authentic contexts for learning |

| | Limited Evidence | Emerging | Accelerating | Advanced |
|---|---|---|---|---|
| **Pedagogical Practices: Learning and Teaching Strategies** | The learning design includes a traditional range of pedagogical practices that may be more teacher directed without taking into account the needs, interests, or voices of students in the learning process. | The learning design includes research-proven pedagogical practices to advance Deep Learning goals.<br><br>The design includes opportunities for active engagement but may not be based on the needs, interests, and abilities of all students or informed by research-proven models.<br><br>Assessment practices are more teacher directed with limited opportunities for peer/self-assessment. They may not represent a broad range of assessment approaches. | The learning design addresses students' strengths, interests, and needs and invites student voice and agency. It includes pedagogical practices that best match the learning goals and needs of the students.<br><br>The learning design uses research-proven models, scaffolds thinking and levels of complexity, and personalizes learning.<br><br>The learning design engages students through choice and authentic tasks to ensure appropriate challenge and maximization of learning potential. Students see themselves as emerging partners in the learning design process.<br><br>The design engages students in a range of assessment approaches with rapid cycles of self and peer feedback to promote metacognition and self regulation. | The learning design reaches each student's strengths, interests, and needs and ensures that each student's voice and agency is activated. Through its design, students fulfil a purpose beyond the learning.<br><br>The most appropriate research-proven pedagogy is facilitated at the right time to respond to learners' needs. It scaffolds thinking and levels of complexity to enable the Deep Learning outcomes to be realized by all students. A broad repertoire of strategies generates authentic experiences, personalized learning, and increased engagement.<br><br>Continuous rapid cycles of self and peer feedback as well as a variety of learning and assessment strategies accelerate metacognition and self-direction. |
| **Leveraging Digital** | Learning design includes limited student access and use of digital and is focused on low-level or shallow use. Digital is often a substitution for traditional learning approaches.<br><br>Use of digital does not yet enable students to interact with each other and does not advance Deep Learning outcomes.<br><br>Digital citizenship and personal safety have not been addressed in the learning design. | The learning design provides access to digital to encourage student motivation, engagement, and connection to local and global sources.<br><br>Digital provides new opportunities for students to reflect, share, communicate, and further develop Deep Learning outcomes.<br><br>The learning design addresses digital citizenship and personal safety | The learning design includes digital to encourage student motivation, engagement, and connection to local and global sources at any time.<br><br>Digital provides explicit and flexible opportunities for students to reflect, share, communicate, and further develop Deep Learning outcomes.<br><br>The learning design is clear about digital citizenship and personal safety and monitors this effectively. | The learning design includes digital seamlessly and authentically to encourage student motivation, engagement, and connection locally and globally.<br><br>Digital amplifies innovation, enabling students to achieve something that was otherwise not possible. Digital normalizes channels for reflection, sharing, communication, and knowledge building in the learning design.<br><br>The learning design incorporates processes to ensure that students exercise a high degree of digital citizenship and personal safety for themselves and others |

DEEP LEARNING DESIGN EXAMPLE
## LEARNING ABOUT LANDMARKS, GRADE 2

**Assess:** What do you already know about your students? (strengths, needs, interests)

These students are tactile, have a lot of energy, and struggle to listen to others. They are a culturally diverse group. They love puzzles and riddles.

**Learning Outcomes:** What do we want students to learn?

### Curriculum Standards

- Language (oral communication): Students reflect and identify strengths as listeners and speakers and identify areas for improvement.
- Math: Describe and represent locations of objects, draw simple maps of familiar settings.
- Arts: Apply the creative process to produce a variety of two- and three-dimensional art works using elements, principles, and techniques of visual arts to communicate feelings, ideas, and understandings.

### Deep Learning Competencies

- Communication—reflection to further develop and improve communication
- Creativity—asking the right questions
- Critical Thinking—meaningful knowledge construction

**Success Criteria Evidence of Outcomes:** How will we know they have learned it?

- Students will learn how to ask good questions and listen for information.
- Students will use maps to communicate in a descriptive way to provide and interpret directions.
- Students will make an Inukshuk and deepen understanding of diverse cultures within Canada.
- Students will make a geocache box, describe it in writing, and present to peers.

### Learning Design Overview

(3 weeks)

1. Students will be asked how they know how to get home from school. What landmarks do they pass along the way?
2. Students will be exposed to different types of landmarks and their practical and symbolic importance in cultures.
3. Students explore a Canadian landmark of their choice and build a small 3D replica and present its significance to the class
4. Students will place their landmarks in hidden locations around the school.
5. They will draw maps for other students to find their landmarks.
6. Explore geocaching. Invite a parent in to explain.
7. Groups create a geocache box.
8. Go on a field trip to a local conservation area to participate in geocaching

### Four Elements of Learning Design

**Pedagogical Practices**

Students work individually, in pairs, and in small purposeful groups.
Students will present their landmarks—use communication and creativity learning progressions.

Assess

Design

| Learning Partnerships | A parent speaker and a park ranger (of conservation area) |
| | School secretary and school caretaker support hiding of the landmarks around the school |
| | Students work and assess in small groups |
| Learning Environments | Use of school (for hiding landmarks) |
| | Conservation area |
| Leveraging Digital | Online maps and geocaching application |

## Implement

### Implement the Learning Design:
Note any adaptations, observations, and insights as you go.

- Student in class presented an Inukshuk and others were fascinated. So we collected rocks and made one for the school yard.
- We could not get to the conservation area for the field trip so we geocached around the neighborhood.
- These students love to build and use manipulatives.

## Measure, Reflect, and Change

### Measure:
What assessments will you use?

Each of these assessments used the same criteria and were used to measure student growth

- Two short presentations
- Being a part of an audience, asking good questions
- Two three-dimensional creations: an inukshuk and a geocache box
- Two maps: one school and the conservation area

### Reflect and Change: Assessing learning
How well did the learning design meet the intended learning outcomes?

- 21/22 improved in Communication (self and teacher assessment)
- 22/22 improved in Creativity (self, peer, and teacher assessment)
- 22/22 improved in Critical Thinking (self and teacher assessment)
- 20/22 were able to reflect and identify strengths as listeners and speakers and identify areas for improvement with proficiency
- 17/22 were able to describe and represent locations of objects, draw simple maps of familiar settings with proficiency
- 22/22 were able to apply the creative process to produce a variety of three-dimensional art works

### Reflect and Change: Assessing learning design
What parts of the learning design worked well, and what can be improved?

Students were very engaged in the task, and their skill in reflecting on their work is improving. However, the teacher designed the tasks. We could have focused more on the Arctic because students were fascinated by the Inuksuit. As well, students struggled with being able to understand maps. More time should have been spent helping them to understand maps of familiar settings before exposing them to online maps and the neighborhood; need to use more manipulatives and visuals when teaching spatial reasoning with this group.

# EXPLORING WORLD PEACE, GRADE 4

## Assess

### Assess: What do you already know about your students? (strengths, needs, interests)

Students are good citizens around the school. They like to help out. However, they live in a sheltered middle class community and are unaware of some of the issues that dominate the world. Some of the girls are bullying each other. Because there are three classes of Grade 4, we want to purposefully mix them up to minimize the cliques.

### Learning Outcomes: What do we want students to learn?

#### Curriculum Standards

- Reading: Integrate information from two texts on the same topic in order to write or speak about the subject knowledgeably.

- Writing: Conduct short research projects that build knowledge through investigation of different aspects of a topic.

- Social Studies: Participate in projects to help or inform others.

#### Deep Learning Competencies

- Creativity—leadership for action

- Critical Thinking—experimenting, reflecting and taking action on their ideas in the real world.

- Communication—communication designed for particular audiences

- Communication—substantive, multi-modal communication

### Success Criteria Evidence of Outcomes: How will we know they have learned it?

- Students will be able to define empathy and citizenship.

- Students will be able to use fiction and nonfiction texts, digital resources, and articles to research equality, equity, and peace.

- Students will be able to propose solutions to complex world problems.

- Students will be able to use different modes of communication to share their understandings with a broad audience.

## Design

### Learning Design Overview

Students will explore issues related to peace around the world. We will use a variety of pedagogical strategies to activate student understanding of complex issues such as race, gender, world conflict, and immigration. Students will choose from a range of picture books (e.g., *A Piece of Home* by Jerry Watts) to adequately prepare and read to a Grade 1 reading buddy. Students will interview diverse groups of people (family members neighbors, school staff, veterans, and kindergartners) to hear different perspectives of what would bring equality among all people. They will use digital resources to find images that challenge and confirm notions of equality, equity, and peace. They will also listen to protest music from the 1960s. After this research, students may create inspiring and hopeful songs, dances, and poems regarding world peace.

### Four Elements of Learning Design

| Pedagogical Practices | Students participate in experiential learning through activities that challenge them to "step into the shoes" of individuals in different situations. Students will choose their topics and express themselves creatively. Teachers and students co-create success criteria for their visuals/poems/presentations. Parents will be informed of the learning goals and expectations. The teacher will monitor progress using digital. |
|---|---|

| | | |
|---|---|---|
| **Learning Partnerships** | Families, community members, and cross-grade groupings will be included in the initial research component. Students from across Grade 4 will partner with each other. Students will present at a school assembly. | |
| **Learning Environments** | The learning environment represents student thinking through their visuals, anchor charts, and student quotes. | |
| **Leveraging Digital** | Sites like Google Drive (to store research and provide peer feedback), PowerPoint, Skype, and email allow students to connect beyond the classroom with partners. Seesaw app allows students to track, share, and reflect on their learning. Animoto allows students to create videos on the iPads and laptops. | |

## Implement the Learning Design:
## Note any adaptations, observations, and insights as you go.

During the interview process, one student encountered a neighbor who was a recent veteran; she came in to share her story of what life was like in Afghanistan. This connection led to a partnership with the local veterans' association. Students interviewed and performed for them. They also prepared baked goods and had tea with the veterans and wrote letters of gratitude. Students also presented a PowerPoint presentation using the visual images they had created. Some students chose to write letters to those serving overseas. Noticing that the girls are treating each other better.

## Measure:
## What assessments will you use?

- Research (oral and written)
- Reading buddy presentation (oral and written)
- Veterans' presentation (oral and written)
- Student follow-up letter to the veteran (written)
- Student reflection and conferencing: Learning progression (oral and written)

## Reflect and Change: Assessing learning
### How well did the learning design meet the intended learning outcomes?

- 57/61 students showed growth in their understanding of the issues.
- 59/61 students used the research process to create and communicate their knowledge.
- 59/61 students demonstrated and could articulate how they grew in the focused competencies: Creativity, Communication, Critical Thinking

## Reflect and Change: Assessing Learning Design
### What parts of the learning design worked well, and what can be improved?

It was good to provide students with a range of choices; they could choose from eight books to read to their reading buddies but had free reign for their presentations to veterans. Coordinating among three teachers with varying levels of understanding of Deep Learning was new but not impossible—our collaboration has led to better insights and relationships. Next time, when an opportunity (like the veteran partnership) comes up, we would slow down to think through the opportunity and scaffold the learning so students are better prepared.

*Margin labels:* Implement; Measure, Reflect, and Change

# EXPLORING POVERTY: A SUSTAINABLE APPROACH, GRADE 6

## Assess
### Assess: What do you already know about your students? (strengths, needs, interests)

Students have developed a keen and shared interest in giving back to wider communities. They lack a depth of understanding of how local contexts vary outside their own community but are excited to learn about others' ways of living and how they can contribute to enhancing quality of life. Students have a genuine interest in becoming changemakers.

### Learning Outcomes: What do we want students to learn?

| Curriculum Standards | Deep Learning Competencies |
|---|---|
| • Geography: Knowledge and understanding-differences in the economic, demographic, and social characteristics between countries across the world. | Citizenship—a global perspective; Empathy and compassion for diverse values and worldviews |
| • English: Language for interaction, Understand how to move beyond making bare assertions and take account of differing perspectives and points of view. | (Although all of the Cs were addressed) |
| • Mathematics: Number and algebra, money and financial mathematics, create simple financial plans. | |
| • Literacy: Creating texts, plan, draft, and publish imaginative, informative, and persuasive texts, choosing and experimenting with text structures, language features, images, and digital resources appropriate to purpose and audience. | |

### Success Criteria Evidence of Outcomes: How will we know they have learned it?

- Students will demonstrate an interest in tackling real-world problems that are unstructured and open ended.
- Students will actively engage in thinking about and taking action, both individually and collectively, on issues with global implications.
- Students will share a thoughtful plan for tackling the problem.

## Design
### Learning Design Overview: How will you sequence the learning?

In collaborative groups, students devised business plans with the emphasis on independence, originality, and cost effectiveness, and made informed decisions on the loans process through Kiva. Design included formative assessment to determine individual knowledge about poverty, whole-class discussions on the topic and student and group conference to assess progress and obstacles; a business plan with a list of criteria was designed with students. Also displayed a WILF (What I am Looking For?) requirement. Students chose to enact their plans either individually or in groups. Students jotted regular reflections and questions in our journal.

### Four Elements of Learning Design

| Pedagogical Practices | • Direct instruction |
|---|---|
| | • Collaborative learning groups, conferencing with students |
| | • Brainstorm ideas for a fund raising project |
| | • Structure and facilitate time for groups to collaborate on business plans |
| | • Create success criteria for class with business plans |

| | |
|---|---|
| **Learning Partnerships** | Kiva microfinance provided the platform to investigate and assign loans.  Some local businesses were contacted.  It was stressed that fundraising would occur in the wider community. The project was featured in the state newspaper. |
| **Learning Environments** | Learning was undertaken in the classroom. We took all of our fundraising activities to the wider community to literally spread the message farther. Most of our communication occurred online. Planning and learning occurred in whole-class and small groups. |
| **Leveraging Digital** | Word processing tools, email, Internet, Kiva (online microfinance platform) |

## Implement the Learning Design: Note any adaptations, observations, and insights as you go.

Some students were really keen to work independently to implement their final business plans. Whilst I had envisaged this to be a group activity, individual application was a viable and impactful outcome. In these individual cases, there was still powerful collaborative feedback and learning taking place. The process of collaborative learning was as important as the outcomes.

As the individual projects took off, I needed to emphasize taking opportunities for collaborative check-ins.

## Measure: What assessments will you use?

- Completed a business plan that addressed cost effectiveness, originality, and independence
- Collaboration to organize and conduct a successful fund raising activity
- Responses with caring and thoughtful comments and questions to *Exploring Poverty Journal*
- Understanding of key concepts presented in a series of lessons from a resource, *What Matters Most? Exploring Poverty with Upper Primary Students*

## Reflect and Change: Assessing learning outcomes
### How well did the learning design meet the intended learning outcomes?

- 24/27 gained a deep understanding/empathy of the challenges of poverty
- 27/27 deepened their global perspective
- 24/27 provided an effective business plan (12 of these students raised money)

## Reflect and Change: Assessing learning design
### What parts of the learning design worked well, and what can be improved?

As a group, we thoroughly enjoyed working on this project and it reaffirmed our initial thinking that education is a very significant, if not the most significant factor, in alleviating poverty.

The crucial question for us was *Who needs the education the most, the poor or those who are living a life free from poverty?*

The answer for us was clear cut. A truly educated wealthy world has all the resources at their disposal to eliminate poverty. Some students were challenged to understand poverty; next time, we would use more fictional texts to build empathy before beginning the projects. Some students struggled to work in groups; I would provide more deliberate and explicit check-ins.

Source: Adapted from Waimea Heights Primary School, Australia

DEEP LEARNING DESIGN EXAMPLE

# SPEED DATING: CRITICAL THINKING AND WRITING, GRADE 10 ENGLISH

## Assess: What do you already know about your students? (strengths, needs, interests)

Students in Eleanor's 10th grade English class need to build strength in persuasive and argumentative styles of writing.

## Learning Outcomes: What do we want students to learn?

### Curriculum Standards

- Write arguments to support claims in an analysis of substantive topics or texts, using valid reasoning and relevant and sufficient evidence.

- Write informative/explanatory texts to examine and convey complex ideas, concepts, and information clearly and accurately through the effective selection, organization, and analysis of content.

- Develop and strengthen writing as needed by planning, revising, editing, rewriting, or trying a new approach, focusing on addressing what is most significant for a specific purpose and audience.

- Gather relevant information from multiple authoritative print and digital sources, using advanced searches effectively; assess the usefulness of each source in answering the research question; integrate information into the text selectively to maintain the flow of ideas.

### Deep Learning Competencies

- Critical Thinking

## Success Criteria Evidence of Outcomes: How will we know they have learned it?

Students will be able to evaluate their own and others' writing and provide focused feedback based on the Critical Thinking Rubric.

## Learning Design Overview

Over five lessons students will be introduced to three dimensions of the Critical Thinking Rubric:

- Evaluating information and arguments
- Making connections and identifying patterns
- Meaningful knowledge construction

We will discuss how these three dimensions will help us focus our writing skills and suggest what each dimension might look like in practice.

Students will then apply the three dimensions to their own work, highlighting strengths and opportunities for improvement.

Students will then engage in a "speed dating" protocol. They will be given a template that includes prompts based on the three dimensions. They will use the prompts to help them analyze other students' work and provide feedback to them. This process will take 15 minutes per round, in which time students will read their peers' work, analyze it, and provide notes and suggestions. This process will be repeated four times, so each student will receive four sets of feedback.

| Four Elements of Learning Design | |
|---|---|
| Pedagogical Practices | Direct instruction on how to use the Critical Thinking Rubric Individual student use of the rubric (application to their own work). |
| Learning Partnerships | "Speed dating" style process through which students evaluate the strengths of others' work and provide feedback. Prior, review norms of collaboration and ways of working together effectively and respectfully. |
| Learning Environments | |
| Leveraging Digital | |

**Implement**

### Implement the Learning Design:
Note any adaptations, observations, and insights as you go.

I was unsure whether there would be enough time across five lessons, but this worked well. We split the speed dating process across two lessons to allow students to reflect on feedback so they were not overwhelmed.

**Measure, Reflect, and Change**

### Measure: What assessments will you use?

- Observations of the quality of feedback
- Whole class and individual discussions about the effectiveness of the processes
- Assessment of the writing product (via rubric)

### Reflect and Change: Assessing learning
How well did the learning design meet the intended learning outcomes?

Students were able to use the rubric to focus on explicit feedback that improved their own and others' writing.

### Reflect and Change: Assessing learning design
What parts of the learning design worked well, and what can be improved?

When my colleagues and I talk about Deep Learning, we talk about critical thinking—it's so important for our students to be critical thinkers across the curriculum. This is what speed dating really allows them to practice. I want them to know that professional journalists revise, re-interview, make mistakes, ask colleagues for feedback, and repeat those processes to make their work shine.

Next time, I would allow extra time between "speed dates" to allow students reflection and processing time.

# VULNERABLE POPULATIONS AND ECONOMIC ACTIVITY, GRADE 12 ECONOMICS

**Assess**

## Assess: What do you already know about your students? (strengths, needs, interests)

Students were interested in the schoolwide campaign against drinking and driving. Many of them are not fully elaborating when they write, although I believe they understand because of the depth of their insights during class discussions. They are not yet making the connections to global economics and daily life in our community.

## Learning Outcomes: What do we want students to learn?

### Curriculum Standards

- Describe ways in which individuals and groups attempt to address problems related to international economic activities.

- Explain how various social movements and social justice organizations address global economic equality.

### Deep Learning Competencies

- Collaboration—working interdependently as a team

- Critical Thinking—experiment, reflect, take action on their ideas in real world

- Citizenship—leveraging digital and solving ambiguous and complex problems to benefit citizens

- Character—empathy, compassion, and integrity in action

## Success Criteria Evidence of Outcomes: How will we know they have learned it?

- Students will critically examine a social justice issue (human trafficking).

- Students will communicate convincingly, sensitively, and appropriately about the issue to relevant audiences.

- Students will use digital to reach audiences and share important messages about personal safety and how they can help alleviate a social justice issue.

**Design**

## Learning Design Overview: How will you sequence the learning?

(intermittently over eight weeks) Students will be presented with contemporary articles related to social justice and human slavery, and they will generate questions about it. They will explore what is currently being done by organizations. We will co-create the learning design, based on student interest, and collaboratively identify global competencies. Students will divide into teams to investigate further, propose plans, and take action to raise awareness across the school and broader community.

## Four Elements of Learning Design

| | |
|---|---|
| Pedagogical Practices | Students will work individually and in small groups throughout the design. Student groups will share their planning at various stages and seek feedback from each other and teacher before launching the product/campaign |
| Learning Partnerships | Students will initiate their own community and organization contacts (e.g., social agencies, experts) |
| Learning Environments | Various virtual and physical environments, within and beyond the school |

| Leveraging Digital | Various (e.g., blogging, web pages, social media, word processing, PowerPoint) |

## Implement the Learning Design: Note any adaptations, observations, and insights as you go

Students were completely unaware that thousands of youth (both domestically and internationally) were being lured into prostitution and forced labor every day in America. They were fascinated by the topic of human trafficking, so we took more time to sensitively explore and address the issue. When they recognized there is not a lot of information out there, they wanted to take matters into their own hands. This led us on a different course than what I expected, but it still related to learning goals and curriculum. So they drove the learning.

Here are examples of the action the groups took:

- A police officer (who specialized in human trafficking) was invited in to meet with parents (and other interested community members) to raise awareness and recognize signs of vulnerability

- An Internet safety guide and presentation was created and shared with the Grade 6 students in neighboring school

- A blog, Instagram, and webpage created with links for Grades 8 and 9 students in the district

- Peer connections initiated with foster students/local service agencies to reach marginalized youth

- Campaign at airport to hand out pamphlets students had created

Students were thrilled when the local media took interest in their initiative. This was a great teaching opportunity because we were able to make links to media and social movements

## Measure: What assessments will you use?

- Critical reviews of three articles/videos on a topic related to social justice
- Persuasive Essay: social justice, economics, and equity
- Group Presentation/Take-Action Campaign
- Summary reflection on their contribution to a social movement

## Reflect and Change: Assessing learning outcomes
### How well did the learning design meet the intended learning outcomes?

- 25/30 Collaboration: self, peer, and teacher assessment—level 3 or higher
- 28/30 Critical Thinking: self, peer, and partner assessment—level 3 or higher
- 30/30 Citizenship: self, peer, teacher, and partner assessment—level 3 or higher
- 30/30 Character: self, peer, teacher, and partner assessment—level 3 or higher

## Reflect and Change: Assessing learning design
### What parts of the learning design worked well, and what can be improved?

Students were very motivated by this task because there is a lack of information, so they felt they were contributing to something larger than themselves. Next time around, I need to be more explicit about success criteria for collaboration. Also, given that it is such an emotionally charged topic, I needed to stop the class several times to teach them about how to communicate sensitively and maturely to appropriate audiences. However, because they were so self-directed, I could easily assume an "activator" stance. We could have dedicated the whole term to this.

>> This shift in values away from standardization and content memorization toward the creation and application of new and powerful knowledge and competencies necessitates a transformative shift in measurement tools and practices. "

*—DEEP LEARNING: ENGAGE THE WORLD CHANGE THE WORLD, P. 139*

# SECTION 05

## Assessment Practices

**"** The power of the process lies in the professional discussion about the learning and the sharing of effective strategies in preparing for the next stage of learning. **"**

# Chapter 09
# Collaborative Assessment

Whether your learning design works or not, your last one will inform your next one. That's why reflecting on our practice is so critical. We need to be able to dig in and wrestle with the brutal facts: the good, the bad, and the challenging. We need to clarify what worked and what didn't and understand why in order to fulfill the needs of all students. This level of scrutiny is hard to do in isolation—it's lonely, and our narrow perspectives can wreak havoc on our efficacy. Time to call for reinforcements—our colleagues!

In this chapter, we address the process of collaborative assessment, now understood as one of the most powerful professional learning strategies for improving instructional practice. It draws from our own meaningful contexts and allows us to roll up our sleeves and problem-solve relevant instructional issues. Just as Deep Learning calls for a shift in teachers' stances, collaborative assessment begs for a redefinition of how we learn as professionals. There's no "sit 'n' git" here. Collaborative assessment calls for all members of the group to fully participate. It is iterative, messy, and tremendously rewarding. Let's now look at what collaborative assessment involves; how to create a safe, collegial, and meaningful platform for reflection and measurement; and how to conduct the process itself.

## The Collaborative Assessment Process

Throughout this book, we have been emphasizing how collaborative inquiry is a powerful mindset to guide Deep Learning. The more we use the cycle of assessing, designing, implementing, measuring, and reflecting, the more we improve our practice. When these phases of the cycle become habitual, iterative, and informal and the way we behave around here—when they are not only visible during professional learning time—you know the cultural shift to Deep Learning is well under way. Collaborative assessment takes that last phase of the cycle (measure, reflect, assess) and applies it to examining student learning and learning design. Within our global partnership, we have adopted this approach to regularly learn together and improve our instructional design practice; we meet virtually (through teleconferencing) with the Deep Learning tools to collectively examine innovative practice. When participants arrive to the session prepared to discuss the learning designs, the whole process can take no more than a half hour. If this can be done effectively across time zones, language and cultural barriers, and borders, we know that teachers within a school or district can allocate a half hour for this enriching experience.

## Establishing Norms

If you want to gather your colleagues together for honest and meaningful collaborative assessment, you will need to set the table for an invisible and sometimes pernicious guest: vulnerability. When we feel vulnerable in a group, we don't contribute our best thinking; instead, we "armor up." The amygdala in our brains grows and allows the more primitive functions to take over. We often resort to one of three behaviors: we freeze, we fly, or we fight. When vulnerability is not addressed up front in a group, we protect ourselves first. Brené Brown knows this topic well and elaborates,

 When our organization rewards armoring behaviors like blaming, shaming, cynicism, perfectionism and emotional stoicism, we can't expect innovative work. You can't fully grow and contribute behind armor. It takes a massive amount of energy just to carry it around— sometimes it takes *all* of our energy.

*—DARE TO LEAD, P. 14*

The best way to address this is to co-construct norms before the work begins and to revisit and collectively review them frequently. In Protocol 29, we introduce some norms that can get you started; these seem to work well within our global partnership but they are not exhaustive. It's important that the group crafts what matters to them to increase their sense of shared ownership.

One principle we hold dear is that we should speak about the task as though the teacher who created it is in the room, observing the discussion, and assume that the teacher has provided his or her best thinking at the time. As a group of professionals, we need to recognize that any learning design shared, no matter how detailed, cannot provide a full picture of what is happening in the learning setting. We know there are hundreds of decisions, moves, interactions, and interpretations at play in any given learning environment. We don't know the students the way the teacher does. We cannot fully know what happened before the learning design was executed or what will follow it. Furthermore, an example a teacher provided a year ago might look very different if shared today; we all grow in this process. So we need to reserve our attributions and resist the urge to jump to conclusions. Honoring teachers' voices and their courage to share is what's at stake here. Only now is the teaching profession coming out of its rabbit hole; sharing our practice is becoming a new normal. Unfair and harsh criticism may risk sending teachers into an isolated retreat once more.

## Managing the Process

As indicated earlier, it's important that colleagues come to the process having already reviewed the learning design. In this way, they have their own perspectives and are not susceptible to groupthink. Questions to ask when you are beginning to examine the design include

- What are you noticing?

- What do you recognize?

- What are you wondering about?

- What are you appreciating?

These questions enable colleagues to speak about the information in front of them, using descriptive voice and specific references. They help to keep the conversation focused on the facts. Encourage the group to ask clarifying questions and refrain from judgment. As they share what they are noticing, they may want to organize their observations according to the Four Elements.

It is important to use the Learning Design Rubric as the common anchor for the next level of discussion (see pages 174–175). The Learning Design Rubric provides the common language and precision that raises the level of professional discourse, especially when we make specific references to the shared example. The Conversation Guide (introduced in Chapter 7) can serve as a skeleton for the analytical conversation. The first two questions are best used at this time: "Where does this learning design fall on this element of the Learning Design Rubric?" and "What is our evidence to support that?" An example may demonstrate evidence at varying levels of the progression for a single dimension. Highlighting or marking the rubric to show at which levels of the progression evidence is present helps to identify areas of strength and areas for growth. Another good question to ask is "What information is unavailable or unclear at this time?" Absence of evidence in an exemplar doesn't necessarily mean it was not present in the Deep Learning experience. Support your thoughts and decisions with direct evidence from the example, and if evidence isn't available, discuss where evidence could be provided. This helps the group to pause and remember that all the information from the learning experience cannot possibly be conveyed in the example.

Here are some more questions to guide the discussion, organized by the Four Elements:

## Learning Partnerships

- Were students partners in designing their learning, and did student voice guide the process?

- How is the teacher acting as an activator of learning?

- Are there opportunities for partnerships to be further explored or expanded?

## Learning Environments

- How did the Deep Learning experience facilitate knowledge and competency development anytime, anywhere, both within and beyond the classroom walls?

- How did the learning spaces (physical, virtual, cultural) contribute to and deepen the learning?

## Pedagogical Practices

- How do the defined success criteria support and measure Deep Learning?

- How was a range of evidence used to measure student learning?

- How did students receive and respond to feedback, including self, peer, teacher, and community?

## Leveraging Digital

- How do the digital tools advance the Deep Learning experience?

Digging even deeper, then, the group asks a central question: How well did the learning design support the intended outcomes? To be able to answer that, the group needs to look over the student learning. How well did students progress in the Global Competencies? How well did they fulfill the learning goals?

Finally, the group reflects on how this example can be further improved. Teachers who generously shared their work will be hungry for feedback. We know effective feedback is the infant of improvement and it needs to be nurtured wisely. Protocol 15 addresses how to provide effective feedback, and we encourage groups to frame feedback as a question so that the teacher is left thinking.

## Final Thoughts

Sometimes when time is tight, groups will not be able to examine a learning design through the lens of all Four Elements. Focusing on one or two elements can still provide rich insight and keep everyone thinking about how they might improve their own practice.

Protocols

 ## Norms for Collaborative Assessment

Explore and co-create ways of working together that allow for deep and trusting collaboration.

Assessing a Deep Learning Task

Using one of the five Deep Learning examples, collaboratively assess the design using the lens of the Four Elements and the Learning Design Rubric.

## For more information:

Read Chapter 9 from *Deep Learning: Engage the World Change the World.*

# 29 Norms for Collaborative Assessment

Purpose: **Understand the professional norms needed to collaboratively assess a Deep Learning Task**

Time: **10–20 minutes**

Process: **Building Understanding and Consensus of Norms**

**1** **Examine** the norms listed on the first column of the Norms for Assessing a Deep Learning Task Organizer.

**2** **Create groups** of four and number off.

**3** **Build Understanding.** Person 1 reads aloud Norm 1 and then explains why that norm is important for the process. The group then brainstorms examples of what the norm would look like, sound like, and feel like.

**4** **Repeat this process** with Persons 2, 3, and 4 until all four norms are understood.

**5** **Consider as a group** what norms to add, edit, or delete. Make suggestions.

**6** **Review the final list** of norms and reach consensus before moving on with the assessing of task.

**7** **Keep your list** of norms visible throughout the process and revisit it regularly.

## Group Norms

**1.** Speak about the task as though the teacher who created it is in the room, observing the discussion.

**2.** Assume the teacher has provided her or his best thinking at the time.

**3.** Presume that all details of the task cannot be shared within this example.

**4.** Assume a learning stance with yourself and group members.

## Norms for Assessing a Deep Learning Task Organizer

| Norm | Why is this important? | What does the norm look like, sound like, and feel like? | Agree |
|---|---|---|---|
| **1.** Speak about the task as though the teacher who created it is in the room, observing the discussion. | | | |
| **2.** Assume the teacher has provided her or his best thinking at the time. | | | |
| **3.** Presume that all details of the task cannot be shared within this example. | | | |
| **4.** Assume a learning stance with yourself and group members. | | | |
| Additional Norm: | | | |

# 30 Assessing a Deep Learning Task

Purpose: **Collaboratively assess a simulated Learning Design**

Process: **Simulation**

Time: **60 minutes**

Resources:
- Tool: Learning Design Rubric
- Learning Design Examples

## Part One

**1** **As a group**, review the norms agreed upon in Protocol 29.

**2** **Choose one** of the five Learning Design Examples.

**3** **Look** at the Learning Design Example and complete the Learning Design Observation Organizer to capture what you are noticing. Do this individually and use the sentence stems provided.

**4** **Collectively share** these observations. Withhold judgment and use clarifying questions only.

## Part Two

**5** **Review** the Learning Design Rubric introduced in Protocol 25 and your observations from the organizer.

**6** **Highlight** the descriptors on the rubric that match what you have observed. Do this individually.

**7** **Share** your highlighted rubrics. Discuss these questions:

- Where would you place this example on each of the Four Elements of the Learning Design Rubric?
- What evidence supports your analysis?
- What information might not be available or unclear at this time?

**8** **Assess** what the students learned

- How well did the Learning Design support the intended learning outcomes?

**9** **Look** at the Four Elements and identify what you could do to improve the quality of the Deep Learning experience.

**10** **Frame** your feedback as though the colleague were in the room. (Refer to Protocol 15 for principles of effective feedback). Phrase feedback as questions where possible.

**11** **As a group**, read over the norms (generated in Protocol 29) and reflect on how they were executed during this simulation. Each individual shares a short self-assessment.

# Learning Design Observation Organizer

## Pedagogical Practices

I noticed . . .
I'm wondering about . . .
I recognized . . .
I appreciated . . .

## Learning Partnerships

I noticed . . .
I'm wondering about . . .
I recognized . . .
I appreciated . . .

## 6Cs

I noticed . . .
I'm wondering about . . .
I recognized . . .
I appreciated . . .

I noticed . . .
I'm wondering about . . .
I recognized . . .
I appreciated . . .

## Leveraging Digital

I noticed . . .
I'm wondering about . . .
I recognized . . .
I appreciated . . .

## Learning Environments

"Making this kind of learning the norm for all schools and classrooms doesn't happen by chance."

SECTION 06

# Building Capacity for Deep Learning

# Chapter 10
# Teacher Capacity for Deep Learning

Young or old, we're all trying to make sense of the world and our place in it. The more we learn about this Deep Learning enterprise, the more we realize that we're all swimming up the same river. The best way to really learn is to dive in yourself. Avon Maitland District School Board, an active contributing member of our global partnership, shared a pivotal "ah-ha!" moment that gets at this very point. Last spring, it invited hundreds of students to a student voice forum and, among other things, asked them what they wanted their learning to look like. The students were clear about what improvements they wanted in their learning experiences. A few months later, the district office brought the staff together and asked them the same question. Remarkably, the staff wanted to learn the way the students wanted to learn. It included agency in their learning, time to learn with peers and passionate experts, authentic learning, and strategies to address teaching needs in a rapidly changing world (see Figure 10.1).

In Fort Wayne, Indiana, the district leadership team had a similar epiphany. They looked at the Global Competencies and asked, "Hang on, if employers are looking for these 6Cs in their graduates, why aren't we looking at developing the 6Cs in our own employees? We all need to get into Deep Learning." We don't need schools where our teachers are simply compliant. Rather, we need schools where teachers jump out of bed in the morning, anticipating the joy that is found in teaching and learning. In this chapter, we explore how to leverage the inquiry conditions to disrupt disengagement, stimulate innovation, and resuscitate the energy of seasoned learners in order to make deep learners of us all.

At the New Pedagogies for Deep Learning (NPDL) global Deep Learning Lab in Toronto in 2017, our critical friend, Alan November, asked us a simple but penetrating question that nearly knocked us out of our banquet chairs. It was this: "Who owns the learning?" We know the importance of providing voice and

FIGURE 10.1
Teacher Voices About Learning

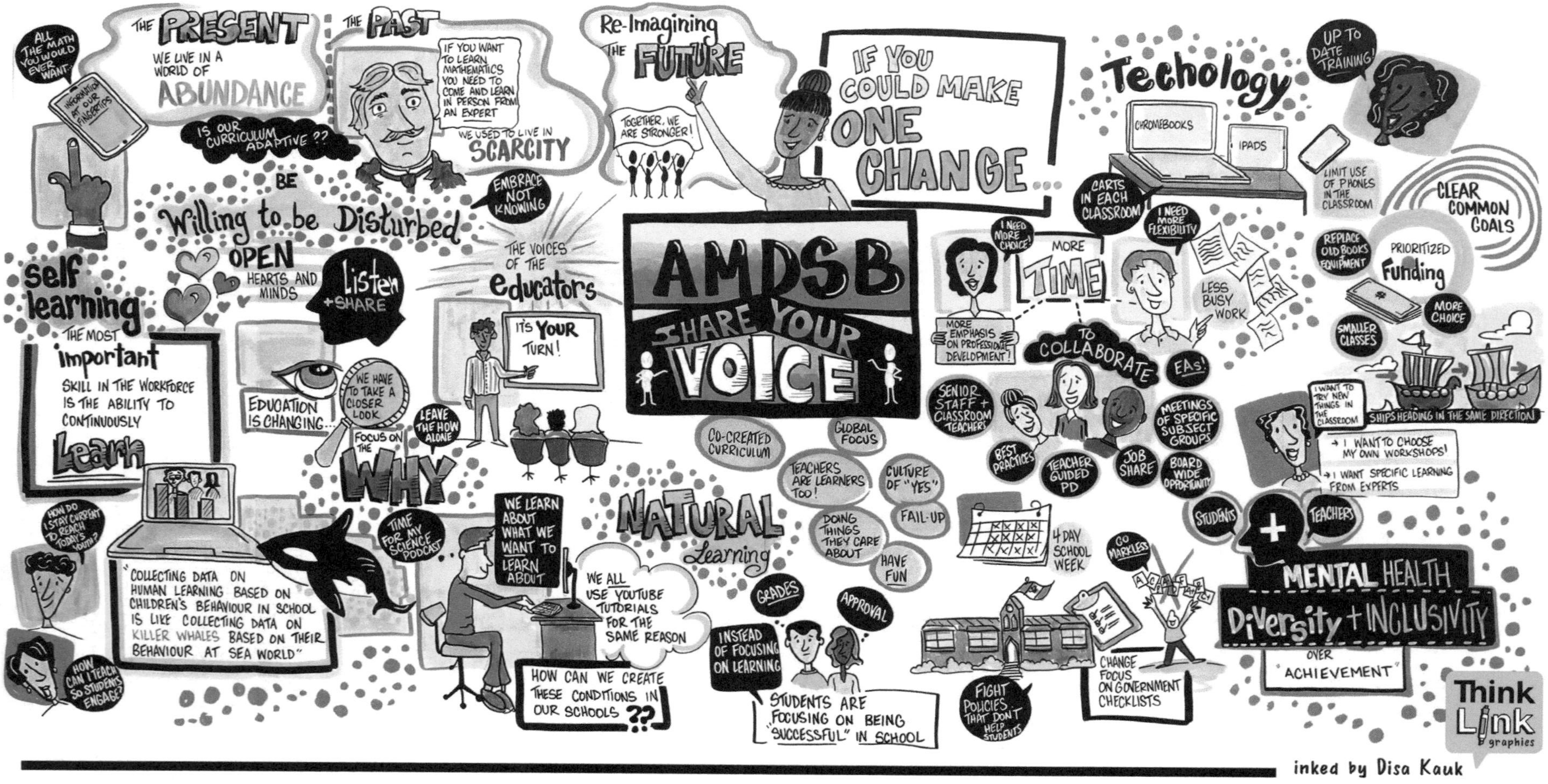

choice to students, but what about our staff? How do we allow the adults to exercise agency—to direct their own learning? Ownership encourages youth to ask questions, take initiative, and be creative—to further develop the six competencies—and it does the same for the adults.

Ownership jars staff out of the comfortable cradle of compliance that too many cultures have settled into. It encourages a shift from "tell me how to do it" to "let's figure out how to do it." Ultimately, teacher ownership restores the profession. It says "You matter and your thinking matters." This isn't a ticket to go maverick. With ownership comes a shared commitment to contribute to the learning of the group. When teachers come together to make sense of the framework and its language, it is important that they are given room to make decisions and try strategies in new and compelling ways. It's even more important to create the safe space for shared reflection—the good, the bad, and the challenges—as we mentioned earlier in the book.

For teachers, becoming deep learners means a shift to "de-front" the classroom, and this can be seismic as teachers give up control from the front of the room. If it were easy, we would all be doing it by now. Recalling all we have said to this point about creating safe conditions for students registers for teachers too. Acknowledge that this shift represents something deeply personal, and therefore, teachers can feel exposed and unsure. Dedicate uninterrupted time for shared reflection with trustworthy colleagues. Let's explore reflective practices and coaching approaches that can support this important shift.

## Reflective Practice

If we want to position the teacher in control of his or her own learning, the Teacher Self-Assessment Tool can be a good place to start. The tool details the shifts in teacher behavior that have been outlined in Chapter 3, namely that the teacher assumes the roles of activator, culture builder, and collaborator. The list of behaviors offers precision but it can also be overwhelming, so it's best to frame the learning as we would any significant habit change. Here's an approach: The teacher chooses only one behavior on the list (or even part of one) to focus on. Then he or she starts small by identifying what that behavior would look like— practically visualizing exactly what it would look like in action. Teachers write out a brief plan and try it out for two weeks. Here is the important part—after two weeks, they share with colleagues and celebrate how that small step went. Protocols 31 and 32 detail a process to develop a plan and get feedback from a peer. A caution: The teacher self-assessment tool should never be used for supervision. No "gotcha" here. If the tool is perceived as threatening, the teacher's behavior will rapidly shift to self-preservation rather than reflection for action.

## Coaching for Success

Using a coaching approach is essential to create the conditions for deep reflective conversations. When each person assumes the role of coach and learner, and when those positions are swapped evenly, everyone is a learner. There are a few conditions to bear in mind when coaching. Effective coaches recognize they are in service of the learner. Good questions cue reflection, contemplation, and insight. These are not drive-by conversations; time is allocated and distractions are limited. Coaches recognize that while they may understand and empathize with the learner's challenges, they can't possibly know every angle of the learner's perspective. And here is where the "Who owns the learning?" question pops in again. When a coach shifts from asking good questions and providing space for reflection to a position of dispensing advice, the learning moment is lost. Or worse, the coach may direct the learner to focus on the wrong problem. Michael Bungay Stanier says that for coaches,

> " Every fibre of your body is twitching to fix it, solve it, offer a solution to it. It's Pavlovian . . . and why people in organizations like yours around the world are working very hard and coming up with decent solutions to problems that just don't matter, and why the real challenges often go unaddressed. "

—*THE COACHING HABIT*, P. 82

If we want teachers to own their next step in improvement, we need to help them unearth the issues as *they* see them, not as we do.

The Learning Design Coaching Tool in Protocol 33 provides some powerful open-ended prompts to get learning conversations going. However, it's not about racing through this, checking off items quickly. We want the learner to fully explore a question before moving on. Get comfortable with the muddle; that's where the thinking thrives. For example, let's say that you ask the question, "How will you create a learning partnership with students and others?" and the learner responds with a simple answer like, "I am going to give them a choice in their assignments." Don't stop there! Bring on the muddle. The next question might be, "What does that look like?" or "Tell me more about that" or "How would you go about doing that?" *Instead of answering their questions, question their answers.* The learner benefits from the learning conversation when details emerge and the learning experience is visualized. Visualizing leads them to their next step.

## Final Thoughts

Much of this chapter has focused on creating conditions for facilitating teacher reflection, and for good reason. Katz and Dack (2013) assert that a permanent change in thinking and behavior comes when teachers have the opportunity to wrestle with the discrepancy between their initial thinking and the new insights that surface from assessment, reflection, and examination of evidence. What if we allocated as much time to shared reflection as we do for shared planning? What if a coaching approach was embedded in the culture and we all assumed the learner stance? Regular reflective practice leads to change.

In the next chapter, we take up the critical issue of the school conditions that are needed if teachers and students are to embrace Deep Learning.

## Protocols

**31** ## The Teacher Self-Assessment Tool

This is a protocol for small groups that generates reflection on teacher practice and supports consideration of strategies for improvement.

**32** ## The Teacher Self-Assessment Tool in Action

This step-by-step planning document allows teachers to choose how they wish to grow as Deep Learning teachers.

**33** ## Using the Learning Design Coaching Tool

Questions within the tool and a video example show how deeper reflection can guide next steps in practice.

## Tools

Teacher Self-Assessment Tool

Teacher Action Plan Organizer

Learning Design Coaching Tool

## For more information:

Read Chapter 7 from *Deep Learning: Engage the World Change the World.*

# 31 The Teacher Self-Assessment Tool

**Purpose: Use the Teacher Self-Assessment Tool**

**Process: Deep Listening Exchange**

**Time: 30–70 minutes**

Resource:
• Tool: Teacher Self-Assessment Tool

## Part One

**1** **Complete** the Teacher Self-Assessment Tool individually.

**2** **Reflect** on your results of the Teacher Self-Assessment Tool and complete Part One of the Deep Listening Exchange Organizer.

**3** **Form groups** of four.

**4** **Share one area** of confidence and describe the practices used regularly. Repeat for each group member. (10 minutes)

## Part Two

**5** **Select an area** where each individual wants to develop more confidence or expertise.

**6** **Person A shares** the area where he or she wishes to develop more confidence and why it is a challenge. The other three members of the group listen, take notes and do not interrupt. (2 minutes)

**7** **The other group members** talk among themselves to discuss what they have heard Person A say, how they understand the challenge, and what might be helpful. The prompts support the discussion. Person A takes notes and listens without interjecting. (5 minutes)

**8** **Person A then responds** to what has been discussed/suggested and identifies key points or strategies that may help to build confidence in the area. Person A also identifies one next step. (3 minutes)

**9** **If time allows,** someone else assumes the role of Person A to share their challenge, and the protocol is repeated.

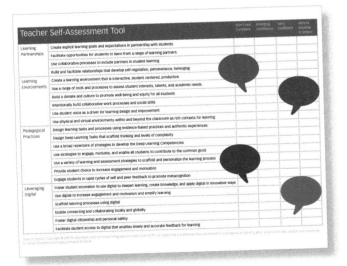

# Deep Listening Exchange Organizer

## Part One: Exploring our confidence

| | |
|---|---|
| What is something I feel confident about? | |
| What do I do in my practice that exemplifies this? | |

## Part Two: Exploring where we want more confidence

- Prompts to support the deep listening exchange:
- What I heard her or him say was . . .
- One assumption I hear him or her making is . . .
- A question that could be asked is . . .
- I'm wondering if he or she has ever tried . . .
- What she or he hasn't mentioned is . . .

| Protocol: | Person A | Rest of the Group |
|---|---|---|
| **Person A shares:** (2 minutes)<br>• Area for confidence building<br>• Why is this a challenge | Area and why is this a challenge | Listening and taking notes |
| **Rest of group:** (5 minutes)<br>• What is the challenge?<br>• What might support Person A? | Listening and taking notes | What is the challenge?<br>What might support Person A? |
| **Person A:** (3 minutes)<br>• What are key points?<br>• What strategies might help?<br>• What is one next step? | Key points and next step | Listening only |

# 32 The Teacher Self-Assessment Tool in Action

**Purpose: Putting the Teacher Self-Assessment Tool into action**

**Process: Using the Teacher Action Plan**

Time: **20 minutes**

Resource:
• Tool: Teacher Self-Assessment Tool

1 **Identify** three areas on the Teacher Self-Assessment Tool where you noticed the need for more confidence.

2 **Choose one** of the three areas you would like to focus on.

3 **Read** the Teacher Action Plan example.

4 **Fill in** the blank Teacher Action Plan Organizer.

5 **Share** your initial plan with a partner before taking action.

6 **Check in** with the colleague within one week of taking action.

7 **Reflect** with a colleague after two weeks. How did it go? What will you do next?

## Teacher Action Plan Organizer: Example

| | |
|---|---|
| What is the one teacher action from the Teacher Self-Assessment that I choose to focus on? | "Use student voice as a driver for learning design and improvement" |
| What does that look like specifically? (3 descriptions) | 1. students having choice in assignments<br>2. asking open-ended questions<br>3. teacher talking less |
| Of those descriptions, pick one that you would like to work on. | teacher talking less |
| Brainstorm: What would that behavior look like/sound like in the classroom? (3–5 descriptions) | • more students talking to each other, relying on each other for support, perspectives, expertise, assessment<br>• more visual cues around the room<br>• wait time: not providing the right answer immediately<br>• allowing three or more students to contribute before I intervene |
| Of those descriptions, pick one small action that you would like to focus on. | • wait time |
| What would success of that small action look like? | • waiting 5 seconds before jumping in to answer student questions<br>• less empty praise: not affirming right or wrong but probing students to elaborate on their thinking<br>• students listening to and respecting each other |
| What would be your plan for two weeks? (Limit your plan to 3–5 strategies.) | • share with the students my intention to use more wait time and how it contributes to their learning<br>• co-create what respectful listening of each other looks like<br>• ask students for help—to remind me to wait using visual cues<br>• ask for feedback mid-way through the week from students<br>• ask a peer to come in and watch me for 20 min. Maybe collect data and feed it back to me? |

Colleague I will check in with is    Alex    on (date)  February 19

Check in: Personal reflection on my progress:
• My own thinking and questions are clearer when I use wait time
• The quality of the student answers is improving
• Two students who have not participated much this semester are now putting up hands to answer
• Students are beginning to give each other wait time when they collaborate

Reflection: Discussion points with colleague:
• Alex noticed that when I am rushed near the end of the lesson or I'm trying to cover too much content I do not respect wait time.
• Alex refers to wait time as "think time" and is explicit with students
• Alex looks at her feet and touches her forehead to signal to students that they need time to think

CHAPTER 10

# 33 Using the Learning Design Coaching Tool

**Purpose: Understand how coaching can strengthen learning design**

**Time: 20 minutes**

**Resource:**
- Video at www.deep-learning.global: Grovedale West PS Library Malaysia

**Process: Simulation**

**1** **Review** the Deep Learning Design Coaching Tool.

**2** **Which questions** do you think are the most helpful in coaching peers (or yourself) around their learning designs?

**3** **As a simulation**, watch the video Grovedale West PS Library Malaysia.

**4** **Jot your notes** in the right-hand column of the tool.

**5** **What are** the three questions that you would like to ask the teacher?

**6** **What questions** from the coaching tool would you use to prompt them to strengthen their learning design?

TOOL
## Learning Design Coaching Tool

| Stage of the Collaborative Inquiry Cycle | Questions/Input to Consider | Notes, Documents, and Links |
|---|---|---|
| **Assess**—use the Deep Learning Competency Framework to identify student progress, strengths, and needs. Combine with student achievement and interests to establish learning goals. | **Deep Learning Competencies**<br>• Where are students on the Deep Learning Progressions? What evidence are you using to make good professional judgments?<br><br>**Achievement and Interest Data**<br>• What are students' knowledge, skills, interests, and needs?<br>• How are you capturing this information?<br><br>**Links to National/Local Curriculum**<br>• What national/local curriculum goals and standards should be incorporated? | |
| **Design**—work with peers, students, and families to use the Deep Learning Progressions to design Deep Learning Tasks steeped in a real-world problem or challenge of relevance to the learners. | **Deep Learning Competencies and Content Areas**<br>• Which Deep Learning Competencies are you targeting for this learning task?<br>• What content areas will provide the problem/challenge context?<br><br>**Deep Learning Task Design**<br>• What is the driving question?<br>• How will students and others be engaged in designing the learning task?<br><br>**Deep Learning Success Criteria**<br>• How will students be engaged in designing/understanding the learning criteria and assessment methods?<br>• Is their role clear?<br><br>**Learning Design Elements**<br>• How will you create a learning partnership with students and others? | |

# Teacher Self-Assessment Tool

| | | Don't Feel Confident | Emerging Confidence | Very Confident | Able to Develop in Others |
|---|---|---|---|---|---|
| **Learning Partnerships** | Create explicit learning goals and expectations in partnership with students | | | | |
| | Facilitate opportunities for students to learn from a range of learning partners | | | | |
| | Use collaborative processes to include partners in student learning | | | | |
| | Build and facilitate relationships that develop self-regulation, perseverance, belonging | | | | |
| **Learning Environments** | Create a learning environment that is interactive, student centered, productive | | | | |
| | Use a range of tools and processes to assess student interests, talents, and academic needs | | | | |
| | Build a climate and culture to promote well-being and equity for all students | | | | |
| | Intentionally build collaborative work processes and social skills | | | | |
| | Use student voice as a driver for learning design and improvement | | | | |
| | Use physical and virtual environments within and beyond the classroom as rich contexts for learning | | | | |
| **Pedagogical Practices** | Design learning tasks and processes using evidence-based practices and authentic experiences | | | | |
| | Design Deep Learning Tasks that scaffold thinking and levels of complexity | | | | |
| | Use a broad repertoire of strategies to develop the Deep Learning Competencies | | | | |
| | Use strategies to engage, motivate, and enable all students to contribute to the common good | | | | |
| | Use a variety of learning and assessment strategies to scaffold and personalize the learning process | | | | |
| | Provide student choice to increase engagement and motivation | | | | |
| | Engage students in rapid cycles of self and peer feedback to promote metacognition | | | | |
| **Leveraging Digital** | Foster student innovation to use digital to deepen learning, create knowledge, and apply digital in innovative ways | | | | |
| | Use digital to increase engagement and motivation and amplify learning | | | | |
| | Scaffold learning processes using digital | | | | |
| | Enable connecting and collaborating locally and globally | | | | |
| | Foster digital citizenship and personal safety | | | | |
| | Facilitate student access to digital that enables timely and accurate feedback for learning | | | | |

Source: Quinn, J., & McEachen, J. Copyright © 2019 by Education in Motion (New Pedagogies for Deep Learning™). All rights reserved. Reproduction authorized for educational use by educators, local school sites, and/or noncommercial or nonprofit entities that have purchased the book.

CHAPTER 10

# Teacher Action Plan Organizer

| | |
|---|---|
| What is the one teacher action from the Teacher Self-Assessment that I choose to focus on? | |
| What does that look like specifically? (3 descriptions) | |
| Of those descriptions, pick one that you would like to work on | |
| Brainstorm: What would that behavior look like/ sound like in the classroom? (3–5 descriptions) | |
| Of those descriptions, pick one small action that you would like to focus on. | |
| What would success of that small action look like? | |
| What would be your plan for two weeks? (Limit your plan to 3–5 strategies) | |

Colleague I will check in with_____

on (date)_____

Check in: Personal reflection on my progress:

Reflection: Discussion points with colleague:

" School leaders model being learners themselves by actively participating in tackling new approaches. They don't simply send teachers to workshops but learn alongside them, and this immersion in learning has the added benefit of building trust and relationships. "

*—DEEP LEARNING: ENGAGE THE WORLD*
*CHANGE THE WORLD, P. 70*

# Learning Design Coaching Tool

| Stage of the Collaborative Inquiry Cycle | Questions/Input to Consider | Notes, Documents, and Links |
|---|---|---|
| **Assess**—use the Deep Learning Competency Framework to identify student progress, strengths, and needs. Combine with student achievement and interests to establish learning goals. | **Deep Learning Competencies**<br>• Where are students on the Deep Learning Progressions? What evidence are you using to make good professional judgments?<br><br>**Achievement and Interest Data**<br>• What are students' knowledge, skills, interests, and needs?<br>• How are you capturing this information?<br><br>**Links to National/Local Curriculum**<br>• What national/local curriculum goals and standards should be incorporated? | |
| **Design**—work with peers, students, and families to use the Deep Learning Progressions to design Deep Learning Tasks steeped in a real-world problem or challenge of relevance to the learners. | **Deep Learning Competencies and Content Areas**<br>• Which Deep Learning Competencies are you targeting for this learning task?<br>• What content areas will provide the problem/challenge context?<br><br>**Deep Learning Task Design**<br>• What is the driving question?<br>• How will students and others be engaged in designing the learning task?<br><br>**Deep Learning Success Criteria**<br>• How will students be engaged in designing/understanding the learning criteria and assessment methods?<br>• Is their role clear?<br><br>**Learning Design Elements**<br>• How will you create a learning partnership with students and others?<br>• Is the learning design steeped in a real-world problem of relevance to the learners?<br>• How will you focus on development of Deep Learning Competencies?<br>• How will you leverage digital to accelerate and deepen the learning? | |

**Implement the Learning**—implement the Deep Learning Task, leveraging digital to accelerate and deepen learning.

- How will you build meaningful collaboration through learning partnerships?
- How are you optimizing the learning environment for success?
- How will you build rapid cycles of student self/peer formative assessment to accelerate the learning?

**Measure, Reflect, and Change**—use a range of evidence to measure the outcomes of the learning and effectiveness of the design so that you can reflect on what works and what can be improved.

**Measure the Learning Outcomes**

- How will products and performances be assessed?
- How will you provide summative feedback and to whom?

**Reflection & Improvement**

- What structures and processes will you use to reflect on the learning task implementation and outcomes—individually and with peers?
- How will you collaboratively go about changing and improving this learning task?

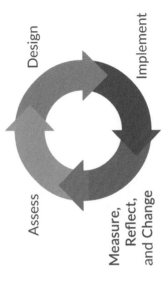

Design

Implement

Measure, Reflect, and Change

Assess

“ Programs don't scale;
culture does. ”

—*DEEP LEARNING: ENGAGE THE WORLD*
*CHANGE THE WORLD, P. XVI*

# Chapter 11
# School Capacity for Deep Learning

Most schools can point with pride to some classrooms where innovative practices result in students who are highly engaged in inventive learning experiences through STEAM (science, technology, engineering, art, and mathematics) approaches or solving real-life problems. However, the bigger challenge is how to move Deep Learning from a few bright spots of innovation to a pervasive shift in thinking and practices that impact *all* learners across the entire school. If the goal is to help all teachers in a school take on the new pedagogies and practices that foster Deep Learning, then we need to create schools as cultures of learning for youth and adults alike.

To that end, our global partnership set out to identify the conditions and practices that need to be in place in schools for Deep Learning to take root. The tools and protocols in this book are essential supports for fostering change, and when they are used in combination with the collaborative inquiry process introduced in Chapter 6, massive shifts in practice result.

In this chapter, we introduce the School Conditions Rubric. This tool describes the conditions that need to be in place for Deep Learning to flourish. We examine how the rubric can be used by school leaders and leadership teams collaboratively to assess current conditions in the school and identify areas of need, design a plan to address the identified gaps or needs, implement and monitor the plan, and measure progress on the condition over time to inform the next cycle of school growth. The same four phases of the collaborative inquiry cycle—assess; design; implement; measure, reflect, and change—used in classroom learning design are mirrored in this reflective process using the School Conditions Rubric.

Remember, though, that a tool is only as good as the mindset using it. You will need to know that collaboration is elusive and can only be achieved through interactive experience, which is an emotional as well as a cognitive phenomenon. Moreover, the field is becoming clear on what *good* versus *superficial* collaboration looks like. Good collaboration is both formal and informal; it is precise without being prescriptive; it is based on evidence of impact; it increases the collective capacity of the group; it embraces both autonomy and collaboration and their reciprocal power; and it requires "lead learners"—principals and teachers—engaging together (Datnow & Park, 2018; Donohoo, Hattie, & Eells, 2018; Fullan 2019; Fullan & Quinn, 2016; Hargreaves & O'Connor, 2018).

## The School Conditions Rubric

Five conditions and their subdimensions contribute to a school culture that diffuses Deep Learning; these are identified in Figure 11.1.

The School Conditions Rubric depicted in Figure 11.2 describes the practices related to each of the five conditions and its subdimensions. The rubric provides descriptors for each of the four levels of progress: limited, emerging, accelerating, and advanced. Protocol 34 will help you dig into the rubric and unpack the conditions and practices.

After establishing norms of trust and transparency to ground the work, school leaders and leadership teams use the rubric to assess current strengths and needs. To build understanding of this tool, use Protocol 35 to simulate analyzing a school that is currently using Deep Learning. Deep dialogue emerges as team

FIGURE 11.1

## Five Learning Conditions That Impact the Diffusion of Deep Learning

FIGURE 11.2
## School Conditions Rubric

| Dimensions | Limited | Emerging | Accelerating | Advanced |
|---|---|---|---|---|
| Vision and Goals | There are no Deep Learning strategies, goals, or implementation supports in place to achieve Deep Learning. Decisions and resources reflect the status quo. | Deep Learning strategies and goals are formally written and articulated. Some decisions regarding resources, processes, and funding reflect a shift toward Deep Learning. | There is a written and understood strategy articulating Deep Learning goals and how they will be implemented. Most decisions are driven by and aligned with Deep Learning. | A concise, well-articulated strategy with focused Deep Learning Goals and implementation support is owned by all members of the school community and used to drive decision making. |
| Leadership | Leaders rely on formal roles and structures and view Deep Learning as an add-on rather than integrator and accelerator of processes. There is no strategy to intentionally develop leaders, and engagement in Deep Learning is restricted to a few early innovators. | Lead learners emerging across the school clearly see their role in developing leaders, structures, processes, and formal and informal opportunities, all committed to fostering Deep Learning. Student, teacher, family, and community engagement in Deep Learning is emerging. | Lead learners have created structures and processes that propel shifts in practice and intentionally develop leaders. There is engagement in Deep Learning across the school and among some students, families, and communities who actively take part in the creation of Deep Learning experiences. | Lead learner capacity exists with a clear strategy to develop, diffuse, and distribute leadership capacity across the school. Students, families, communities, and all members of the school community are informed, engaged, and influential in Deep Learning for all students. |
| Collaborative Cultures | Collaboration between and among leaders, teachers, and learners occurs through formal structures without challenging "the way we do things around here." Inquiry is practiced inconsistently, and low levels of trust are reflected in an unwillingness to share practices and ideas. Capacity-building support often focuses on individual needs and is not explicitly linked to Deep Learning. | There is an emerging collaborative culture developed around Deep Learning and collective capacity building. Leaders and teachers are using collaborative inquiry to reflect on existing practices, and there are some structures and processes for building vertical and horizontal relationships and learning across the school. Resourcing to support collaboration is emerging but may not always be focused, connected, or consistently used to foster Deep Learning. | A culture of learning and collaborative inquiry exists in which most teachers and leaders reflect on, review, and adjust their teaching and leadership practices. Capacity building is designed based on teacher and student needs and is clearly focused on the knowledge and skills needed to mobilize and sustain Deep Learning. Through vertical and horizontal relationships, collaboration and trust are growing, and practices are becoming more transparent. School-level inquiry and learning involves teachers from all levels, who may also be collaborating across schools. | A powerful culture of collaborative Deep Learning pervades the school. Learning collaboratively is the norm and includes structures and processes to build collective capacity. The culture uses the group to change the group by fostering strong vertical and horizontal relationships that support innovation and risk taking. Capacity building focuses comprehensively and consistently on precision in pedagogy and incorporates cycles of learning and application within and across the school. |

*(Continued)*

CHAPTER 11

FIGURE 11.2 (Continued)

| | | | |
|---|---|---|---|
| **Deepening the Learning** | The relationship between school curriculum and Deep Learning competencies is unspecified.<br><br>A framework for Deep Learning is beginning to develop but is not understood by all or used consistently to guide learning. Individual teachers and leaders are innovating independently.<br><br>Few coaches and personnel are dedicated to supporting Deep Learning. Collaborative practices such as collaborative inquiry and moderation are not well understood and are used infrequently. | The relationship between Deep Learning and local curriculum is beginning to be articulated.<br><br>Some goals to improve precision in pedagogy have been identified, but the strategy for improvement may be unclear or implemented inconsistently.<br><br>Deep collaborative practices such as collaborative inquiry and protocols for examining student work may be used by some teachers, but there is not consistency of practice or support. | Learning and pedagogical goals are articulated and the link between Deep Learning Competencies and core curriculum standards is visible. A comprehensive framework for Deep Learning is used widely to design and assess Deep Learning experiences.<br><br>Resources and expertise for creating collaborative learning structures are becoming more consistent across the school, as are deep collaborative practices such as collaborative inquiry and protocols for examining student work. | Learning goals for Deep Learning competencies, goals to improve precision in pedagogy, and requirements of core curriculum standards are clearly articulated and integrated consistently with visible impact.<br><br>A comprehensive framework for Deep Learning is understood by all and used consistently across the school to design and assess effective Deep Learning experiences.<br><br>Collaborative inquiry is used to monitor progress in impacting learning at all levels, and protocols for examining student work are used consistently across the school. |
| **New Measures and Evaluation** | Evaluation of student success and achievement continues to rely on a narrow range of indicators (e.g., tests and a small number of work products) to measure and track success.<br><br>Teachers and school leaders may be using the New Measures to develop a shared language and understanding of Deep Learning, but Deep Learning conditions, design, and outcomes are not yet measured or assessed. | Mixed-method assessment practice is beginning to develop as a wider and more diverse range of evidence sources is used to measure and track progress and success.<br><br>Capacity-building supports for using the New Measures and designing meaningful assessments are beginning to develop.<br><br>Some teachers and leaders are beginning to use the New Measures to design Deep Learning experiences, measure student outcomes, and measure conditions for Deep Learning. | Teachers and leaders demonstrate the capacity to assess, develop, and measure<br><br>• student growth on the Deep Learning Progressions,<br>• conditions that enable Deep Learning to occur and<br>• the effectiveness of Deep Learning design in facilitating Deep Learning outcomes<br><br>Local/national priorities and curricula are linked to and accelerated by Deep Learning experiences, which are moderated through a structured process.<br><br>Teachers are beginning to design new assessments for Deep Learning that more clearly demonstrate Deep Learning as it occurs. | The development and measurement of Deep Learning is pervasive throughout the school and used to focus capacity-building efforts. Measures are compared across years and time periods and demonstrate consistent growth.<br><br>Deep Learning experiences demonstrate clear alignment between curriculum and Deep Learning goals and are formally moderated both within and between schools to establish reliability. Feedback is shared and leveraged to deepen learning design.<br><br>Assessment practice reflects a deep knowledge of students' interests and needs and uses a wide range of evidence to determine progress and learning. |

members look for evidence of the conditions and match it to the descriptors of the rubric cells. The simulation deepens understanding of the content of the rubric while building trust and confidence for sharing opinions and perspectives prior to analyzing your own school data.

Once teams feel comfortable with the content of the rubric, Protocol 36 provides a process for assessing the conditions in their own schools. After highlighting their current status, they can look to higher levels on the rubric to inform their next steps for growth. Protocol 37 offers an organizer and process for developing a School Deep Learning Plan. Schools most often use the rubric at the beginning and end of each year to assess progress and make plans for the coming cycle.

## Getting Started With Deep Learning

Schools that are on the move toward building precision in Deep Learning begin by cultivating a culture of learning for both the educators and the students. If the teachers and leaders are not thinking deeply, then it's unlikely they will create these conditions for their students. Schools moving most quickly with Deep Learning

- establish norms and relationships that foster transparency of practice,

- build common skills and language using evidence-based pedagogy,

- create intentional mechanisms for identifying and sharing innovative practices, and

- provide sustained opportunities for teachers to build their capacity— knowledge and skills—in using the new practices with feedback and support.

Principal Andrea Green described her approach to bringing the four strategies to life in this way: "Lead by doing. . . . Choose one competency and have all staff explicitly teach the competency in all classes." For example, record students collaborating, observe the video with students, and co-create a Y chart. What does collaboration look like and sound like? Observe and reflect on the change in culture for students and teachers. Sustain the competency and explicitly teach a second competency. Listen and observe the familiar language, expectations, and knowledge of all students across all grades. Deep Learning and planning within the four dimensions is possible for all teachers when students understand the expectations and possible growth in the six competencies.

## Planning for Deep Learning

We have noticed new, dynamic changes emerging in schools and systems that are moving toward Deep Learning. A shift away from an implementation mindset of "rolling out" to a more organic process of co-learning and co-development (where you learn from the work and adjust plans and strategies) is taking root. It is crucial to note that learning occurs laterally (within and across schools, districts, and systems), much more so than in traditional hierarchical schooling. The three phases of change we have observed as schools, districts, and countries have taken up Deep Learning are described in the following excerpt adapted from *Deep Learning: Engage the World Change the World* (pp. 123–125).

FIGURE 11.3

## Phases of the New Change Dynamic

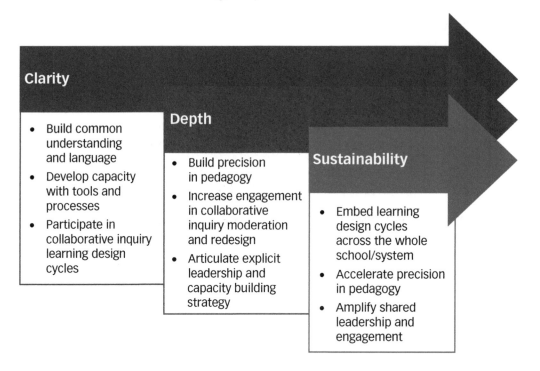

**Clarity**

- Build common understanding and language
- Develop capacity with tools and processes
- Participate in collaborative inquiry learning design cycles

**Depth**

- Build precision in pedagogy
- Increase engagement in collaborative inquiry moderation and redesign
- Articulate explicit leadership and capacity building strategy

**Sustainability**

- Embed learning design cycles across the whole school/system
- Accelerate precision in pedagogy
- Amplify shared leadership and engagement

# Phase I: Clarity

The first phase of Deep Learning work involves establishing clarity of focus, shared understandings, and expertise. Principal Em DelSordo noted, "Align your work and thinking around a school vision that fuels curiosity and creativity. Build the conditions for collaboration and passion and guide the work around the 6Cs [six Global Competencies]." Grassroots efforts often emerge from the passion of teachers or leaders who are ready to embrace different ways of working. Everyone has a different starting point. Rapid cycles of innovation are fostered and feed into establishing a clear, shared vision of what Deep Learning might look like and sound like in the classroom. As teachers and leaders begin to use the new approaches and share results, they need a mechanism to learn from the work. The focused discussions and examination of current and future practice reinforce the new vision for learning. The collaborative inquiry process begins to guide the examination of pedagogical practices and assessment of student progress. Teachers need to feel safe and free from judgement as they share their successes and challenges. As the sharing evolves, schools often need to reorganize structures to create time and space for teacher collaborative inquiry. Teachers engage in rich dialogue, examine pedagogical practices that deepen learning, and look carefully at how well students are learning and how to improve this learning. One of the most powerful impacts during this early stage is the visible changes in their students' engagement, curiosity, collaboration, and excitement.

Leaders who wish to encourage Deep Learning

- give teachers risk-free opportunities to talk, plan, and collaborate with peers about Deep Learning;

- make time for teachers who have experienced the power of Deep Learning in their classrooms to share their stories;

- encourage visits to other classrooms and schools where this new approach is taking root;

- facilitate connections with other schools and practitioners who are a few months further on the journey; and

- engage parents as partners in understanding the elements of Deep Learning.

## Phase II: Depth

The second phase usually evolves 6–12 months into the learning journey. Teachers and leaders have developed a working, collective vision of the competencies and the initial skills in using the Four Elements to design Deep Learning experiences. Mechanisms are needed to intentionally learn from the work, to gain precision in collaborative examination of practice, and to increase precision in pedagogy. In this phase, teachers and leaders have participated in at least one collaborative inquiry cycle and, as a result, are motivated to develop even greater precision in selecting pedagogical practices and in scaffolding experiences so their students will move to higher levels of progress in acquiring the competencies. Collectively, they begin to engage in more frequent collaborative inquiry cycles to design new learning experiences and also to moderate the progress of their students. Teacher leadership grows as teachers seek opportunities to learn within and outside the school. Capacity building for teachers and leaders is embedded in their jobs, with external inputs as needed. This increased precision and intentionality is observed in both student and adult learning experiences.

## Phase III: Sustainability

Once a level of expertise is attained, usually in the first two years, the focus shifts to deepening the work and diffusing it across and beyond the school. Schools consider how to integrate their strategies to build schoolwide coherence. Globally, we have observed that once teachers develop confidence and expertise in designing and assessing Deep Learning and in working effectively in collaborative inquiry cycles, they shift their focus to helping others to grow and change. This happens in two ways. First, the focus moves to going deeper—building greater precision in learning designs and moderation cycles. Second, districts and clusters move to embed the collaborative practices across more schools and, ultimately, the entire system. Strong teacher and school leadership evolves to guide the next steps. They continue to explore the best ways to develop and measure the six competencies but also set internal targets for the school or system. In effect, all of this amounts to continuous professional learning the way it should be—an integral part of the school and district culture.

## Final Thoughts

Schools do not operate in a vacuum; they are impacted by the policies of districts and systems. But they should not wait for the system to get its act together; in fact, proactive schools contribute to district improvement. The good news is that innovative schools "go outside to get better inside." They take advantage of the ideas and resources of the system to make headway and, as they make progress, they begin to influence upward change to policies and structures. They seek connections with other schools in their jurisdictions in person or virtually to share practices. These intraschool and interschool connections accelerate progress.

Diffusing Deep Learning is complex work because it depends on building new relationships between and among students, teachers, families, leaders, and communities. Our advice is this: *Go slow to go fast*—take time to build norms of trust that support innovation, but don't wait for conditions to be perfect. Build a team of innovation pioneers, use the School Conditions Rubric to assess your starting point, get started, use rapid cycles of doing and reflecting to adjust your strategy, and celebrate gains. At the same time, begin to approach parents as partners, finding ways to listen to and respond to their concerns while also engaging them in the new learning practices. Remember, we learn more by reflective doing than by thinking about doing, so get started! If you want to accelerate quality change, then have a good framework, employ good tools, start the journey with others, overcome setbacks, and gather momentum. Success will not be simply linear, but you will gain and consolidate success using our frameworks and tools along with the ingenuity and energy of you and the group.

The diffusion of Deep Learning can be further accelerated and amplified when the district takes on a role of catalyst and integrator, as we explore in Chapter 12.

## Protocols

###  34 Understanding the School Conditions Rubric

Build a shared understanding of the conditions that support Deep Learning and innovation in schools and the use of the School Conditions Rubric.

### 35 Assessing School Conditions: A Simulation

Engage with teams in a simulation to develop your skills in the process of using the School Conditions Rubric to assess the conditions that support Deep Learning.

### 36 Assessing Your School Conditions

Use the School Conditions Rubric to assess the conditions in Deep Learning in your school.

Developing a School Deep Learning Plan

Use the four phases of the collaborative inquiry cycle to create a plan to support Deep Learning in your school. The data generated through your analysis of the School Conditions Rubric will inform the consensus-making process.

## Tool

School Conditions Rubric

## For more information:

Read Chapter 8 from *Deep Learning: Engage the World Change the World.*

# 34 Understanding the School Conditions Rubric

**Purpose: Build understanding of the school conditions that foster Deep Learning and innovative practice**

**Process: Graffiti Organizer and Jigsaw**

**Time: 45–60 minutes**

**Resource:**
• Tool: School Conditions Rubric

**1** **Work in a group of five** using the Graffiti Organizer.

**2** **Record** in your assigned section the important conditions that need to exist for schools to support Deep Learning.

**3** **As a group,** review the ideas and look for commonalities. Reach consensus on the most important and record those in the center box section.

**4** **Read** your assigned dimension of the School Conditions Rubric.

- Person 1  Vision and Goals
- Person 2  Leadership
- Person 3  Collaborative Cultures
- Person 4  Deepening the Learning
- Person 5  New Measures and Evaluation

**5** **Formulate** the key ideas from your dimension and jot notes in the organizer. Prepare to share with your group.

**6** **Discuss** ways this rubric might be useful in your school.

# GRAFFITI ORGANIZER

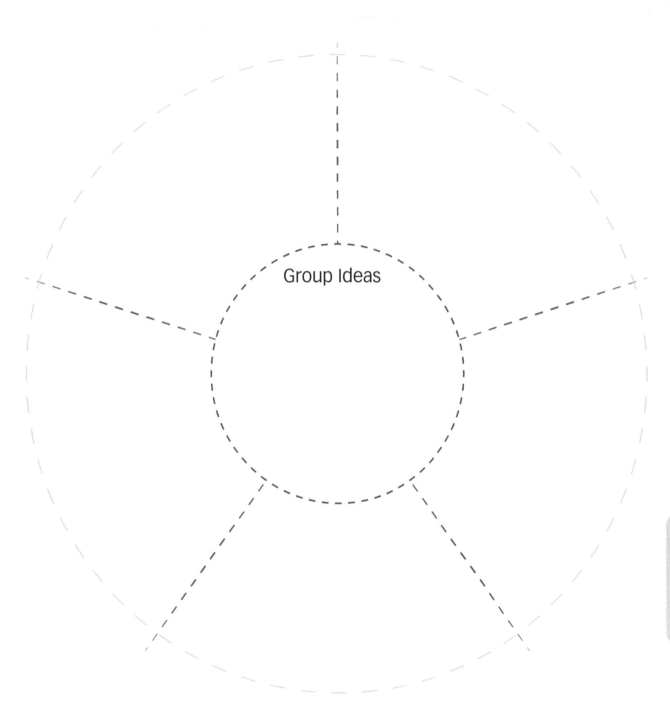

Group Ideas

## School Conditions Rubric: Key Ideas Organizer

| Dimension | Key Ideas |
|---|---|
| Vision/Goals | |
| Leadership | |
| Collaborative Cultures | |
| Deepening the Learning | |
| New Measures and Evaluation | |

> ❝ Go deep or go home. And be pervasive (system minded) or stand aside. ❞

—*DEEP LEARNING: ENGAGE THE WORLD CHANGE THE WORLD, P. 9*

# 35 Assessing School Conditions: A Simulation

**Purpose: Develop skill in using the School Conditions Rubric to assess a school**

**Time: 60–75 minutes**

**Process: Simulation**

**1** **Form a group** of four and watch one video listed.

**2** **One pair** will look for evidence of the Deepening Learning dimension. The second pair will look for evidence of Vision and Goals dimension.

**3** **Record evidence** on sticky notes—one idea per note.

**4** **Share the evidence** on the sticky notes.

**5** **Place the notes** (evidence) on the School Conditions Rubric.

**6** **As a team**, review the sticky notes and reach consensus on where the school should be positioned on each dimension. Use highlighters to note specific points where the evidence matches the Rubric.

**7** **Discuss**

- What are the strengths and needs of this school?
- What focus would you suggest for this school?
- What specific actions might the school take to further develop this school condition?

**Resources:**

- Tool: School Conditions Rubric Videos at www.deep-learning.global:
- Wooranna Park Part Three— online resources (www .deep-learning.global)
- Bray Park High School (Queensland)
- School Implementation, Flourishing in a Complex World

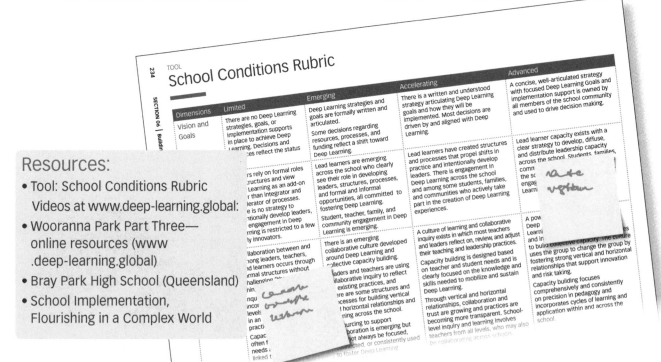

# 36 Assessing Your School Conditions

**Purpose: Assess the conditions that support Deep Learning in your school**

**Time: 30–90 minutes**

Process: **Clustering Process**

Resource:
• Tool: School Conditions Rubric

**1** **Create** a wall chart that includes the dimensions and levels of the School Conditions Rubric.

**2** **Select** one dimension of the School Conditions Rubric to review as a team.

**3** **Individually** reflect on ways that the school fosters that dimension.

**4** **Record** evidence on sticky notes—one idea per note.

**5** **Place** all sticky notes on the School Conditions wall chart.

**6** **As a team**, review the sticky notes (evidence) and discuss areas of agreement as well as different perspectives for the dimension.

**7** **Reach consensus** for where to position your school on the dimension and your reasons for that placement.

**8** **Repeat** for other dimensions as needed.

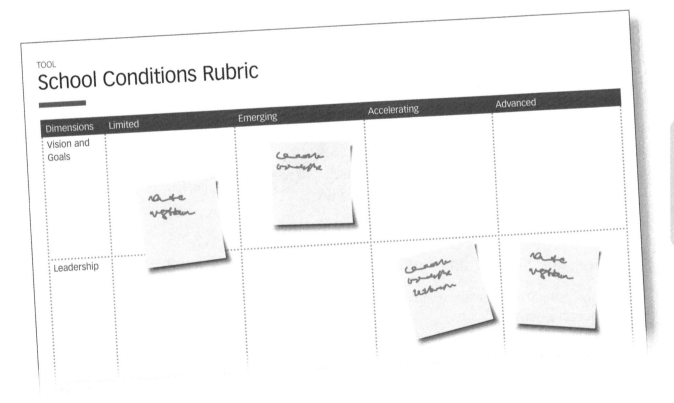

TOOL
## School Conditions Rubric

| Dimensions | Limited | Emerging | Accelerating | Advanced |
|---|---|---|---|---|
| Vision and Goals | | | | |
| Leadership | | | | |

# 37 Developing a School Deep Learning Plan

Purpose: **Use the School Conditions Rubric to inform the Deep Learning Plan**

Process: **Planning Forward With the Collaborative Inquiry Cycle**

Time: **60–120 minutes**

Resource:
• Tool: School Conditions Rubric

**1** **Establish** a team that brings together various perspectives and experiences. This may include staff representing various roles, parents, and students.

**2** **Review** the four phases of the Collaborative Inquiry Cycle as a team.

**3** Assess ▶

a. Review the results of the School Conditions Rubric. Use that data and consider the following questions:

• What evidence did you have for making the rating for each dimension?

• What does the collated data from the School Conditions Rubric tell you?

• What other evidence do you need? How will you get it?

• What are your strengths?

• What are your needs?

b. Identify 1–3 action areas that are most crucial to improve conditions for Deep Learning in the school.

**4** Design ▼

a. Identify key actions needed. Use the next levels on the dimensions to provide ways to move along the dimension.

b. Record key actions, who will be responsible, and time frames on the 100-Day School Deep Learning Plan.

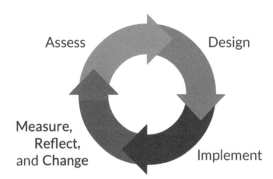

**6** Measure, Reflect, and Change ▲

a. Identify how you will measure success

b. Use the conditions rubrics at regular intervals to assess progress on the dimension

c. Adjust the plan based on evidence

**5** Implement ◀

a. Take action on the plan

b. Monitor by gathering feedback and data for status updates.

## 100-Day School Deep Learning Plan

| Goal Area | Key Actions | Lead | Time | Status |
|-----------|-------------|------|------|--------|
| | | | | |
| | | | | |
| | | | | |
| | | | | |
| | | | | |
| | | | | |
| | | | | |
| | | | | |
| How will you measure success? | | | | |

# School Conditions Rubric

| Dimensions | Limited | Emerging | Accelerating | Advanced |
|---|---|---|---|---|
| Vision and Goals | There are no Deep Learning strategies, goals, or implementation supports in place to achieve Deep Learning. Decisions and resources reflect the status quo. | Deep Learning strategies and goals are formally written and articulated. Some decisions regarding resources, processes, and funding reflect a shift toward Deep Learning. | There is a written and understood strategy articulating Deep Learning goals and how they will be implemented. Most decisions are driven by and aligned with Deep Learning. | A concise, well-articulated strategy with focused Deep Learning Goals and implementation support is owned by all members of the school community and used to drive decision making. |
| Leadership | Leaders rely on formal roles and structures and view Deep Learning as an add-on rather than integrator and accelerator of processes. There is no strategy to intentionally develop leaders, and engagement in Deep Learning is restricted to a few early innovators. | Lead learners are emerging across the school who clearly see their role in developing leaders, structures, processes, and formal and informal opportunities, all committed to fostering Deep Learning. Student, teacher, family, and community engagement in Deep Learning is emerging. | Lead learners have created structures and processes that propel shifts in practice and intentionally develop leaders. There is engagement in Deep Learning across the school and among some students, families, and communities who actively take part in the creation of Deep Learning experiences. | Lead learner capacity exists with a clear strategy to develop, diffuse, and distribute leadership capacity across the school. Students, families, communities, and all members of the school community are informed, engaged, and influential in Deep Learning for all students. |
| Collaborative Cultures | Collaboration between and among leaders, teachers, and learners occurs through formal structures without challenging "the way we do things around here." Inquiry is practiced inconsistently, and low levels of trust are reflected in an unwillingness to share practices and ideas. Capacity-building support often focuses on individual needs and is not explicitly linked to Deep Learning. | There is an emerging collaborative culture developed around Deep Learning and collective capacity building. Leaders and teachers are using collaborative inquiry to reflect on existing practices, and there are some structures and processes for building vertical and horizontal relationships and learning across the school. Resourcing to support collaboration is emerging but may not always be focused, connected, or consistently used to foster Deep Learning. | A culture of learning and collaborative inquiry exists in which most teachers and leaders reflect on, review, and adjust their teaching and leadership practices. Capacity building is designed based on teacher and student needs and is clearly focused on the knowledge and skills needed to mobilize and sustain Deep Learning. Through vertical and horizontal relationships, collaboration and trust are growing and practices are becoming more transparent. School-level inquiry and learning involves teachers from all levels, who may also be collaborating across schools. | A powerful culture of collaborative Deep Learning pervades the school. Learning collaboratively is the norm and includes structures and processes to build collective capacity. The culture uses the group to change the group by fostering strong vertical and horizontal relationships that support innovation and risk taking. Capacity building focuses comprehensively and consistently on precision in pedagogy and incorporates cycles of learning and application within and across the school. |

| | | | | |
|---|---|---|---|---|
| Deepening the Learning | The relationship between school curriculum and Deep Learning competencies is unspecified.<br><br>A framework for Deep Learning is beginning to develop but is not understood by all or used consistently to guide learning. Individual teachers and leaders are innovating independently.<br><br>Few coaches and personnel are dedicated to supporting Deep Learning. Collaborative practices such as collaborative inquiry and moderation are not well understood and are used infrequently. | The relationship between Deep Learning and local curriculum is beginning to be articulated.<br><br>Some goals to improve precision in pedagogy have been identified, but the strategy for improvement may be unclear or implemented inconsistently.<br><br>Deep collaborative practices such as collaborative inquiry and protocols for examining student work may be used by some teachers, but there is not consistency of practice or support. | Learning and pedagogical goals are articulated and the link between Deep Learning Competencies and core curriculum standards is visible. A comprehensive framework for Deep Learning is used widely to design and assess Deep Learning experiences.<br><br>Resources and expertise for creating collaborative learning structures are becoming more consistent across the school, as are deep collaborative practices such as collaborative inquiry and protocols for examining student work. | Learning goals for Deep Learning competencies, goals to improve precision in pedagogy, and requirements of core curriculum standards are clearly articulated and integrated consistently with visible impact.<br><br>A comprehensive framework for Deep Learning is understood by all and used consistently across the school to design and assess effective Deep Learning experiences.<br><br>Collaborative inquiry is used to monitor progress in impacting learning at all levels, and protocols for examining student work are used consistently across the school. |
| New Measures and Evaluation | Evaluation of student success and achievement continues to rely on a narrow range of indicators (e.g., tests and a small number of work products) to measure and track success.<br><br>Teachers and school leaders may be using the New Measures to develop a shared language and understanding of Deep Learning, but Deep Learning conditions, design, and outcomes are not yet measured or assessed. | Mixed-method assessment practice is beginning to develop as a wider and more diverse range of evidence sources is used to measure and track progress and success.<br><br>Capacity-building supports for using the New Measures and designing meaningful assessments are beginning to develop.<br><br>Some teachers and leaders are beginning to use the New Measures to design Deep Learning experiences, measure student outcomes, and measure conditions for Deep Learning. | Teachers and leaders demonstrate the capacity to assess, develop, and measure<br><br>• student growth on the Deep Learning Progressions,<br>• conditions that enable Deep Learning to occur and<br>• the effectiveness of Deep Learning design in facilitating Deep Learning outcomes<br><br>Local/national priorities and curricula are linked to and accelerated by Deep Learning experiences, which are moderated through a structured process.<br><br>Teachers are beginning to design new assessments for Deep Learning that more clearly demonstrate Deep Learning as it occurs. | The development and measurement of Deep Learning is pervasive throughout the school and used to focus capacity-building efforts. Measures are compared across years and time periods and demonstrate consistent growth.<br><br>Deep Learning experiences demonstrate clear alignment between curriculum and Deep Learning goals and are formally moderated both within and between schools to establish reliability. Feedback is shared and leveraged to deepen learning design.<br><br>Assessment practice reflects a deep knowledge of students' interests and needs and uses a wide range of evidence to determine progress and learning. |

" We are seeing system change because we have a strong mechanism—a partnership with powerful frameworks, strategies, and tools—to invite, propel, and support progress. "

—*DEEP LEARNING: ENGAGE THE WORLD CHANGE THE WORLD, P. 118*

# Chapter 12
# District Capacity for Deep Learning

Deep Learning doesn't just happen by chance. Districts play a vital role by enabling the conditions that foster a shift to Deep Learning mindsets and practices while removing barriers to promote the spread of best practices across whole systems. The role of the district is to legitimize, support, and enable schools to engage and embrace Deep Learning. Districts that are on the move have a *whole system change* mindset; we define *whole system change* in education as a transformation in the culture of learning. Districts with this mindset see Deep Learning as a way of rethinking the learning process. They determine how they will begin and how they will expand this rethinking but do so with the perspective that, ultimately, this is for 100% of the schools in the district.

Two critical clarifications: While we use the term *district* to denote the local organization of schools, it is not only districts that form the local entity. It can be municipalities (Finland), local networks (New Zealand), or clusters within a state system (Australia). What is essential is the connection and mutual co-learning of the schools with a mindset that says, "Go outside to get better inside." Secondly, we are talking about a change in culture—in this case, of the local authority. This means that the local authority has to work on coherence relative to Deep Learning within its own culture as well as in relation to local schools and, indeed, upward with respect to state policy. All this time, we are talking about system change within and across levels.

We have identified the components that must be addressed and what districts need to do to stimulate and support the evolution of Deep Learning. Districts propel change when they

- articulate Deep Learning as a valued goal,

- focus on Deep Learning with a whole system mindset,

- cultivate a culture of innovation and collaboration where students and adults feel safe and supported in taking risks,

- have rich mechanisms to learn from the work,

- intentionally build precision in pedagogy through collective capacity building, and

- establish assessment systems for measuring success aligned with Deep Learning.

They operationalize this by facilitating vertical relationships within schools through the grade levels and between schools and district leaders as well as horizontal relationships that connect schools to each other and cross role boundaries. These may include capacity building opportunities, use of coaches and networks, and virtual connections such as collaboration platforms. They actively support partnerships with other community groups and find ways to reallocate resources to support the learning work. They integrate the thinking seamlessly into all decisions in the organization. The work of the collaborative cultures is focused on Deep Learning, thus supporting the district goals and creating coherence. The changes to the learning process are perceived as connected. Common language and purpose evolve and spread; thus, the change is systemic, not piecemeal.

In this chapter, we examine the District Conditions Rubric as a tool for districts to assess their current conditions that support Deep Learning; design plans to address needs or gaps; implement changes; and use as a mechanism to measure progress, reflect, and adjust for continuous improvement.

## The District Conditions Rubric

Transforming practice requires a multidimensional approach. The District Conditions Rubric identifies five conditions and the related practices and systems needed to stimulate and support the evolution of Deep Learning.

The District Conditions Rubric describes the practices related to each of the five conditions and their subdimensions (see Figure 12.1). The rubric provides descriptors for each of the four levels of progress: limited, emerging, accelerating, and advanced. District leaders may want to use the rubric as a team or may create a cross-role team with representation from across the district to ensure that many perspectives are included. As noted in Chapter 11, it is essential to create norms of transparency and trust to ground this work. Protocols 38 and 39 will help you dig into the rubric and unpack the conditions and practices based on your district context.

Once teams feel comfortable with the content of the rubric, Protocol 40 provides a process for assessing the current conditions in the district. After highlighting their current status, districts can look to higher levels on the rubric to inform their next steps for growth.

Districts on the move toward Deep Learning are strategic in their decision making. Examine the strategic thinking and strategies used by one of our partner districts using Protocol 40. Ottawa Catholic School Board embraced the Deep Learning agenda and used our Deep Learning framework to craft a whole system strategy for change. In the mini-case, district leaders describe the conditions that have contributed to their journey and how they moved over a four-year

FIGURE 12.1

## District Conditions Impacting Diffusion of Deep Learning

**Collaborative Culture**
- Culture of learning
- Collaborative work
- Capacity building
- Vertical and horizontal relationships

**Leadership**
- Lead learners as culture builders
- Leadership development strategy
- Innovation mobilization
- Students, families, and community engaged

**Deepening Learning**
- Global competencies
- Comprehensive framework
- Precision in pedagogy
- Collaborative inquiry processes shift practice

**New Measures and Evaluation**
- New tools and methods of measurement
- Mechanisms to measure impact

**Vision and Goals**
- Goals drive decisions on policies, practices and resource allocation
- Clarity of strategy

period from an initial engagement of seven schools to engaging all 84 schools using Deep Learning. The simulation asks you to rate the district on the rubric. Deep dialogue emerges as team members look for evidence of the conditions and match it to the descriptors of the rubric cells. The simulation deepens understanding of the content of the rubric while it builds trust and confidence for sharing opinions and perspectives prior to looking inward at your own district.

## Developing a District Deep Learning Plan

Protocol 42 offers an organizer and process for assessing district needs using the School Conditions Rubric. Collating a comprehensive profile of where schools see themselves on the School Conditions Rubric feeds into the district analysis and plan.

Once all the sources of data are collected, Protocol 43 provides a process for developing a District Deep Learning Plan. Districts most often use the District Conditions Rubric at the beginning and end of each year to assess progress and make plans for the upcoming cycle.

## Leveraging the Power of School Visits

Developing a district plan is the first step in changing learning, but the relationships cultivated within and across schools will be at the heart of shifting practice. One effective method to build common language, focus, and culture is to use the School Conditions Rubric as a focus during school visits by district leaders with principals and school teams. Protocol 44 provides a Simple Conversation Guide to promote focused, intentional dialogue. The conversation deepens trust and transparency as district leaders develop a better understanding of the needs and successes of each school and ways to support them.

## Final Thoughts

Diffusing Deep Learning across a whole district or system of schools is complex work because it depends on building new relationships and a new culture for the learning of adults and students alike. Foster the early innovators and explicitly connect them across the schools so that they learn from each other and create a mechanism so that the early insights can be shared more widely. Don't wait for the district to be perfectly aligned; get started and use rapid cycles of doing and reflecting to adjust your strategy and celebrate gains. Remember, we learn more by reflective doing than by thinking about doing, so get started! If you want to accelerate quality change, use a common framework, employ effective tools, start the journey with others, overcome setbacks, and gather momentum. Success will not be simply linear, but you will gain insights and consolidate gains using our framework and tools, along with the ingenuity and energy of you and the group.

Leading for the future means that leaders must foster cycles of innovation by attracting and nurturing talent, providing a culture of trust and exploration, synthesizing the learning from innovation, and cultivating the pathways vertically and horizontally across the district to make meaning in the organization. Leadership at any level of the system is essential, but districts and regions have a special linking role because they are in the middle. Such leaders must be able to see the trees and the forest and their interconnections—what Fullan calls *nuance leaders* (2019). Five years ago, we decided to take our own advice and get started with eight partner countries who became a knowledge-building partnership to mobilize Deep Learning.

 All in all, given the disruption of the change we are talking about, it has had a rapid start. We would call it a *go slow to go fast* proposition—lots of questions at the beginning, a sense that there is great new value accompanied by a burst of energy. Like most social movements, and because of the strategy we employ, there is a strong contagion factor— locally and globally. **""**

Together, we are forging a new frontier of learning and invite you to dive into Deep Learning and join the movement!

## Protocols

### 38  Examining District Conditions for Deep Learning

Use the three-step interview process to ensure that all voices are part of the conversation as you build a shared understanding of the conditions in your district that currently support Deep Learning and innovation in schools.

### 39  The District Conditions Rubric

Engage with teams in a simulation to develop a shared understanding of the dimensions and purpose of the District Conditions Rubric.

### 40  Assessing District Conditions for Deep Learning

Engage with leaders and teams to use the District Conditions Rubric to assess the current level of conditions that support Deep Learning in the district.

### 41  Mobilizing Districtwide Change

Examine a case study of districtwide change to analyze the strategic thinking and strategies used by leaders to mobilize Deep Learning across all 84 schools over a three-year period.

### 42  Collating Information to Support the District in Deep Learning

Explore a process to gather and synthesize data on the needs of your schools. Use this profile of school needs to inform capacity building, resource allocation, and policy decisions that will support Deep Learning.

## 43 Strategizing a District Deep Learning Plan

Engage with the leadership team to assess the data generated by the District Conditions Rubric and the synthesis of school conditions to think strategically and develop a plan to support Deep Learning in the district.

## 44 Leveraging the Power of School Visits

Use the School Conditions Rubric and the Simple Conversations Guide as a foundation for discussions during interactions with school leaders and teams. This process of learning from the work builds common language and surfaces needs that can be incorporated into the district plan.

## Tool

District Conditions Rubric

## For more information:

Read Chapter 8 from *Deep Learning: Engage the World Change the World.*

# Notes

_____

_____

_____

_____

_____

_____

_____

_____

_____

_____

_____

_____

_____

_____

_____

_____

_____

_____

_____

_____

_____

_____

# 38 Examining District Conditions for Deep Learning

**Purpose:** Build a shared understanding of the district conditions that foster Deep Learning

**Time:** 45–60 minutes

**Process:** Three-Step Interview

**1** **Form groups** of three and designate A, B, and C. Begin the cycle with Person A as the interviewer, B as the respondent, and C as the recorder. Think about the three questions on the organizer and complete your responses.

**2** **Provide 5 minutes** for the interview and then rotate roles. Continue the cycle until all three have been interviewed.

**3** **Discuss the commonalities** that emerged across the interviews. Synthesize a list of the conditions that will be most critical to fostering Deep Learning in your district.

**A** Interviewer
**B** Respondent
**C** Recorder

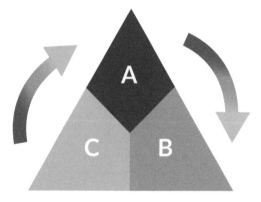

**C** Interviewer
**A** Respondent
**B** Recorder

**B** Interviewer
**C** Respondent
**A** Recorder

## Three-Step Interview Organizer

| Question | Person A | Person B | Person C |
|---|---|---|---|
| 1. What conditions currently exist in the district that would support Deep Learning? | | | |
| 2. What other conditions would need to be in place? | | | |
| 3. What could you do in your role to support Deep Learning? | | | |

# 39 The District Conditions Rubric

**Purpose: Build understanding of the dimensions and purpose of the District Conditions Rubric**

**Process: Three-Step Interview Extension Activity**

**Time: 30–90 minutes**

**Resource:**
• Tool: District Conditions Rubric

**1** **Read** the rubric independently.

**2** **Compare** the conditions of the rubric to the ones you generated during the three-step interview in Protocol 38.

**3** **Select** one dimension from the rubric (e.g., Vision and Goals) and discuss the key concepts.

**4** **Repeat** for each of the dimensions.

**5** **Discuss** ways the rubric might be useful in the district.

> " Individuals can buck the system; groups are needed to upend it. "
>
> —*DEEP LEARNING: ENGAGE THE WORLD CHANGE THE WORLD*, P. 25

# 40 Assessing District Conditions for Deep Learning

**Purpose:** Assess the current level of district conditions that foster Deep Learning

**Process:** Gathering Perspectives on the District Conditions Rubric

**Time:** 1–3 hours

**Resources:**

Tools:
- District Conditions Rubric
- School Conditions Rubric

**1 Establish** a diverse team to gather perspectives. Identify the roles that need to be engaged in this task to ensure a comprehensive view of the organization (district leaders, principals, teacher leaders, board members, union members, etc.)

**2 Select** one dimension of the District Conditions Rubric to review as a team.

**3 Review** the descriptions in the dimension and highlight what best captures the current situation in the district. Do this silently and be ready to share evidence for your rating.

**4 Share** your ratings and rationale for the dimension.

**5 Consider**

- What might explain the range of perspectives of the ratings?
- What other evidence/data do you need to make the rating or to validate the rating?
- How will you get that information?

**6 Reach** consensus for where to position your district on the dimension and your reasons for that placement.

**7 Repeat** for other dimensions.

**8 Review** the profile to determine patterns and areas of greatest strength and greatest need.

**9 Use this data** along with a synthesis of the school conditions ratings (see Protocol 36) and other data to develop a district strategy for Deep Learning.

**10 Use the District Conditions Rubric** at regular intervals to assess progress and plan for continuous improvement.

# 41 Mobilizing Districtwide Change

**Purpose:** Examine the strategic thinking and strategies that lead to districtwide Deep Learning, and apply the District Conditions Rubric to a simulated case

**Process:** Case Analysis

**Time:** 60–120 minutes

What?
So what?

**1** **Extract** information about a district's implementation of Deep Learning from two sources:

- Case Study: Mobilizing a Districtwide Shift to Deep Learning: The Case of Ottawa Catholic School Board (OCSB)
- Video: Deep Learning: System Level Implementation—Flourishing in a Complex World

**2** **Identify** two to three key strategic moves that were critical in leading a successful districtwide transformation to Deep Learning. As individuals, write the strategic moves on sticky notes (one per note).

**3** **Form a small group** to read the strategic moves you have identified. Merge any duplications.

**4** **Using the "What? So What?" Template,** consider each strategic move:

- Match it to the dimension on the District Conditions Rubric. (Place in the *What*? column.)
- Explain the significance it had for districtwide growth in the *So What*? column.

**5** **Now consider** ways that the district was proactive in addressing the following principles in order to avoid common barriers to whole system change:

- sustainability
- shared ownership
- internal competition
- equity of outcomes
- wise use of resources

**6** **Analyze** where you would place the district on each dimension.

- Where would you place this district on the continuum?
- What is your evidence to support that position?
- What might be one next step for the district?

**Resources:**

- Tool: District Conditions Rubric
- Case Study: Mobilizing a Districtwide Shift to Deep Learning
- Video at www.deep-learning .global: Deep Learning: System-Level Implementation— Flourishing in a Complex World

# What? So What? Organizer

| Dimension | What?<br>What strategies/actions were catalyst for change? | So What?<br>What were the implications of those strategies? |
|---|---|---|
| Vision and Goals | | |
| Leadership | | |
| Collaborative Cultures | | |
| Capacity Building | | |
| New Measures and Evaluation | | |

# Mobilizing a Districtwide Shift to Deep Learning

## The Case of Ottawa Catholic School Board Ottawa, Canada

Walk into schools and you see students working with their own personal devices and using space purposefully for collaborating or moving.

They may be using green walls scattered throughout the building to create videos so that they can add backgrounds and audio later. Walls are covered with colorful student-made products and art. There is a buzz of engagement, and students taking responsibility for their learning is the norm. But it's not just the students who are learning in new ways. Teaching and learning are highly visible, with teachers meeting in teams by grade or cross panel to plan learning activities or examine the depth of student learning and work. Teacher learning isn't restricted to planning, because you will see schools where teachers are learning alongside or directly from students as they explore ideas, new digital devices, or resources that are not familiar to the teachers. Principal and district leaders are also visible learners because they attend student-led workshops or tutoring sessions to learn how to leverage digital to enhance their own learning or pedagogical practice. Participation in learning walks, where teams of teachers, leaders, and sometimes students visit classrooms with an observational purpose, sharpens skills of both observing classroom practice and providing feedback to deepen student learning. At the same time, monthly meetings of all principals and district leaders are opportunities to focus on sharing and developing solutions to problems of practice.

### About the District . . .

The Ottawa Catholic School Board in Ottawa Canada is a publicly funded urban school district serving over 41,000 students in 84 schools. The district joined the global partnership in 2014 to extend and enhance its work on 21st-century learning and in four years has spread the Deep Learning practices to all 84 schools to better serve their multicultural population. Consider the strategic actions that moved this innovation to a foundation for learning for ALL.

### Setting the Stage . . .

Innovation and well-being were already at the heart of change in this district. Beginning in 2010, a collaboratively created blueprint for change focused on a cultural shift across the board while the creation of a digital ecosystem focused more on staff and student collaboration, creativity, critical thinking, and communication. Simultaneously, the district improved infrastructure, including Wi-Fi in all schools, conversion of school libraries to learning commons, laptops for all educators, and integrated software and hardware supports. Governance issues were integrated with the creation of a social media policy as well as the first plan in the province to integrate yearly instruction on digital citizenship into the curriculum. Leaders were intentional in building on these foundations to strategically craft a coherent plan for whole system change over three years (2014–2017) and to divert funds to directly support this new direction. It is important to note that the strong implementation was achieved without new money by focusing direction and realigning resources to support it. A whole system mindset was intentional.

## The First Year 2014–2015

The district senior leadership team recognized early on that NPDL was aligned with the board's focus on pedagogy as a driver and leveraging technology to create new learning and teaching opportunities. Strategically, they selected seven schools to participate in NPDL. Schools were selected so that one was from each academic superintendent's family of schools. This was to ensure that all superintendents were part of the leadership process and that each school board member had a school in their zone. Each superintendent selected a school that had a supportive principal and a staff that had demonstrated a commitment to the change process that had been initiated with the creation of a digital ecosystem.

To build capacity, each school was matched with one central staff member and also with one teacher from another school that was already part of a learning network called *learning connections*. Learning connection teachers were taking part in a provincial learning network that supported educators with access to applications, technology, professional learning, and collaboration opportunities. In this way, they were able to gain synergies by connecting multiple learning networks. Two teachers from each school were released for the cross-district capacity sessions. A central staff member was assigned to lead, support, and promote this new NPDL learning network and became the board champion for Deep Learning.

> To build capacity, each school was matched with one central staff member and also with one teacher from another school that was already part of a learning network . . .

## The Second Year 2015–2016

In the second year, the district built on the early successes by expanding from seven to 15 schools and by creating a virtual connection with five intermediate schools for a total of 20 participating schools. Leadership from the middle became important, as the work of staff involved in Year One schools was leveraged to spread the work in new schools. The model of connecting schools with one central staff member and with one teacher from another school was continued.

Capacity building continued to connect teachers across schools and a leadership program for Deep Learning was introduced. The Inquiry Cycle model was used and culminated in a successful learning fair where staff celebrated and shared their successes using the NPDL framework.

An important system structure was created in that year—the central coherence committee. Previously, district leaders had encouraged interdepartmental work to try to align initiatives including the NPDL learning network. The creation of the central coherence committee proved that function trumps structure because a more nimble and strategic committee focused on coherence across the district rather than simple alignment.

## The Third Year 2016–2017

In Year Three, the district made a strategic decision that NPDL was no longer a network but that Deep Learning would be the district's learning framework. It expanded the approach from 20 to all 84 schools. The capacity building that had taken place in Years One and Two was a crucial foundation for engaging all schools. The natural transfer of teachers as well as the strategic expansion of the network had created both an interest and capacity across most schools.

All district staff built their capacity in using the Deep Learning Framework with a specific focus on the terminology of the Four Learning Design Elements and the six Global Competencies of Deep Learning. Learning networks such as numeracy, literacy, and kindergarten continued, but each used the framework of Deep Learning and a common language in its practice.

The whole system focus was based on collaborative inquiry. Superintendents used the School Conditions Rubric as a discussion point for reflecting on school innovation when they met with the school principals they supported. The existing NPDL champion remained involved but used her expertise to bring the Deep Learning process to all new teachers and to the various coaching and professional learning groups throughout the district. All staff throughout the district received a Deep Learning reference guide so that they would see the language of Deep Learning and the coherent approach to the district focus on literacy and numeracy achievement. The director of education included Deep Learning as a focus in all systemwide addresses and in the monthly meeting with school principals and system leaders. Each learning network used a Deep Learning Rubric to monitor and reflect on the system impact of their work. Educators involved in Year One or Year Two of NPDL had an opportunity to participate in a Deep Learning Certificate Program where they mentored educators from another school through an Inquiry Cycle, taking advantage of the toolkit of rubrics for teaching and measuring global competencies. The early adopters were rewarded with digital badges in recognition of their work. A separate Introduction to Deep Learning course was created for staff who wanted to accelerate their implementation of Deep Learning in their classrooms.

> We are successfully "using the group to move the group."

At the district level, leaders saw greater coherence because departments were working together and implementing their collective work using the same teaching and learning network. School staff has the same common framework that enables them to work collaboratively and connect learning networks. Leadership is coming from all areas of the organization, and school visits and learning walks are focusing on the Four Elements and six Global Competencies.

Ottawa Catholic has not only changed within but also offered leadership to global partners by hosting visits to its classrooms and sharing a range of resources it has created. In its own words, "Students and staff are energized with the Board focus on Deep Learning. We are successfully 'using the group to move the group'" (personal communication, December 2016).

## The Fourth Year 2017–2018

In the fourth year of implementing Deep Learning to scale, the district continued to build capacity across the system. They clearly signaled the importance of understanding the Deep Learning Framework by updating the principal and vice principal promotion interview process to incorporate interview questions and portfolio presentations that reviewed potential leader's understanding of the Deep Learning Framework. Supervisory officers also worked with central principals to update the Board Improvement Plan and School Improvement Plans to focus on the Four Elements and the Global Competencies. Presentations and discussions were added to a newly created principal learning series and central educator learning series that included reference to the Deep Learning Framework. Staff were introduced to new strategic commitments—"Be Well," "Be Community," and "Be Innovative"—and the language incorporated the Deep Learning Framework. Monthly staff meeting resources for Deep Learning were provided to each school, and monthly Twitter contests were held to highlight staff use of the elements and competencies. An innovation fund was established for staff to collaborate with other educators in any area that included the use of the Deep Learning Framework. Both the central coherence committee and an interdepartmental leadership committee met on a regular basis with a meeting agenda that included monitoring the system implementation of Deep Learning and looking for coherence opportunities.

In order to celebrate the accomplishments of many staff across the system who were now teaching and learning using the Deep Learning Framework, a series of videos was created to highlight staff and student use of the elements and competencies. In addition to a digital badge, staff that successfully completed their Deep Learning Certification Program received a letter of recognition and a copy of *Deep Learning: Engage the World Change the World* as a means to celebrate and continue in their mentoring role.

> They clearly signaled the importance of understanding the Deep Learning Framework by updating the principal and vice principal promotion interview process to incorporate interview questions and portfolio presentations that reviewed potential leader's understanding of the Deep Learning Framework.

## Looking Ahead to 2018–2019

For the 2018–2019 academic year, the Ottawa Catholic School Board began the implementation of new Board strategic commitments: "Be Community," "Be Well," "Be Innovative." At the first meeting of the year, the district leadership team (all principals, managers, district leaders) heard the director of education speak of the coherence between the Deep Learning Framework, the new strategic commitments, and the Board spiritual theme.

Moving into Year Five, the task of monitoring the systemwide implementation was moved to both the central coherence committee and the interdepartmental leadership team from a steering committee focusing solely on Deep Learning. This strategic move helps to reinforce that Deep Learning is not another initiative but rather a foundation for all that they do in the district. An additional change was the shifting of the two Deep Learning champions into other roles in the district, one leading the math focus and the other moving into a vice principal role. The success of the implementation is reflected by the focus continuing systemwide, despite the change of the key leads. Two new coordinators who are part of the Interdepartmental leadership team now assume the additional responsibilities of Deep Learning leads.

The logical progression of providing staff meeting resources also is evidence of the success of the systemwide implementation, since stand-alone resources related to the four elements and the global competencies are not provided but are the framework incorporated into all systemwide resources, such as "How to use the Deep Learning Framework to support students with a learning disability profile." Staff look forward to continuing a coherent approach to systemwide implementation of the Deep Learning Framework in the Ottawa Catholic School Board.

# 42 Collating Information to Support the District in Deep Learning

**Purpose:** Develop skill in using the School Conditions Rubric to collate data on school needs to inform district planning

**Process:** Collect, Collate, Review

**Time:** 30–90 minutes

**Resource:**

• Tool: School Conditions Rubric

1. **Collect** the self-assessment ratings of each school on the School Conditions Rubric.

2. **Collate** the ratings on the District Profile of School Conditions Rubric Ratings Organizer. Use color coding to identify different levels (e.g., blue for Limited Evidence, green for Emerging).

3. **Review** the profile that emerges. Use these questions to fuel the discussion into the District Plan for Deep Learning.

## Questions

• What patterns emerge?

• What are the surprises?

• What are the strengths?

• What are the high needs?

• What will be the focus for capacity building?

• How will you differentiate to meet diverse needs?

• How can schools support one another?

# District Profile of School Conditions Rubric Ratings Organizer

| Dimension | Vision and Goals | Leadership | Collaborative Cultures | Deepening Learning | New Measures and Evaluation |
|---|---|---|---|---|---|
| School A | | | | | |
| School B | | | | | |
| School C | | | | | |
| School D | | | | | |
| School E | | | | | |

# 43 Strategizing a District Deep Learning Plan

**Purpose:** Develop a district plan to improve conditions that support Deep Learning

**Process:** Planning Forward Using the Collaborative Inquiry Cycle

**1** **Establish** a team that brings together various perspectives and experiences. This may include staff from a range of roles, union representation, students, and parents.

**2** **Review** the four phases of the Collaborative Inquiry Cycle as a team.

**3** **Assess** ▶

a. Review the results of the District Conditions Rubric and the collated results from School Conditions Rubric. Use that data to consider the following:

- What evidence did you have for making the rating for each dimension?
- What does the collated data from the School Conditions Rubric tell you?
- What other evidence do you need? How will you get it?
- What are your strengths?
- What are your needs?

b. Identify 1–3 action dimensions that are most crucial to improve conditions for Deep Learning in the district.

**4** **Design** ▼

a. Identify key actions needed to move toward the goals. Use the next levels on the dimensions to provide ways to move along the dimension.

b. Specify who will be responsible and time frames.

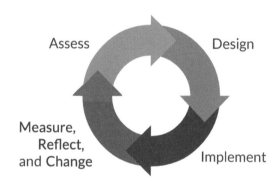

**6** **Measure, Reflect, and Change** ▲

a. Identify how you will measure success.
b. Use the Conditions Rubrics at regular intervals to assess progress on the dimension.
c. Adjust the plan based on evidence.

**5** **Implement** ◀

a. Take action on the plan.
b. Monitor by gathering feedback and data for status updates.

## District Deep Learning Plan

| Goal Area | Key Actions | Lead | Time | Status |
|---|---|---|---|---|
| Dimension 1.0 | | | | |
| | | | | |
| | | | | |
| Dimension 2.0 | | | | |
| | | | | |
| | | | | |
| Dimension 3.0 | | | | |
| | | | | |
| | | | | |
| How will you measure success? | | | | |

# 44 Leveraging the Power of School Visits

**Purpose:** Develop common language and practices about Deep Learning across the district

**Process:** The Simple Conversation Guide

**Time:** 30–60 minutes

**Resource:**
- Tool: School Conditions Rubric

**1** **Establish** and review norms for emotional safety and deeper thinking during the conversation:

- Attend fully, listen to understand, avoid interrupting
- Ask open-ended exploratory questions (avoid yes/no)
- Paraphrasing allows the protégé to hear his or her own thoughts
- Pose positive presumptions, be non-judgmental

**2** **Use the question prompts** on the Conversation Guide to focus the conversation.

**3** **Repeat the process** in future visits/conversations to reflect on progress made and set next steps for that dimension.

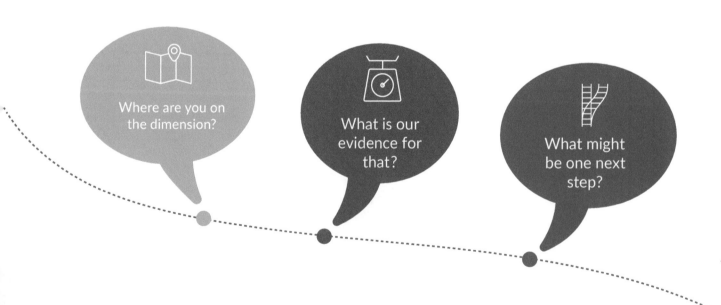

Where are you on the dimension?

What is our evidence for that?

What might be one next step?

# Simple Conversation Guide

**Where are you on the dimension?**

What dimension would you like to focus on today?

When you refer to the language on the continuum, where would you see yourself currently?

What are some examples of how that is playing out?

**What is our evidence for that?**

What are you specifically seeing, noticing, and experiencing that speaks to that hunch?

What are you observing about your learners? Teachers?

What might be some other perspectives that would give this a fuller view?

What, if any, patterns seem to be emerging?

What might have been some reasons for that outcome?

What information is still missing, hidden, or unclear to you?

**What might be one next step?**

How might this next step lead you forward on the continuum?

What would it look like, feel like, or sound like, if it was effective?

What strategy or approach might you use?

How might you know it's effective?

What bumps are you anticipating?

What strategies have you used before that worked well?

How can I support you? What might be some resources to tap?

TOOL

# District Conditions Rubric

New Pedagogies for **Deep Learning**™
A GLOBAL PARTNERSHIP

| | Limited | Emerging | Accelerating | Advanced |
|---|---|---|---|---|
| **Vision and Goals** | There are no Deep Learning strategies, goals, or implementation supports in place to achieve Deep Learning.<br><br>Decisions and resources reflect the status quo. | Deep Learning strategy and goals are formally written and articulated. The goals may be unclear to some, and there may be competing priorities.<br><br>Some decisions regarding resources and processes reflect the shifting of the status quo to Deep Learning. | There is a written and understood strategy articulating Deep Learning goals and how they will be implemented. There is a strategy to reduce competing priorities.<br><br>Most decisions are driven by and aligned with Deep Learning. | A concise, well-articulated strategy with focused Deep Learning goals and implementation support is owned by all members of the district community and used to drive decision making and resource allocation. Regular collective questioning assesses how well decisions are serving Deep Learning for all students. |
| **Leadership** | Leaders rely on formal roles and structures and view Deep Learning as an add-on rather than integrator and accelerator of processes.<br><br>Engagement in Deep Learning is restricted to a few early innovators. | Lead learners are emerging across schools who see their role in developing leaders, structures, processes, and formal and informal opportunities, all committed to fostering Deep Learning.<br><br>Student, teacher, family, and community engagement in Deep Learning is emerging. | Lead learners have created structures and processes that build a culture to propel shifts in practice and shared understanding. They intentionally develop leaders at all levels and make Deep Learning a priority by being visible and dedicating resources.<br><br>Strategies to identify and mobilize innovation are emerging.<br><br>There is engagement in Deep Learning across many schools and among some families and communities. | Lead learners consistently serve as culture builders developing shared purpose, understanding, and belonging. Lead learner capacity exists at *all* levels with a clear strategy to develop and distribute leadership capacity.<br><br>The district uses challenges as opportunities to grow capacity. It sees internal expertise as a driver of innovation; it identifies and mobilizes talent.<br><br>Students, families, and community are informed, engaged, and influential in Deep Learning for all students. |
| **Collaborative Cultures** | Collaboration between and among leaders, teachers, and learners occurs through formal structures without challenging the status quo. Low levels of trust are reflected in an unwillingness to share practices and ideas.<br><br>Capacity-building support often focuses on individual needs and is not explicitly linked to Deep Learning. Inquiry and reflective practice are used inconsistently across the district. | A collaborative culture is developing around Deep Learning and collective capacity building. Collaboration and trust are emerging within schools but may be inconsistent across the district.<br><br>Capacity building is moving from individual to collaborative learning.<br><br>Collaborative inquiry is beginning to be used to reflect on existing practices. Some structures exist for building vertical and horizontal relationships across the district. Resources to support collaboration are emerging but may be inconsistent. | A culture of learning and collaborative inquiry exists in which most teachers and leaders reflect on, review, and adjust their teaching and leadership practices.<br><br>Capacity building is based on assessed needs across the schools and is clearly focused on the knowledge and skills needed to mobilize and sustain Deep Learning.<br><br>Through vertical and horizontal relationships, collaboration and trust are fostering risk taking and innovation in many schools. School-level inquiry and learning involve leaders and teachers from all levels and collaboration across schools. | A powerful culture of collaborative Deep Learning pervades the district. Learning collaboratively is the norm and includes formal and informal structures and processes for building collective capacity.<br><br>Capacity building focuses comprehensively and consistently on precision in pedagogy and incorporates cycles of learning and application within and across the schools.<br><br>The district consistently fosters strong vertical and horizontal relationships that support innovation and risk taking. |

## Deepening the Learning

| | | | |
|---|---|---|---|
| The relationship between school curriculum and Deep Learning competencies is unspecified.<br><br>Individuals may be innovating independently. Few coaches and personnel are dedicated to supporting Deep Learning.<br><br>Collaborative practices such as collaborative inquiry and moderation are not well understood and are used infrequently. | The relationship between Deep Learning and local curriculum is beginning to be articulated.<br><br>A district framework for Deep Learning is beginning to develop but is not understood by all or used consistently to guide learning. Some goals to improve precision in pedagogy have been identified but the strategy for improvement may be unclear or implemented inconsistently.<br><br>Deep collaborative practices such as collaborative inquiry and protocols for examining student work may be used by some schools, but there is not consistency of practice, shared language, or support. | Learning and pedagogical goals are articulated and the link between Deep Learning competencies and core curriculum standards is visible.<br><br>A comprehensive framework for Deep Learning is used widely to design and assess Deep Learning experiences across the district. Shared language and understanding are fostered regularly.<br><br>Resources and expertise for creating collaborative learning structures are becoming more consistent across the district, as are deep collaborative practices such as collaborative inquiry and protocols for examining student work. | Learning goals for Deep Learning competencies, goals to improve precision in pedagogy, and curriculum standards are clearly articulated and integrated consistently with visible impact across the district.<br><br>A comprehensive framework for Deep Learning is understood by all and used consistently across the district to design and assess effective Deep Learning experiences.<br><br>Shared language is developed to build common understanding of Deep Learning concepts and practices. Shared language is consistently used to design and measure Deep Learning.<br><br>Collaborative inquiry is used to monitor progress at all levels, and protocols for examining student work are used consistently across the district. |

## New Measures and Evaluation

| | | | |
|---|---|---|---|
| Evaluation of student success and achievement continues to rely on a narrow range of indicators (e.g., tests and a small number of work products) to measure and track success.<br><br>Schools are beginning to use the New Measures to develop a shared language and understanding of Deep Learning, but Deep Learning conditions, design, and outcomes are not yet measured or assessed.<br><br>The district has not yet begun to use the New Measure to consider organizational health, well-being, and equity. | Assessment practice reflects a diverse range of evidence and tracks progress and success. The New Measures are beginning to be used across the district.<br><br>Capacity-building supports for using the New Measures and designing meaningful assessments are beginning to develop.<br><br>Schools and departments are beginning to use the New Measures to design Deep Learning experiences, measure student outcomes, and measure conditions for Deep Learning, but use is inconsistent.<br><br>Measures of student performance are beginning to inform well-being and equity as well as addressing Deep Learning outcomes. | Teachers and leaders demonstrate the capacity to assess, develop, and measure<br>• student growth on the Deep Learning Progressions,<br>• conditions that enable Deep Learning to occur, and<br>• the effectiveness of Deep Learning design in facilitating Deep Learning outcomes<br><br>Processes such as collaborative assessment of student work and collaborative inquiry are used by many schools Deep Learning experiences are moderated through a structured process between and within many schools.<br><br>Some measures of organizational health, student learning, and well-being and equity are monitored. | The development and measurement of Deep Learning is highly valued and pervasive throughout the district. It is used to focus capacity-building efforts and make informed decisions.<br><br>The district uses a system of measures compared across time and demonstrates consistent growth.<br><br>Processes such as collaborative assessment of student work and collaborative inquiry are used consistently and are embedded in the district culture. This information is monitored for impact across the district. Deep Learning experiences demonstrate clear alignment between curriculum and Deep Learning goals and are formally moderated both within and between all schools.<br><br>Varied measures of organizational health, student learning, and well-being and equity are monitored. |

" The invitation to join the social movement of Deep Learning could not be clearer or more compelling. Yes, start-up will not be easy and facing down inertia is not pleasant. But the ideas and people are there and ready to tackle the status quo. Armies of young people are potentially available if we can find the right starting point; then, deep change will take hold and accelerate. "

# Epilogue: Act Now

There are three big reasons to take action now. The first is that society is worsening on the big indicators: inequity, climate, jobs, the economy, levels of trust, anxiety and stress among all age groups, predictability, the paradox of technology—being simultaneously closer and farther apart from others—and the overall bewilderment about the future. Where in the universe are we heading? Nobody knows, and people of all ages are worried.

The second reason to act is that the way forward is becoming clearer through our Deep Learning work. *Deep Learning: Engage the World Change the World* and our tools for engagement provide ideas, clarity, confirmation, kindred spirits, and much more. The invitation to join the social movement of Deep Learning could not be clearer or more compelling. Yes, start-up will not be easy and facing down inertia is not pleasant. But the ideas and people are there and ready to tackle the status quo. Armies of young people are potentially available if we can find the right starting point; then deep change will take hold and accelerate.

Third, public education is one of the few domains that has the power to transform society. Can we think in 2020 in the same way that George Counts (1932) did almost 100 years ago when he asked, "Dare the school build a new social order?" Deep Learning shifts the role of education. No longer is the main role of education the transmission of knowledge and values. Instead, we need to learn about a world that is changing faster than we can know it. Deep Learning is the avenue to understand and thereby change the evolving world for the better. It is not a case of "to know him/her is to love him/her" but more to understand the magical dynamics, danger, and drama of what humankind and mother nature are creating together—both destructive and prolific.

Get to know the world for selfish and altruistic reasons. In Deep Learning, teachers and students together treat the world as the living laboratory it is. Use any subject or any theme and join up with others to learn more about the world and yourselves. The more you learn, the more you will change the world and yourselves. Education just became a lot more interesting and meaningful!

You have all you need to get started: the Deep Learning text, tools for engagement, and others willing to join you in a learning journey that will have immediate payoff and long-term

 The fundamental shift that Deep Learning signifies is that subject-based learning is not detached from the world; the world is the subject!

impact. We know from experience that Deep Learning accelerates with just a few favorable circumstances: some leaders and willing joiners, good ideas and tools that enable start-up, hands-on learning, and a commitment to making a difference in a specific area or domain. You will then find others: locals and far-flung others who are on similar quests.

We can also pay attention to the basics: literacy, numeracy, science, the arts, and more. Subject-based learning immerses with Deep Learning to the benefit of both students and teachers. The fundamental shift that Deep Learning signifies is that subject-based learning is not detached from the world; the world is the subject! Having said all of this, you don't need to position yourself to save the world. Start by saving yourself and those around you.

Who said this and when? (And yes, *troublous* is a legitimate word.) George Counts wrote this passage in 1932 (p. 31) as he was lamenting that education had become a victim of the very forces that are transforming the rest of society—for the worse. This is the situation that we now find ourselves in—education on the receiving end of destructive societal trends. Deep Learning has the power to reverse this trend. Students, teachers, and other educators become agents of change not only for the own good but for the good of all. It can be this big and this exciting.

> " We live in troublous times; we live in an age of profound change; we live in an age of revolution. Indeed, it is highly doubtful whether man ever lived in a more eventful period than the present. "

The next 10 years and more will be a period of transition in education. This means ambiguity, frustration, innovation, and an opportunity to be part of a movement. You will need (and have) three supports: our Deep Learning Framework, the tools for engagement, and at least a small support group of fellow collaborators. You need to learn through action, consolidation, and more action. Look for and cultivate engagement in purposeful learning and the fruits of better learning: kids who can handle (and, indeed, want to lead) complex change; teachers who deeply realize why they came into teaching; principals and leaders at all levels who weave in and out of apprenticing and becoming experts at enabling change; parents and caregivers who become less worried and more proud of their young people; growing equity as all rise, with some blowing the lid off learning; and a public who, for the first time in their lives, feel and see that trust in society is on the ascendancy.

Of course, this is a big request of education. For the past 75 years, education has been tidying up and trying to make life better for an increasingly diverse population. It is now losing ground in most of the Organisation for Economic Co-operation and Development (OECD) countries. In the Global South, young people are restlessly milling around, realizing that being stuck with one's lot in life is not for them but not knowing what to do. Sooner than later, they will break out, for better or worse.

Increasingly we are coming to the conclusion that purported examples of Deep Learning are not Deep Learning if they do not encompass understanding and improving the world. In the short run, we must address individual and subgroup problems; for example, pertaining to inequities. Ultimately, however, if the vast majority of students do not engage in the "change the world" agenda, we will lose our planet. The goal is to achieve the broad unity of the human race, not just to address local issues.

Choose wisely and choose now! A better world is within grasp as we engage the world, change the world together.

# References

Brown, B. (2018). *Dare to lead*. New York, NY: Random House.

Bungay Stanier, M. (2016). *The coaching habit: Say less, ask more and change the way you lead forever.* Toronto, Canada: Box of Crayons Press.

Connection through relationship: The key to mental health. (2017, June 13). [Seminar] . Toronto, Canada.

Counts, G. (1932). *Dare the school build a new social order?* New York, NY: The John Day Company.

Datnow, A., & Park, V. (2018). *Professional collaboration with purpose*. London, UK: Routledge.

The Deming Institute. (n.d.). *The Deming system of profound knowledge*. Retrieved from https://deming.org/explore/so-p-k

Donohoo, J., Hattie, J., & Eells, R. (2018). The power of collective efficacy. *Educational Leadership, 75*(6), 41–44.

Fullan, M. (2019). *Nuance: Why some leaders succeed and others fail.* Thousand Oaks, CA: Corwin.

Fullan, M., & Quinn, J. (2016). *Coherence: The right drivers in action for schools, districts, and systems.* Thousand Oaks, CA: Corwin.

Fullan, M., Quinn, J., & McEachen, J. (2018). *Deep learning: Engage the world change the world.* Thousand Oaks, CA: Corwin.

Hargreaves, A., & O'Connor, M. T. (2018). *Collaborative professionalism: When teaching together means learning for all*. Thousand Oaks, CA: Corwin.

Katz, S., & Dack, L. A. (2013). *Intentional interruption: Breaking down learning barriers to transform professional practice.* Thousand Oaks, CA: Corwin.

Papert, S. (1994). *The children's machine: Rethinking school in the age of the computer.* New York, NY: Basic Books.

Petrone, P. (2019, January 1). The skills companies need most in 2019—and how to learn them. *Linked In Learning*. Retrieved from https://learning.linkedin.com/blog/top-skills/the-skills-companies-need-most-in-2019-and-how-to-learn-them

Stringer, K. (2018, August 30). Citizenship as a classroom priority: New Gallup poll shows 74 percent of superintendents say "preparing engaged citizens" has become a major challenge for their districts. *Newsfeed.* Retrieved from https://www.the74million.org/citizenship-as-a-classroom-priority-new-gallup-poll-shows-74-percent-of-superintendents-say-preparing-engaged-citizens-has-become-a-major-challenge-for-their-districts/

Wiggins, G. (2012). Authentic education: Seven keys to effective feedback. *Educational Leadership, 70*(1), 10–16.

# Index

# Acknowledgments

We are engaged in an exciting innovation partnership involving hundreds of schools in eight countries and have thousands of people to thank. We are privileged to learn from inspiring teachers and leaders who are on the journey to Deep Learning. We want to thank all of these people, among others, in schools, districts, municipalities, and governments for being co-learners with us over the past five years.

We thank the Hewlett Foundation, particularly Barbara Chow and Marc Chun for their support of our Deep Learning work, and the Stuart Foundation for its long-term funding of our work in system change and support of Deep Learning in California and Washington.

We are blessed with committed quality all around us, including the country and cluster leaders in each country: Lynn Davie, Mary Coverdale, Wendy Macpherson, Anna Antonijevic, Scott Millman, Kelly Borg, and Rosemary Vellar (Australia); Tom D'Amico and Debbie Frendo (Canada); Vesa Åyrås, Tomi-Pekka Miukkanen, and Tarja Tuomainen (Finland); Marlou van Beek (Netherlands); Margot McKeegan and Greg Carroll (New Zealand); Miguel Brechner, Claudia Brovetto, and Ramon Silveira (Uruguay); Larry Thomas and Pam Estvold (US); and Trish Oliver (Hong Kong).

Thanks to the scores of schools, teachers, and administrators who contributed their stories in exemplars, videos, and vignettes: Denise Andre, Frank Bradica, Andrew Bradshaw, Tom D'Amico, Ryan Dufrane, AnneMarie Es, Jennifer Flinn, Debbie Frendo, Angelina Glynn, Andrea Green, Kevin Hall, Michelle Howe, Aki Kukkonen, Kahukura Cluster, Terry Kirkey, David McCully, Jane Morris, Pamela Newton, Janne Niemine, Madeline Parthum, Parmatta School Team, Jussi Roms, April Smith, St. Louis School, Kenora Catholic School Board, Lisa Walsh, Laura White, and J. Wilkinson.

Next, we thank our global team, a powerhouse of dedicated leaders: Cecilia de la Paz, Bill Hogarth, Catie Schuster, Matt Kane, and Mary Meucci. Special recognition goes to Jean Clinton, who has added insights to the connections between well-being and Deep Learning. We work with a host of thought leaders: Eleanor Adam, Peter Hill, Jal Mehta, Daan Roosegaarde, Andreas Schleicher, Michael Stevenson, and more.

There has been great support for the production of this book. Special thanks to Trudy Lane for her inspired graphic designs that capture the essence of the concepts. Finally, we thank our fabulous publisher, Corwin: fast, flexible, and fastidious about quality; Arnis, Gail, Erin, and Melanie and the Corwin infrastructure: We can't thank you enough.

In this book, we hope we have contributed to the capacity to foster Deep Learning so that all may flourish. This book is dedicated to all the deep learners who inspired the work and the students who will guide the future. It's time to engage the world and change the world!

# About the Authors

**Joanne Quinn** is an international consultant and author on system change, leadership, and learning. As co-founder and global director of New Pedagogies for Deep Learning, she leads the capacity building of a global innovation partnership across eight countries focused on transforming learning. Joanne has provided leadership at all levels of education as a superintendent of education, implementation advisor to the Ontario Ministry of Education, and Director of Continuing Education at the University of Toronto. Recent books include *Coherence: The Right Drivers in Action for Schools, Districts, and Systems*; *The Taking Action Guide for Building Coherence in Schools, Districts, and Systems*; and *Deep Learning: Engage the World Change the World*. Joanne's diverse leadership roles and her passion to open windows of opportunity for all give her a unique perspective on influencing positive change.

**Joanne McEachen** is an internationally recognized education leader, founder and CEO of The Learner First, and the Global New Measures director for New Pedagogies for Deep Learning (NPDL). Joanne led the development of a system of tools and measures for Deep Learning, which supports educators and leaders at all levels of the system as they assess and measure Deep Learning conditions, designs, and outcomes. Joanne's expertise spans every layer of the education system. She has been a teacher, principal, regional manager, and a national change leader in

New Zealand and around the world. With firsthand experience addressing the issues faced by schools and education departments, Joanne provides tools, processes, measures, and thinking that combine with leveraging digital technologies and deepen learning for every learner.

**Michael Fullan**, PhD, Order of Canada, Professor Emeritus, Ontario Institute of Education, University of Toronto, has had a long and distinguished career as a researcher and developer, senior administrator, and policy advisor to premiers and other senior politicians. He served as dean of education for the University of Toronto from 1988 to 2003, leading the development of a world-renowned faculty of education. Professor Fullan is currently engaged in developmental work in over 10 countries in the Global North and South. He has written several award-winning books that have been translated into many languages. He is co-director of the New Pedagogies for Deep Learning global initiative. His latest books are *Nuance: Why Some Leaders Succeed and Others Fail* and *The Governance Core*.

**Mag Gardner** is a global capacity-building facilitator with New Pedagogies for Deep Learning and education coach. She supports districts in Canada, Finland, Netherlands, New Zealand, and the United States as they work to transform their classrooms, schools, and systems. Formerly, Mag was a superintendent, secondary school principal, and teacher in a range of settings in Ontario. She was also a pioneering force in Ontario's student success movement. Mag earned her doctorate in education from OISE/UT, focusing on professional collaboration and leadership.

**Max Drummy** has more than 25 years of experience as a teacher and school and system leader in Australia, southern China, and the United States. Max co-led the Australian New Pedagogies for Deep Learning Cluster between 2013 and 2016, establishing and enabling a powerful national network committed to reimagining education. Max is a member of the NPDL Global Capacity Building team and is based in Seattle, Washington. He supports schools and systems across the United States, Australia, New Zealand, Uruguay, and Hong Kong as they strive to create educational environments and practices that foster Deep Learning so that all learners can contribute to the common good, address global challenges, and flourish in a complex world.

# *Leadership* That Makes an Impact

### MICHAEL FULLAN, JOANNE QUINN, & JOANNE MCEACHEN

This book defines what Deep Learning is, and takes up the question of how to mobilize complex whole-system change.

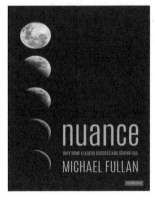

### MICHAEL FULLAN

How do you break the cycle of surface-level change to tackle complex challenges? *Nuance* is the answer.

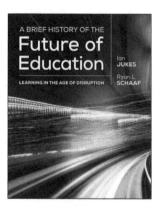

### IAN JUKES & RYAN L. SCHAAF

The digital environment has radically changed how students need to learn. Get ready to be challenged to accommodate today's learners.

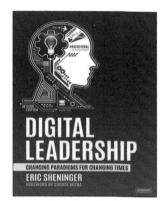

### ERIC SHENINGER

Lead for efficacy in these disruptive times! Cultivating school culture focused on the achievement of students while anticipating change is imperative.

### JOANNE MCEACHEN & MATTHEW KANE

Getting at the heart of what matters for students is key to deeper learning that connects with their lives.

### LEE G. BOLMAN & TERRENCE E. DEAL

Sometimes all it takes to solve a problem is to reframe it by listening to wise advice from a trusted mentor.

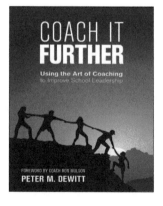

### PETER M. DEWITT

This go-to guide is written for coaches, leaders looking to be coached, and leaders interested in coaching burgeoning leaders.

### ANTHONY KIM & ALEXIS GONZALES-BLACK

Designed to foster flexibility and continuous innovation, this resource expands cutting-edge management and organizational techniques to empower schools with the agility and responsiveness vital to their new environment.